Who Killed Detroit?

Who Killed Detroit?

✦

Other Cities Beware!

Johannes F. Spreen
and
Diane Holloway, Ph.D.

iUniverse, Inc.
New York Lincoln Shanghai

Who Killed Detroit?
Other Cities Beware!

iUniverse books may be ordered through booksellers or by contacting:

iUniverse
2021 Pine Lake Road, Suite 100
Lincoln, NE 68512
www.iuniverse.com
1-800-Authors (1-800-288-4677)

ISBN-13: 978-0-595-35798-7 (pbk)
ISBN-13: 978-0-595-80267-8 (ebk)
ISBN-10: 0-595-35798-9 (pbk)
ISBN-10: 0-595-80267-2 (ebk)

Printed in the United States of America

Contents

Acknowledgements

I thank my wonderful wife, Sallie Ann Spreen, for her love and for much support and encouragement throughout our sixteen years of marriage. Her understanding of my writing, and not begrudging the time necessary, I much appreciate.

I must also thank Elinor, my deceased wife and the mother of my only child, who strengthened me as I struggled with New Detroit and Common Council in Detroit as well as standing beside me and even serving with me as a police officer in New York City.

I thank my daughter, Betty, for her love and strong belief in me. She is the light of my life.

So much thanks goes to Dr. Diane Holloway, my co-author. Without her tremendous help and expertise, this book would never have been.

My special thanks go to Bob Cheney for his brilliant work in proofreading and reviewing the book before publication.

Also thanks to all the people and police officers I have met and worked with during my career, both the good and the bad. One can learn from both.

Preface

Life is certainly interesting. As we travel our road of life, we all realize there are forks in that road. That brings to mind Yogi Berra's comment: "When you come to a fork in the road, take it!"

Sometimes we decide to take one road. Sometimes others make the decision for us. I often wonder what my life would have been like if I hadn't taken certain forks in the road.

The first big fork in my life was taken by my mother and father. They brought me to America in 1923 when I was four years old. We settled in Brooklyn. I went to school and learned to speak proper English.

When I was 18, a knock on the door by a friend, Freddy Bogens Berger, brought me to the second fork. He said, "Let's study to become police officers." I agreed and then I passed the exam but Freddy didn't.

I became a police officer in the New York City Police Department (NYPD) at age 21. I stayed on that road and never wavered till I reached the top, but there was a detour.

After two years as a cop, a big fork in the road loomed with World War II. The road to war was a decision made by others. But I did choose to enlist as an aviation cadet in the U.S. Army Air Corps. I became a lieutenant bombardier, and then an instructor (then in B-29s). Remember the Enola Gay? That B-29 plane dropped the bomb on Hiroshima. I often wonder what if the Enola Gay had failed or if the war had not ended after August 6th. I was lead bombardier for our group. Would I have had to drop the atom bomb? I'm glad I didn't have to face that road.

We defeated Germany—our enemy then. I often wonder what if my mother and father had remained in Germany. Things would have been quite different for me. I remember the Olympics in 1936. They were held in Berlin, Germany, and Hitler was there. I was 17 then. What would I have been doing then? Probably I would have been forced into the Hitler Youth (like our new Pope Benedict), marching and shouting "Heil Hitler". Then I probably would have been a soldier in the German Army, goose-stepping in parades. Or maybe I would have been an S.S. officer—Achtung! Or Hitler's bodyguard—or worse!

But thankfully, after the war I went back to policing in 1946. I studied and went up in the ranks. I finally started college at age 35. After 12 years, I achieved a bachelors degree, then a master's, and did considerable work on my doctorate—all but my dissertation.

I retired from the NYPD in 1966. I became a professor at John Jay College in New York. But then another fork in the road appeared. One sign pointed to college professor. The other sign pointed to Detroit. I chose Detroit and became their Police Commissioner in 1968. I saw it both as a challenge and an opportunity.

Then after serving as Police Commissioner, another fork in the road led me to become the Sheriff of Oakland County in Michigan for 12 years.

I ended all this in 1985 but still keep abreast of the law enforcement (policing) field as a concerned citizen. After a lifetime in law enforcement, I've seen and learned a lot and formed many opinions about policing and about the decline of Detroit, a city which I came to love.

I have kept file cabinets full of information, letters, reports, news articles, and documents which scream to be shared with the public. So it is not my memory as much as my files that enable me to report so accurately on the life and times of Detroit after 1967.

At my age of 85, I do have definite opinions and I am not afraid to state them and never have been. I will present the truth as I know and feel it for the benefit of police professionalism and my fellow citizens of Detroit and of America.

My co-author, former psychologist Dr. Diane Holloway, will present information on the many destructive forces at work in the City of Detroit from WWI to the present time.

This book is intended to help Detroiters, people across the country, city planners, police executives, and especially those who want to avoid another Detroit.

The world is a dangerous and fascinating place. To plan perpetually for safety is as ridiculous as dodging lightning in a thunderstorm. We have, in fact, only one real concern in life: to live, live dangerously since we must, but at any rate to use all the time that fate allows us.

Foreword

"Johannes Spreen has extraordinary credentials and a range of knowledge that will achieve great results."

Dr. Isaiah "Ike" McKinnon, Former Detroit Chief of Police, and Professor, University of Detroit, Mercy.

"It's almost incredible the task you faced coming to Detroit as Police Commissioner exactly one year after the disaster which this little book describes. The fact that a year later you had achieved such major breakthroughs in building a bridge between the police and Detroit citizens, and healing many of the wounds within the Department, makes your tenure as Detroit's Police Commissioner one of the most significant in the city's history. We remember you with gratitude."

Rev. Dr. Hubert Locke, author of *The Detroit Riot of 1967*.

"I was accorded the priceless gift of serving with Commissioner Spreen as a New York City Police Department officer, sergeant, lieutenant and captain. As we studied together for higher rank, I was most impressed with his ability to speak and write in a manner that produced understanding and other beneficial results. These attributes are certain to bring forth a book which, in the light of Commissioner Spreen's broad experiences, will enrich the lives of readers who are part of, or in support of, the field of criminal justice."

William J. McCullough, Colonel, U.S. Army; President, Loose-leaf Law Publications; and author of *Minuteman/Activist* and *Hold Your Audience*.

"Johannes Spreen was a police officer extraordinary; a man who helped restructure and develop New York City Police Academy training leading to a college program, a West Point for police officers—now John Jay College for Criminal Justice. Johannes Spreen is a man of enthusiasm, indeed a prophet; always ahead of his time and a friend for over 60 years."

Rudolph P. Blaum, Retired Captain, New York City Police Department, served in the operation and development of the New York Police Service College Program, now John Jay College. He is Former President of the American Education Association in Center Moriches, New York.

"I felt an obligation to tell you that I think you performed an outstanding service for the community of Detroit. So many times people in public service seem to get nothing but abuse. To me you gave every indication of dedication to your profession.

The causes of crime are pride, greed, envy and lust. To eradicate these is more in line with my work than yours and if there is greater love of God among our people then crime will lessen. Once a man looks upon his fellow man as a person created by God and knows he must live that way then he will treat his neighbor as one of noble birth regardless of the color of his skin or the size of his bankroll. Poverty of this world's goods may be one thing which helps a person to find riches in crime but I do know for certain that poverty of the love of God causes crime."

Father William Breandan of St. Dominic's Church, Detroit.

"I want to take this opportunity to thank you very sincerely for the help you have given me and our own Police Chief while you were in office in Detroit. The scooter patrol innovation that you instituted in the 12th precinct worked effectively for you, and based upon your recommendations, we here in Flint utilized it to a great advantage."

Mayor Donald R. Cronin of Flint, Michigan.

"We have always felt here at the Greater Detroit Chamber of Commerce, that you were the man to guide us out of the wilderness of law and order problems. Our committees and the members of the staff have enjoyed greatly their association with you. We have admired your work and hope the new innovations you introduced and ideas you developed will continue to contribute effectively to the situation here in Detroit."

Dwight Havens, President of the Greater Detroit Chamber of Commerce.

1

The Great Riot: Detroit July 23, 1967

o o o o o o o o o o o o o o o o o o o o o o o o o o o o o o o o o o o

"In the violent summer of 1967, Detroit became the scene of the bloodiest uprising in a half century, and the costliest in terms of property damage in U.S. history. At the week's end, there were 41 known dead (actually 43), 347 injured, and 3,800 arrested. Some 5,000 people were homeless (the vast majority Negro), while 1,300 buildings had been reduced to mounds of ashes and bricks, and 2,700 businesses sacked. Damage estimates reached $50 million." B. J. Widick in *Detroit: City of Race and Class Riots.*

The Great Riot: Detroit July 23, 1967

On June 20, 1968, on a boat on the Detroit River, I shook hands with Detroit's Mayor, Jerome P. Cavanagh. The next day, the mayor announced me as the new police commissioner. After setting up a residence in the Park Shelton Hotel, I finished a vacation at the New York Police Recreation Center in the Catskills. On July 22, one day before the anniversary of the Riot of 1967, I was sworn in as Detroit's Police Commissioner at police headquarters.

The Detroit Riot of 1967, which began on July 23, was the most destructive of the urban riots of the 1960s. It has had important consequences for the city of Detroit, in fact, for the entire state of Michigan, which are still ongoing. It has been described by some writers as the greatest tragedy of all the long succession of Negro ghetto outbursts.

Because 1967 witnessed a total of 164 eruptions in 128 cities across the United States, much recent scholarship has suggested that it was precisely this sort of urban upheaval that sounded the death knell for America's inner cities.

Sidney Fine, in his thoroughly researched book *Violence in the Model City*, pointed out that the tragedy was not just the deaths, the injuries, and the looted and burned property which constituted major tangible losses for the city of Detroit and its inhabitants. The city also suffered an intangible loss, the death of its notable reputation as a model city in the area of race relations.

Much was written about Detroit *after* the riots by reporters, professors, historians and sociologists with very interesting theories on what went wrong. Someone needs to tell the story from the law enforcement perspective because it hasn't been told correctly yet. I can tell that story.

Yes, I went there, worked hard, and did a lot, and I will describe some of those things in this book. I stayed in Michigan after leaving office and did not go back to New York. I was very concerned about Detroit.

Who killed it? I feel we all may be responsible: police, political leaders, and people. Me first, because I did not fight to keep my position even though I knew the Detroit Police Department was improving. But you will hear about that later.

Details of the Riot

Many people learned about the riot as they tuned in to see the Detroit Tigers play the New York Yankees the evening of July 23, 1967. I couldn't miss it—that's my team! Willie Horton and Earl Wilson were black Detroit Tiger players, but generally black baseball players were not altogether welcome in those years. Little did I know then that I would participate in a game with Willie Horton not that far in the future.

As the game progressed, black clouds of smoke and fire appeared on the horizon. The Tigers split a double header with the Yankees. Buildings and homes began burning that night over a 25 square mile area. Baseball concession stands closed early. Airlines cancelled flights. The Mayor issued a curfew.

I woke up on the morning of July 24, 1967, to find every television station reporting on a riot that was developing in Detroit. The morning newspapers didn't have the story yet but the evening newspapers did. Over the next four days the horror of death and destruction in one of our major American cities dominated everyone's attention.

The news reporters said that a crowd became agitated by a police raid and began to attack policemen who were hauling in those arrested. As police retreated under the attack, more were called in and soon a full-blown riot was occurring.

History professor Heather Ann Thompson at the University of North Carolina, in *Whose Detroit*, wrote about what triggered the riot.

> In the wee hours of July 23, 1967, Detroit police officers engaged in a routine raid on a "blind pig" in the city, where a party was taking place to celebrate the return of a black veteran from Viet Nam. But when these officers arrested 82 people, they touched a nerve in the black community. In the one hour that it took to make its arrests, the DPD attracted the attention of more than 200 local residents (Thompson, 46).

I should explain that a "blind pig" is where alcohol is sold without a liquor license by people greedy for profit who just turn a blind eye to illegalities. These routine "blind pig" raids for liquor violations were familiar operations in New York and other places.

Later I came to know more of the details of how the riot developed. On Twelfth Street, an after hours club run by a group called "United Community League for Civic Action" was selling alcohol without a license and sold to minors as well. A tip led a sergeant to the site on Sunday morning and officers were surprised to find over 80 people there. During the next hour, squad cars and a paddy wagon ferried the arrested to the police station but not fast enough, as a crowd began to gather.

The first day of the rebellion, Hubert Locke, a black administrative assistant to Detroit's police commissioner, called together several of the city's responsible black leaders. In pairs, they spread across the Tenth Precinct to plead with the crowds to disperse. One pair was Deputy School Superintendent Arthur Johnson and U.S. Representative John Conyers, Jr., the latter being quite popular in his district.

Authorities allowed Conyers to stand on a car with a bullhorn to try to get the crowd to disperse. He was the wrong man. He shouted such things as, "We're with you but please, this is not the way to do things. Please go back to your homes."

The crowd chanted such things as "No, no, no! Don't want to hear it! Uncle Tom!" One man in the crowd hollered, "Why are you defending the cops and the establishment? You're just as bad as they are!" Rocks and bottles flew toward the car, one of them hitting a policeman nearby. The crowd became uglier and Johnson urged Conyers, "Let's get out of here."

As Conyers climbed down from the hood of the car, he remarked to a reporter in disgust, "You try to talk to those people and they'll knock you into the middle of next year" (Blonston, 1967).

The Mayor requested Michigan State Troopers by 2:00 p.m. the first afternoon. Some 360 State Police Troopers arrived in the late afternoon and the National Guard committed to send troops. The Mayor issued a proclamation for a curfew from 9:00 p.m. to 5:50 a.m. Bars and theaters were ordered to be closed across the city.

By July 25th, 14 had been killed, damage was estimated at $150 million, 731 fires had broken out, over 300 were injured, 1,663 people had been arrested, and snipers, looters, pillagers, fires and destruction continued.

In light of these casualties, President Lyndon Johnson ordered 4,700 Army paratroopers into Detroit riot areas Monday night as mostly black but some white snipers launched an offensive that stretched from the West Side to Grosse Pointe borders.

The President ordered Defense Secretary Robert McNamara to take all appropriate steps to disperse all persons engaged in acts of violence and to restore law and order.

Johnson's personal emissary, Cyrus Vance, immediately ordered 1,800 federal troops to aid Michigan National Guardsmen and State and Detroit police, who were running dangerously short of ammunition in gun battles with entrenched snipers.

The nation watched these events unfold on television and read newspapers in stunned disbelief for four days. Newsmen had to run the gauntlet of snipers and police battles and some were injured.

Pressure built up in Congress on the fourth day for a bipartisan Senate-House investigation of the riot. The President stayed in close contact with Cyrus Vance.

The press reported that Mr. Johnson slept only five hours and was awakened three times with riot reports.

Michigan Governor George Romney reemployed his original state of emergency on the fifth day and ordered a curfew to keep "spectators, gawkers and amateur photographers" from impeding the usual flow of traffic and efforts to clean and restore public facilities in the west side riot area.

The Algiers Motel Incident

Then came the Algiers Motel incident, made famous by Pulitzer Prize winner John Hersey. Hersey wrote that policemen killed three young black men and beat up several other people at a Detroit motel.

On Wednesday, July 26, 1968, just after midnight, an entry in the police log was made at 2:21 a.m. It read: 8301 Woodward (Algiers Motel) "check for dead person".

The Algiers Motel was frequented by prostitutes and narcotics dealers. Two days earlier, the police had received tips that quantities of loot taken in the early hours of the riot (on July 23) were being sold at the motel (Locke, 46).

The initial police report in these deaths was that some persons had been killed at the Algiers Motel on Woodward Avenue (Widick, 183).

According to Hubert Locke, during the week following the riot at least five independent investigations of the Algiers Motel incident were underway. None, however, was as extensive as that of the police department itself. When its investigation was completed, the department presented its findings to William Cahalan, Wayne County prosecutor, who issued first degree murder warrants against three Detroit police officers.

Warrants were issued for only two of the three deaths—there was a possibility that one of the three deaths had occurred prior to the arrival of the police:

"For those poised for charges of police brutality, the Algiers incident became a horribly valid *cause celebre*. For the rest of the city, including many career officers then in the police department, it was a disgusting moment in a tragic week" (Locke, 46).

The Inner City Voice, whose masthead reads, "Detroit's Black Community Newspaper" and "the Voice of the Revolution", reported on the incident using the comment, "...such as the outrageous acquittal of police officers who were charged with murdering black teenagers at the Algiers Motel during the 1967 uprising" (Thompson, 83).

As a matter of fact, the day after I was sworn in, the first thing I noticed on my desk was a copy of John Hersey's book, *The Algiers Motel Incident*. Of course, I read it later but I had so many other things to do that I couldn't read it right then, and it was in the hands of the court at that time. The trial concluded in December, 1968, after I had become police commissioner.

President Johnson made a radio-television address to the nation the fifth evening on the subject of civil disorders. United Auto Workers President Walter Reuther pledged the help of 600,000 Detroit labor union workers in removing the scars torn in Detroit by four days of rioting.

Meanwhile, Lt. Gen. John Throckmorton, in command of federal troops in Detroit, said that he hoped to complete the job in the very near future and phase out the military.

On the sixth day, Governor Romney demanded full integration of metropolitan schools and open housing to prevent new riots in Detroit "or something even worse".

I would like to say that on the seventh day, everyone rested. But that was, of course, impossible.

Immediate Reactions to the Riot

Senator Robert Kennedy said that the nation's welfare system had broken down and called for a private enterprise attack on ghetto housing. He said that wherever violence and mob action break out, it must be stopped forthwith.

I believe that Kennedy was right. The mob action needed to be stopped forthwith.

The Detroit Police could have called back their Tactical Mobile Unit that had gone off duty. That would have brought a quicker response at the very outset of the riot. If they had quickly arrested the original few agitators before it festered, things might have been quite different for the last 35 years. Instead, they followed rules forbidding males and females to be transported in the same patrol wagon, thus extending the time to take in the arrestees as they awaited more vehicles.

Having served as police lieutenant in the well-known Bedford-Stuyvesant district of Brooklyn, and later as captain of the Brooklyn morals squad for over three years, I led many such raids with my officers.

Detroit's police made an unfortunate mistake in allowing some of the participants and hangers-on to remain in the area on that fateful Sunday morning. From the police perspective, that was not good police tactics.

In New York City, we quickly removed participants from raided "after hours" joints to the police station for booking and incarceration. Yes, it was a technical violation of rules and regulations forbidding males and females to be placed in the same patrol wagon. But that practice gave no stage for malcontents on the streets. No time or opportunity for them to preen, prance or mouth off!

However, the Detroit police stuck to the rules which allowed more time for the crowd to gather. The crowd began to taunt the police and jive with friends arrested, who were awaiting a paddy car ride. Suddenly, as a vehicle pulled away, a bottle smashed a squad-car window.

Police Commissioner Girardin had ordered police not to use guns. Soon looters knew they would not be shot at and took advantage of the situation. Rocks, bottles, looting, arsonists, Molotov cocktails, snipers, and hoodlums attacked police and firemen trying to restore order.

Police and firemen were under heavy fire from snipers. The Fire Chief believed that arsonists telephoned some bogus reports of fires to lure his men into gun ambushes. Even black policemen were shot, including the mother of religious writer Stephanie Mitchem, who was one of the few black female Detroit cops at the time.

Mayor Cavanagh looked at the city from a rooftop toward the end of the riot and said it looked like Berlin in 1945.

Absenteeism at auto plants was so high that it nearly stopped production, but the tension among workers and supervisors did not erupt into violence. After surveying the Detroit rubble, Henry Ford II, chairman of Ford Motor Company, said, "It is my feeling that this country may turn out to be the laughing stock of the world because of situations such as we've had in Detroit. I don't think there is much point in trying to sell the world on emulating our system and way of life if we can't even put our own house in order" *(Automotive News)*.

President Johnson decided not to come to Detroit the first week in August 1967 to address the National Association of Counties after the riot. Earlier both Mayor Jerome Cavanagh and Gov. George Romney predicted that Detroit would be safe for convention delegates. By July 28, only a few cancellations were made by more than 3,000 delegates for the convention.

A reporter for the *Detroit Free Press*, Gary Blonston, wrote an article called "How Detroit's Militants Are Changing" on October 1, 1967. He spent several weeks talking to black and white leaders to prepare his story as Detroit groped toward a new existence. Some excerpts from his article show the changes wrought by the riot.

The Negro in Detroit is finding a new voice.

He is emerging from ghetto facelessness and into the forums of white decision making, product of a sudden, profound, riot-wrought change in the pat-
tern of city race relations...

For, as militant Detroit Negro leader Rev. Albert G. Cleage puts it: "Black
militants in every city in the nation are watching Detroit."...But at levels of
power and decision, determined Negroes—especially the militants—have
found voice and influence in Detroit that they have never known before
within the cautious councils of local white leadership.

The New Detroit Committee, charged with coordinating renovation and
social development of riot areas, already has outdone city hall in its willingness
to hear the wishes of Negro organizations. Committee chairman Joseph L.
Hudson, Jr. has asked at least one militant Negro leader to suggest people
from his ranks for New Detroit Committee staff work.

The Greater Detroit Board of Commerce and a number of other Michigan
business organizations, responding to requests from NAACP head Robert
Tindal, have begun a search for 10,000 jobs to accommodate Inner City
unemployed....

Rev. Allen, Detroit Council of Organizations chairman, considers Rev.
Cleage's Citywide Citizens Actions Committee methods and some of its aims
irresponsible, and he says, "Somewhere down the line, we're going to have to
say: Do we want to work with people who try to frighten the power structure
into doing things or do we want to negotiate? There are two things I can't be
with Rev. Cleage on—separation of communities, all white and all black, and
guns, talk of killing, blood running in the streets and the destruction of property."

Rev. Cleage views the Detroit Council of Organizations as a creature of the
white establishment, the United Auto Workers and City Hall, and he says:
"The Reuther men are immobilized by their own past position...It would be
tremendous if the newspapers would not take what I say out of context and
make me sound dangerous, but they could destroy me even faster if they made
me sound like an Uncle Tom."

After the 1967 riot, black and white support for Mayor Cavanagh plunged.
Gun sales rose 90% from 1966 as whites bought weapons to protect themselves.
Rumors that blacks intended to be violent to whites became particularly strong in
the days after the murder of Martin Luther King in April 1968. Conot and Locke
wrote that they were so strong, the Mayor established a rumor control center.

The Police Perspective Is the Untold Story about Detroit

One of the reasons I'm writing this book is that police were and are often the
point of first contact between whites and blacks in Detroit. Rumors tend to run
rampant, and I have been unsatisfied with the lack of attention to the police per-

spective in all the books I've read about the troubles in Detroit. Rev. Dr. Hubert Locke has come the nearest to presenting that perspective, but it has not been adequately covered.

I felt it was important to include some background about what law enforcement agencies had to contend with prior to and immediately after the 1967 riot. So many people have written about Detroit but they have neglected the criminal element and emphasized the revolutionary forces among the blacks rising up against the whites. A good example of this is historian Thomas Sugrue who spoke with the *Detroit Free Press* in 1998. He talked about the conditions that created present-day Detroit. But he did not emphasize conflicts between police and citizens. He told the media that Detroit's woes began in the 1950s with deindustrialization, the flight of jobs away from the city, racial discrimination in labor markets, and then residential segregation into two metropolitan areas: one black and one white. He said it wasn't the riot that led to disinvestment from the city of Detroit—disinvestment had been going on for years. He believed that the solution requires Detroiters to deal with the reality of economic and residential division.

The story of who and what killed Detroit is not complete without the law enforcement perspective. That is a story which I can tell because I was police commissioner during those hard times immediately after the riot and was privy to what actually happened.

2

Where Did All That Rage Come From?

○ ○
"It looked as if a night of dark intent
Was coming, and not only a night, an age.
Someone had better be prepared for rage.
There would be more than ocean-water broken
Before God's last *Put out the light* was spoken."

—*Robert Frost*

Where Did All That Rage Come From?

Detroit is unique. It has possibly the most unusual combination of elements of any American city. I want to show how these unusual elements created an atmosphere of hatred and race issues in Detroit since the Civil War.

An excellent summary of Detroit's history can be found on the internet published by *The Detroit News*. The first riot was a race riot. It occurred during the Civil War when a black man was accused of attacking a child. He was pardoned after a review of the evidence. However, his trial incited an uprising which ended up in widespread arson and attacks on blacks in general.

The small force of 25 white men authorized to maintain order by the police commission was poorly organized, ill-trained and unable to cope with the race riot. A city alderman, John J. Bagley, appealed to the State Legislature, which eventually passed the Metropolitan Police Act, founding the present police department in 1865.

A city charter written during World War I dictated the present organization with an appointed civilian commissioner overseeing a department headed by a professional chief, the superintendent of police.

The black population of Detroit had in a little over a decade increased from some 10,000 to 75,000 or more. Blacks fled the unemployment of the South to the jobs available in the mechanized industries of Detroit. This had brought about an actual physical pressure in their housing conditions.

The Ku Klux Klan was keeping itself busy in Detroit in the early twenties as whites tried to make things difficult for the blacks. There was a membership of only 300 in 1921 but by 1923, the membership had swelled to 3,000. Blacks were looking for help from every possible direction to offset their persecution. The newly formed NAACP branch had their work cut out for them.

James Weldon Johnson, national secretary of the NAACP in the 1920s, wrote about an important case of racial discrimination in Detroit housing in his autobiography, *Along This Way*.

Dr. Ossian Sweet, a black physician, had bought a house in a modest white neighborhood of mechanics, clerks, and small tradesmen. But he hesitated for several months about moving in because of the assaults that had been made on the homes bought by other blacks in white neighborhoods. Finally, in September 1925, he asked for police protection and with his wife moved in. With his household goods, he took in guns and a supply of ammunition.

There also went in with Dr. Sweet his two brothers and some of his men friends, making eleven in the house. The police guarded the house that night and the next day. Later in the afternoon a crowd began gathering, and the police guard was increased; but the police did not disperse the crowd. As darkness came on, the street became jammed with people and others constantly arriving.

Later, stones began to hit the house. There was no interference from the police. A rifle cracked, and Leon Breiner, a white man in the crowd, fell dead. All of the inmates of the house, with the exception of the doctor's wife, were taken to jail and held without bail.

The NAACP branch there called the national office for counsel and assistance. Walter White was dispatched immediately to Detroit and there he took the first steps to allay passions and arrange for legal defense. The NAACP engaged a staff of six lawyers, headed by Clarence Darrow and Arthur Garfield Hays. The eleven defendants were indicted for first-degree murder.

The issue was segregation by mob violence and the simple question was: Does the common axiom of Anglo-Saxon law, that a man's house is his castle, apply to a black American citizen?

The NAACP undertook to raise money for the defense of the case. Within four months, $75,000 was raised.

The trial of the eleven resulted in a disagreement. A second trial began a few months later and each defendant demanded to be tried separately. The state elected to proceed first against Henry Sweet, the doctor's youngest brother, who admitted that he had fired the shot from the house.

On the last day when Mr. Darrow addressed the jury, the courtroom was so jammed that not another person could have been squeezed in. Darrow talked for nearly seven hours. The veteran criminal lawyer, psychologist, philosopher, human, the apostle of liberty, brought every bit of skill and knowledge he possessed into play that day.

The jury brought in a verdict of "Not guilty". That was an exception to the usual judgment of guilty. It served only to increase the ire of whites and the Ku Klux Klan operated in Detroit with little control.

Lynchings, tortures and burnings of blacks continued in Detroit as they did in the South. Mobs assumed the role of the government in capturing blacks merely on hearsay and condemning them to suffering and death as they carried out their executions.

Stalin Sent Communism to Detroit

In 1922, Stalin approved of spending $300,000 to spread communist propaganda among blacks. In 1925, 12 blacks were selected to be trained in Russia. Delighted to find receptive ears among black workers, in 1928, Stalin sent Hungarian communist leader Joseph Pogany (alias John Pepper, John Schwartz, John Swift, etc.) to America and thus divide the Americans into blacks against whites. Pogany was to stir blacks up with the desire to create their own republic within America.

This was not an entirely new idea. Many blacks in the South had been lured by pamphlets to Oklahoma after the Civil War. The pamphlets dangled the promise of setting it up as the first completely black state. Eventually 27 black towns grew to encompass 10 percent of the Indian Territory's population by the time Oklahoma joined the union in 1907.

Stalin's goal, of course, was to set blacks and whites against each other, increase the number of communists, and disrupt the America government. In 1928, Pogany (using the name of John Pepper) distributed a pamphlet to blacks for the Communist Party of the United States of America (CPUSA) called *American Negro Problems: A Program of Racial Strife for the United States.*

The pamphlet urged blacks to use violence if necessary in their struggle for national self-determination. It suggested propaganda to smear the emerging black middle class with terms such as "Uncle Toms" and agents of the "white capitalist". Its proposal to establish a black separate government within the U.S. stated:

> Self-determination means the right to establish their own state, to erect their own government, if they choose to do so...
> The Negro Communists should emphasize in their propaganda the establishment of a Negro Soviet Republic.

By 1928, Henry Ford's assembly line and fame in car production put Detroit on the world map. Josef Stalin was trying to undermine this country, and he was no dummy. Pogany had found that blacks and other workers felt oppressed by capitalist bosses. But he also told of the superior technology in the automotive industry.

So Stalin sent a group of Russians to meet with Ford in Detroit. Stalin wanted Ford's help to establish a Russian car manufacturing company to make the Model A.

A contract was signed between Edsel Ford and the Russians to build two plants, one in Novgorod and the other in Moscow. Russians were sent to Detroit to learn the automotive industry and Americans were sent to Russia to build the plants and assemble some 70,000 cars and trucks.

Even before the beginning of this strong communist influence in Detroit, American blacks as well as whites had a great attraction to the promises of the communist party for the lowly working man, oppressed by big business capital-ists.

In 1930, only 7.7% of Detroit's population was black. The crime rate was fairly low for a large city with 70 homicides and 1629 robberies.

Despite the Great Depression, Mexican painter Diego Rivera, a life-long Marxist, was invited by Henry Ford to paint the famous murals on the walls of the Detroit Institute of Art. Rivera's work depicted industrial life in the United States and concentrated on the car plant workers of Detroit. From April 1932 to March 1933 Diego painted, accompanied by his wife, Frida Kahlo. He visited workers' homes, neighborhoods, salt mines, railroad cars, chemical plants, blast furnaces and the Ford Rouge plant to paint his murals. He found racial diversity and depicted the "yellow, red, black and white" races in his paintings. He sought to glorify the dignity of workers as well as industry and technology (Baulch & Zacharias, *The Detroit News*).

His politics and therefore his art were criticized in later years but Edsel Ford, Henry's son, always defended the art works. Rivera's paintings provided the first inspiration for Franklin Roosevelt's Works Projects Administration (WPA) pro-gram in later years.

The construction of "Soviet Detroit" in Novgorod and Moscow by Ford's engineers and workers became bogged down by Russian ineptitude, unmotivated workers, and awful living conditions for the Americans transferred there. By 1932, Stalin had ordered the Russians to break the contracts and place orders for cars in Europe and Russia, rather than America.

However, the communist influence lingered in the Detroit automotive plants, and especially in the labor unions. Coleman Young was influenced early by com-munism. He is one of many who participated in the decline of Detroit by being influenced by the negative forces at work in this city from the 1930s. He later became Detroit's first black mayor, after I finished my post as police commis-sioner. But in those early days, Young was fired by Ford Motor Company for his union activities during the 1930s. UAW's Walter Reuther led the union to dis-miss those with communist connections or leanings, and Young was ejected. About ten years after he was fired by Ford for his disruptive union activities, he was in the Congress of Industrial Organizations (CIO) in Wayne County.

Perhaps it should be added that Reuther knew what he was talking about. He was let go by Detroit's Ford Company because of his union activities in 1933. He traveled with his brother to Russia where he worked in the Molotov Auto Works in Novgorod (called Gorky then) for two years in an *unheated* plant. After learn-ing about the working conditions there, he went on to China and Japan for a short time to see the working conditions there. When he returned in 1935, he became reinstated in Detroit union activities where he soon led the UAW, and became thoroughly anti-Soviet!

Another person in Walter Reuther's UAW was John Conyers, Sr., father of John and Nathan Conyers who both are still active in the car dealership business and politics in Detroit today. The elder Conyers led strikes for equal wages with whites in the 1930s and 1940s.

Detroit Was the Birthplace of Muslim Movements

Now let me describe a little about the Nation of Islam (NOI), one of the many truly unusual organizations that were to create problems for law enforcement during my term and after.

The Nation of Islam was organized about 1933 by W. D. Fard in Detroit. After he left, it was directed by Elijah Poole, also known as (aka) Elijah Muhammad, until his death in 1975. Then it was then taken over by Louis Farrakhan.

Obviously Detroit spawned many odd movements and odd characters due to being a large industrial city with eclectic political and racial factions. Perhaps one of the strangest characters was W. D. Fard who claimed to be from Mecca or Arabia, who may have been from California, and arrived in 1930 as a door to door silk clothing salesman. Some say he was Wallace Dodd Ford who served time in San Quentin for drug dealing.

Wallace Fard also claimed to be the reincarnation of a black man named Timothy Drew, aka Noble Drew Ali. Drew had converted to Islam during a visit to Saudi Arabia and taught that blacks were "Moors" who were superior to whites. He claimed that Jesus was such a Moor. When Drew disappeared after being arrested for murder, Wallace Fard showed up in Detroit as if to take his place.

As Fard sold his silks, clothes and artifacts, he told stories to black customers of their national origins and stressed the supremacy of blacks over whites. He could also perform magic tricks. He included symbolic meanings in his stories and his tricks. This attractive olive-skinned man who spoke many languages came to the attention of Elijah Poole.

Elijah had started a family and moved from Georgia to Detroit in search of work. He found it and worked six years in the Chevrolet auto plant. He joined the Universal Negro Improvement Association (UNIA) in Detroit. The UNIA is another organization that was created to instill black pride but wound up causing some amount of conflict between blacks and whites. I could say a lot about it but I'll just skim the surface. It had been formed by Jamaican Marcus Garvey during WWI. A branch started in Detroit about 1919.

Poole met Fard in 1930. Fard helped Poole change his name to Elijah Muhammad, shedding his slavery name of Poole and taking a Muslim name. Elijah was the first to call Fard "Allah". For this Elijah was appointed as the Chief Minister of Islam in the NOI order.

To be honest, Fard developed a following by those attracted to the hatred of whites, and this number was growing among the blacks in Detroit. In 1931, he rented a hall and the first Temple of Islam was launched. By 1933, he had 8,000 followers in the Detroit area. He taught that the writings of the white race were symbolic and only he could interpret them properly. He began as a teacher but became known as a prophet, but many claim he was just a con man.

C. Eric Lincoln wrote about Fard in 1961 before I came to Detroit. Lincoln described how in September 1931, the FBI, then called the Bureau of Investigation under Hoover, investigated Fard, but could not charge him with anything. Lincoln wrote that the Detroit Police arrested him on 11/23/32 when Fard was leaving his room in a hotel at 1 West Jefferson Avenue. He was a suspect when one of his own followers was murdered. This arrest took place in the same year that Diego Rivera was painting the murals for Henry and Edsel Ford.

The *Detroit Free Press* issued a story about Fard's arrest. Lincoln stated that the news story described Fard as not resisting arrest, smiling, and telling officers at police headquarters that he was the "supreme being on earth" and the "supreme ruler of the universe" which he also told the judge at his arraignment.

With these bizarre comments, he was placed in the Psychiatric Unit of a hospital in Detroit. Was he conning again to avoid going to jail or was he really crazy? Two weeks later, two Detroit police officers (Oscar Berry and Charles Snyder) were assigned to pick him up upon his release from psychiatric observation. Since he was not given a prison sentence, they put him on a train to Chicago and told him never to return.

Like a bad penny, he turned up again in Detroit, wrote Lincoln. He was arrested at Detroit's Traymore Hotel on 5/25/33. He was held for a while pending investigation of why he returned. He was soon released and fled to Chicago again, where he was arrested in 9/26/33.

By 1934 he disappeared, perhaps died or was murdered. I'd like to say that was the end of the NOI but it wasn't. Elijah (Poole) Muhammad carried on the Nation of Islam until his death in 1975 (Lincoln, 1961).

Now here is where some of these blacks ran into trouble with the law. They objected to the draft, claiming their ancestors were brought to America against their will and they shouldn't be drafted. A good example of this was when Elijah Muhammad (who wound up taking many different names such as Bogans and

Rassoull) was arrested on May 8, 1942 for failing to register for the draft. He was investigated by the FBI. The following FBI memo of 11/9/43 was obtained under the Freedom of Information Act. It was issued in regard to why Elijah refused to serve in World War II. Sorry about the blacked out portions of FBI memos.

> Allah Temple of Islam, et al
> Selective Service
>   (Two blacked out short paragraphs.)
>   Several years later in 1931 while walking down the street in Detroit, according to Bogans, he met "Allah." This person was known to him as Wallace D. Fard and "the living God." Allah has proved to be very much of a human being since he has an arrest record in the Identification Division of the FBI.
>   W. D. Fard taught Elijah that the negroes were Moslems as were all of the dark races and that by registering with the nation of Islam the colored people would be given their correct names from Mecca and their slave names would be taken from them. Members discard their slave names and use symbols such as "X" until they receive their names from Mecca. Fard also instructed that Moslems were not to participate in military matters since they are registered and are citizens of the nation of Islam. In 1934 Fard disappeared and none of his followers will admit having seen him since that time. In his absence Elijah Poole, now known as Gulan Bogans or Mohammed Rassoull, and his helpers have been carrying on the leadership of the group. Temples of Islam have been opened in Milwaukee, Chicago and Washington, D.C., in addition to the original temple in Detroit.
> (One blacked out short paragraph.)

While in prison for evading the draft, Muhammad taught classes on the doctrines of the Nation of Islam. He was released in 1946 and returned to Chicago.

Another follower who rose to leadership in the NOI was Malcolm Little. Although he wasn't in Detroit, the Nation of Islam began there and its presence was a powerful force among blacks in that town.

While in prison for hustling, drug dealing and pimping, Malcolm Little, aka Malcolm X, learned about the Nation of Islam and converted. He wrote to Elijah Muhammad. From Muhammad and the NOI propaganda, he "learned" that the white race was responsible for all the problems faced by nonwhites. He took the last name "X" signifying that he did not know his true identity since his ancestors had lost their original names when sold into slavery in America. When he was released from prison in 1952, Malcolm became a recruiter for the Nation of Islam.

As he rose in power, he strayed from Elijah Muhammad by teaching the *unity* of the races. Thus he became a threat to Muhammad and the beliefs of the NOI. He was assassinated on 2/12/65, perhaps by Muhammad's followers.

The Unions Created Black-White Friction

In 1940, only 9.2% of Detroit's population was black and there were 80 homicides and 1,887 robberies. With easy access to iron resources and good railroad transportation, Detroit was the perfect setting for the automotive industry. Henry Ford's generous wages, assembly line and management style kept union membership low until the outset of World War II. But the unions began to pick up steam during World War II.

The unions were damned if they did include blacks and damned if they didn't. They wanted both black and white members, but whites didn't want them to be part of the union, and certainly not part of its leadership. So the UAW made a show of including blacks, but black members knew they had little say in the union.

In 1941, the UAW faced a tough situation at Ford Motor Company. White workers had called a wildcat strike in response to the UAW's announced plan to include more blacks in their membership drive. The strike could have halted progress in automobile and war machine production. Black workers objected to the white pickets marching around the plant, threatening not to work if blacks were union members. Tension was high.

Paul Robeson, singer, actor, orator, athlete, communist-sympathizer and son of a former slave, came to Detroit. He worked tirelessly, singing, speaking and building one-to-one rapport at the plant picket line to dissolve animosities. Blacks and whites displayed wartime unity and returned to work, sparing the company and the country from a major productivity loss.

Robeson returned to Detroit other times, sometimes just to perform. When he was denied accommodations at the Statler Hilton, a picket line of blacks *and* whites surrounded the hotel.

During the war, the automobile industry produced military equipment and war machinery. Detroit was said to be transformed into an Arsenal of Democracy. Recruiters toured the south, convincing whites and blacks to head for Detroit war factories and high wages. Blacks and whites responded and the flood of workers and their families streamed into Detroit. Those recruiters are partly responsible for the creation of a city which had not sufficiently planned how to handle all the newcomers.

The influx strained housing, transportation, education and recreation facilities. Men and women, black and white, including a variety of other ethnic groups, worked at breakneck speed to provide American military forces with what they needed.

Stalin would later say that Germany had been "defeated by Detroit." Russia, as an ally of the U.S. during World War II, benefited from Detroit directly. Their Red Army tanks as well as American tanks were products of Detroit's technology and Stalin knew it.

But WWII years created severe problems as blacks rushed in to fill "white jobs". Whites would not permit housing integration. So often it is those who fear competition for their very own jobs and lifestyle who object most strongly to integration. Thus despite decent wages, blacks were forced to live in deteriorating houses, segregated from whites, often with no indoor plumbing.

A housing project named Sojourner Truth to accommodate blacks was opened in 1942. However, white picketers wanted the project for themselves and so set a cross on fire near the project. Crowds of whites with weapons prevented blacks from moving in. Blacks had signed leases, paid rent, and given up their shelters in anticipation of moving into the project. They had to be temporarily housed in other sites.

According to Doris Kearns Goodwin, the event was covered by the press across the world. Unfortunately, this included enemy countries like Germany and Japan. So Eleanor Roosevelt convinced President Franklin Roosevelt that the blacks must use the housing. Some months later they did move in to the project. The Detroit mayor ordered police and state troops to keep peace during the move.

Not only did whites object to living near blacks, they also objected to working with them. Early in June, 1943, 25,000 Packard plant workers stopped work in protest to the promotion of three blacks. The strikers shouted, "I'd rather see Hitler and Hirohito win than work beside a nigger on the assembly line."

Women workers tried unsuccessfully to get men to walk off the job to protest against black female workers using the white restrooms. "They think their fannies are as good as ours," screamed one woman.

The Ku Klux Klan with their white hoods and the Black Legion with black hoods and weapons became active by harassing minorities in this hateful Detroit atmosphere. The Black Legion was even more militant than the Ku Klux Klan in keeping foreigners, blacks and communists out of factories. Humphrey Bogart played in a 1937 movie called *Black Legion* about this destructive group which had its origins in Detroit.

The Detroit unions were in the news daily as their influence grew. In July, 1943, Eleanor Roosevelt met UAW leader Walter Reuther. She wrote her daughter that he was "the most interesting labor leader I've met". Doris Kearns Goodwin described their meeting in her book *No Ordinary Time* about the Roosevelts, saying that Reuther expressed views that excited Eleanor such as these.

> As long as the man behind the machine was viewed as "the worker," standing in a class apart from management, the illusion would persist that he had no ideas to contribute to the successful operation of the plant....
>
> But if labor could be seen as something more than skill and brawn hired by the hour, if the workers could be given a measure of responsibility for generating new ideas, then there was no limit to the productivity of the American economy (451).

The Race Riot of 1943

In 1943, there were 200,000 blacks in Detroit and racial tension grew to the point where blacks were deliberately bumping into whites on the streets, bumping them off the sidewalks or nudging them in elevators.

One night, two blacks, angered that they had been ejected from a park, began fighting police and others who tried to suppress them on Belle Isle, separated from the mainland by Belle Isle Bridge. By 10 p.m., more than 200 people had become involved in a free-for-all race riot.

Rumors flew that whites had thrown a black woman and her baby off the bridge, and that blacks had raped and murdered a white woman. Angry whites began to beat blacks as they got off street cars.

The violence escalated and six Detroit policemen were shot, another 75 people were injured, 20 cars belonging to blacks were burned and stores were looted. The 2,000 police officers and 150 state police troopers were overwhelmed. The 36 hours of rioting resulted in 34 deaths, 25 of whom were black. More than 1,800 were arrested, the vast majority of whom were black.

In so many of these racial confrontations, blacks didn't face white citizens as much as they faced the representatives of white citizens—white cops. Had more blacks been police officers, would it have been different? Many believe so and so do I.

I will add one more idea to consider about black-white conflicts from James Weldon Johnson's autobiography, *Along This Way*. The great James Weldon Johnson (1871-1938), a black man, became a celebrated educator, lawyer, diplomat, editor, novelist, poet and reformer. He wrote that the basis of much racial strife, often triggered by incidents involving black men and white women, stems from the white man's fear that black men are sexually superior. Johnson wrote:

> Through it all I discerned one clear and certain truth: in the core of the heart of the American race problem the sex factor is rooted; rooted so deeply that it is not always recognized when it shows at the surface.... It may be innate; I do not know. But I do know that it is strong and bitter; and that its strength and bitterness are magnified and intensified by the white man's perception, more or less, of the Negro complex of sexual superiority (76).

The Mayor and Governor asked President Roosevelt for help. Federal troops in armored cars and jeeps with automatic weapons drove down the main streets and cooled the fervor of the rioters, and mobs dispersed.

As an aside, it is my own feeling that the 1943 riot could have been contained if Detroit's police commanders had blocked off the Belle Isle Bridge, thereby containing the incident to Belle Isle and not allowing it to spread to the mainland and the streets of the city.

The city's white citizenry criticized their police force for its restraint. This was true even though they had killed 17 blacks. They said that Police Commissioner John Witherspoon should have issued shoot-to-kill orders. He defended his actions saying, "All of those killed would not have been hoodlums or murderers. Many would have been victims of mob psychology or innocent bystanders. If a shoot-to-kill policy was right, my judgment was wrong"(Baulch and Zacharias, *The Detroit News*).

The police chief was not only criticized by whites but by blacks. Thurgood Marshall, then with the NAACP, later to become Supreme Court Justice, said, "This weak-kneed policy of the police commissioner coupled with the anti-Negro attitude of many members of the force helped to make a riot inevitable" (Baulch and Zacharaias, *The Detroit News*).

Following the riot, the Mayor asked a black Detroit minister to help search for 200 qualified blacks to join the police force to increase trust in police by black leaders.

The surge of blacks into Detroit during the war brought another figure to the forefront of prominence, George Crockett, Jr. I would interact with him on the worst day of my administration, over the murder at the New Bethel church and his role in releasing the suspects arrested.

He had been the first black lawyer in the U.S. Department of Labor in the 1930s and then made a name for himself as head of the UAW's Fair Practices Committee where he tried to root out auto factory racism. Even though UAW leader Walter Reuther spoke out against racism, in 1946 Crockett questioned why so many of Reuther's supporters were racists. When Reuther emerged as president of the union, he replaced Crockett, whom he probably regarded as a thorn in his side.

Detroit's New Breed of Religious and Government Representatives

In the late 1940s, the charismatic Rev. Clarence LeVaughn Franklin (known as C. L. Franklin) moved to Detroit to found the New Bethel Baptist Church. It was moved from its original location to 8430 Linwood in 1961. Franklin had a very distinctive preaching style. It was so unusual that tapes and CDs of his sermons were made and have been used to train preachers. In the mid-1950s, he preached accompanied by a group of gospel singers including his daughter, Aretha Franklin, who went on to become a well-known singer.

Coleman Young was the U.S. Senate candidate for the communist-backed Progressive Party in 1948, which ran former Vice President Henry Wallace against Democrat Harry Truman and Republican Thomas Dewey. Young was removed from the C.I.O. union office supposedly because of his support for Wallace, who espoused communist doctrines. The appeal of communism was waning in many places across the country but not in Detroit.

After being ousted from the UAW by Reuther, George Crockett helped found Detroit's first integrated law firm. He went on to defend a black man accused of being a communist. Crockett and four other lawyers were sentenced to prison for four months for defending one of 11 people charged in the Smith Act trial in New York in 1949 and 1950. This was the anti-communist McCarthy era and being a communist sympathizer was deemed as bad as being a card carrying communist, plotting to overthrow the U.S. government.

Coleman Young and Rev. Charles Hill were called before the House Un-American Activities Committee (HUAAC) in 1952. Young was interrogated regarding his ties to the Communist Party. He accused the Committee of being "un-American" because they were not doing more for the voting rights of blacks living in the South. He said that if it was communism to defend the rights of workers, then he was a communist.

The account of his interrogation built him an outstanding reputation as a union and civil rights organizer. Crockett supported Young and Hill, and managed to keep them out of jail even though Young mocked the HUAAC (Crockett's obituary in the *Detroit Free Press*).

Coleman Young was apparently not a card-carrying member of the Communist Party of the USA (CPUSA) but one of his close associates, Detroit City

Councilwoman Erma Henderson, admitted being a member of the CPUSA youth group. Some said that Young shared a Detroit home with a black CPUSA leader, James Jackson, who led communist auto workers at Ford's Dearborn plant.

In post-war America, the desire to own a home and a car, the development of Detroit's freeway system in 1950, and low gas prices drove the automotive economy to new heights in Detroit. The big three giants in the car industry, Chrysler, Ford and General Motors, all developed in Detroit. High wages and the proliferation of unions, especially the United Automotive Workers (UAW), drove wages and benefits even higher.

By 1950, Detroit was the country's fifth largest city. The results of black migration from the South for unskilled jobs and high wages in the automotive industry swelled Detroit's black population to 16.4%. That year, there were 113 homicides and 2,320 robberies. In the mid-1950s, Detroit's population hit its highest point with just over 1.8 million and has declined ever since.

In 1953, Congregational minister Albert Cleage, Jr., and a group of followers left the United Church of Christ denomination to form the Central Congregation Church. He had grown up in Detroit, earned his B.A. from Wayne State University in 1942, and his Bachelor of Divinity from Oberlin Graduate School of Theology. He would become influential in 1967 when he developed a radical approach to Christianity intended to reverse black oppression. This man caused me and Detroit law enforcement officers no end of problems because he supported armed and militant groups.

Coleman Young headed the National Negro Labor Council from 1951 to 1956, an organization which was also said to be influenced and possibly backed by communists. But in the amazing revelation of Stalin's crimes against citizens in Khrushchev's famous "secret speech" of 1956, the CPUSA collapsed along with communist movements in many parts of the world.

Young then left the Labor Council and ran for office as a state representative for the Democratic Party in 1959.

John Conyers, Sr., who had worked for the UAW to bring equal wages for blacks and whites, was a founding figure of the Trade Union Leadership Council in 1957. This group campaigned for the ouster of Detroit Mayor Louis Miriani, because the mayor was openly hostile to blacks. (House of Representatives, November 30, 1995.)

Shortly before I went to Detroit, Miriani was defeated by Jerome Cavanagh for mayor and served on the City Council during my term as Commissioner. Miriani and I often wound up on opposite sides of issues, as you will hear later.

In 1957, the Detroit Branch of the NAACP issued a report on police brutality entitled: "Analysis of Police Brutality Complaints Reported to the Detroit Branch of the National Association for the Advancement of Colored People in the Period from January 1, 1956 to July 30, 1957." It brought about some internal changes within the police department. In fact, under the next police commissioner, Herbert Hart, on January 28, 1959, Detroit police rode in integrated patrol cars for the first time.

Blacks wanted to live near their work, only to find that whites refused to accept mixed neighborhoods. So they moved into downtown Detroit. That really precipitated white flight to the suburbs and I blame the real estate profession, housing authorities in Detroit and the Common Council for maintaining such extreme segregation in housing.

In addition, social scientists have often pointed out that an influx of unskilled blacks into a community of unskilled whites evokes extremely strong reactions because the whites fear that their very jobs and income might be in jeopardy. These paranoid reactions among white workers are as much to blame as anything else in the self-destruction of Detroit as it set whites against blacks.

In 1960, the population of Detroit was beginning to shrink. By this time, 29.2% of the city was black. In that year, there were 172 homicides and 3,988 robberies.

The Loss of Automotive Jobs

Heedless of small, well-built fuel-efficient foreign cars, Detroit's carmakers paid little attention to competition until it was too late. With careless disregard for quality redesign or fuel efficiency, new gas guzzlers with minor aesthetic changes in each year's new models spurred the industry on. Profit-oriented car companies must certainly share the blame for Detroit's demise. They began to outsource work to areas with lower wages to maintain their profits without concern for the many who had moved in to work for them. They moved some plants to suburbs and other areas, leaving the blacks in the center of the city, unemployed, surrounded by closed, vacant and burned out buildings as whites moved out. This was the Detroit that was ripe for riot.

Various splinter groups of socialist and communist persuasion were welcome among the working class of Detroit. Just as Walter Reuther and other Detroiters earlier visited Russia to observe communism first hand, so did some Detroiters and members of the Socialist Workers Party join the Fair Play for Cuba Committee and visit Cuba. Speaking of Cuba, I must describe a man whom I never met in Detroit, but I dealt with his presence.

The Emergence of Black Militants

Robert Williams, who would become a hero among black nationalists during my administration, had worked at the Ford Motor Plant in Detroit from 1942 to 1944, when he was drafted into the Army. Upon discharge, he moved to Monroe, North Carolina, and led a group of 40 armed blacks to oppose a parade of the Ku Klux Klan displaying the dead body of a black veteran. Not a shot was fired but Williams became convinced that armed self-defense of blacks was necessary.

He went to college, rejoined the military (Marines) and after an early discharge because of his agitation, returned to Monroe. He became a leader of the local NAACP branch. When he was accused of a kidnapping, he fled to Cuba. Robert Williams had supported the Cuban Revolution, and was welcomed by communists and Fidel Castro in 1961. In Cuba, he ran Radio Free Dixie.

While there, he wrote *Negroes with Guns* in 1962 about the need for blacks to arm themselves for defense from the Ku Klux Klan and the white police forces. Eventually he had a falling out with Cuban leaders and, still dodging arrest in the United States, went to China where he was welcomed by Mao's communists. He was there when he was named the first president of the Republic of New Africa (RNA). This militant group which originated in Detroit became the bane of my administration in the New Bethel Church shootout. I will describe them in more detail later.

Meanwhile, Coleman Young ran for the Detroit Common Council in 1960. In 1961, he won election as a delegate to the state constitutional convention. Jumping ahead, in 1964, he won a seat in the Michigan state senate, where he served as floor leader for the Democrats in 1966. Even though his communist leanings had been opposed by the UAW, he was now allowed to work for the state AFL-CIO union offices.

In 1962, Rev. Cleage (who would eventually form the Shrine of the Black Madonna) denounced the traditional black leadership. He claimed the "Uncle Toms" who cozied up to white bosses betrayed black Detroit. This set blacks against blacks and stirred further the pot of hatred in the city.

Rev. Cleage and Rev. C. L. Franklin were up to more than spreading the word of God. They held an organizational meeting of black power groups at New Bethel church in May 1963. The groups included the NAACP, Group for the Advancement of Leadership, UHURU (founded by Wayne State students), Detroit chapter of the Student Non-Violent Coordinating Committee, and the Revolutionary Action Movement (RAM).

Meanwhile Detroit attorney Milton Henry and his brothers were forming another black movement. Milton had been given a dishonorable discharge when he complained about segregation of black officers in the military. However, he was accepted at Yale Law School where he studied law and became an attorney. Milton and his brother Lawrence (a reporter) met with Malcolm X and introduced their younger brother Richard to Malcolm X. This would prove important to the eventual formation of a new and militant black nationalist group.

The Henry brothers formed a Detroit group called Group on Advanced Leadership (GOAL) and invited Malcolm X to speak. He delivered his famous "Message to the Grassroots" speech just before President John Kennedy's assassination in November, 1963. Some 700-800 people were there, mostly black workers. Malcolm X was cheered as he presented his revolutionary views: support for the Cuban revolution, the Chinese revolution, the colonial revolution, and opposition to the "rulers" in this country.

Next Rev. Franklin came up with a huge media event to increase the intensity of civil rights and black freedom in Detroit. Rev. Franklin invited Rev. Martin Luther King, Jr., to Detroit for a "Walk to Freedom" on June 23, 1964. Rev. Franklin, Rev. King, Walter Reuther and Mayor Cavanagh led the march, which was followed by the "I Have a Dream" speech (*I Have a Dream: Writings,* 1992).

In March 1965, the executive board of the CCEO (Citizens' Committee for Equal Opportunity) was concerned that the Detroit blacks might follow the lead of "less responsible" black leadership. There had been challenges to the established black organizations. There was heightened racial consciousness and group movements to increase racial pride.

Demands were made—sometimes unreasonable or unable to be met immediately. Unrest in the black community followed.

A black man who became my friend, Hubert Locke, was then attached to Police Commissioner Girardin's office under Mayor Cavanagh's administration. In 1965, he wondered whether the city would be able to move fast enough to allay the frustrations, the unrest and the fears of its Negro citizens.

Militant blacks called traditional black leaders "Uncle Toms". Even though benefits had occurred for the Civil Rights Movement and their leadership, militants claimed that they were out of touch with those blacks in the ghettos who were less fortunate. Lower class blacks resented the success of those in the black middle class who were concerned about the extremist blacks. Those extremists called successful blacks "Oreos", black on the outside, white on the inside. Blacks were at odds with each other.

There were voices who claimed the city administrators, the NAACP and the Detroit Urban League were too busy feathering their own nests to care about the voices from the slums. These voices felt no one really spoke for or understood their problems. Thus they were among those responsible for the "spontaneous protests" and other actions that sparked the 1967 riot.

In Locke's book, *The Detroit Riot of 1967,* he described the uncertainty of racial dilemmas in big cities. In an interesting analogy, he said it was irrelevant whether black men or white men made decisions because it was like arguing over who will be on the bridge or at the helm when the ship sinks.

His recognized that his analysis bore the seeds of cynicism and despair, but at least he realized that big cities in America were the most physically, socially and economically vulnerable structures in contemporary society.

Detroit Militants Required Law Enforcement Surveillance

Detroit was attracting increased FBI and police surveillance for black groups and radical organizations that advocated bearing arms.

After a May, 1965, open-housing rally supported by Michigan State University (MSU) students, 59 students were arrested by the nearby East Lansing Police Department and the MSU Department of Public Safety. FBI and police surveillance had been used to gain information about students who planned the rally to integrate housing. The magazine *Vietnam* in August 1995 wrote about those arrests. They called the police "Red Squads" when they used surveillance and other repressive activities to disrupt groups identified as planning to upset the status quo.

Perhaps the largest big city "Red Squad" was by my former employer, the New York City Police Department. The surveillance and undercover police sent to cover and disrupt radical and militant groups was under the Bureau of Special Services (BOSS) and operated during the 1960s and 1970s.

I was trying to move in a better direction, toward citizens rather than against them, which caused me to come up with the idea of putting police on motor scooters. It was so different that it attracted attention to the New York City Police Department in many ways including an article in *The New Yorker* in Appendix I.

Meanwhile, in Detroit on the political scene, the elder John Conyers' son, John Conyers, Jr., became a lawyer and was moving up in visibility and influence. He was elected to Congress in 1965, where he still serves. He became a frequent agitator on the Detroit scene complaining of police repression and brutality.

In 1966, George Crockett won a seat on the Recorder's Court in Detroit. He had begun to criticize judges and lawyers for perpetrating by law the American doctrine of racism and said they used the law as a "handmaiden of the propertied class" in repressing blacks.

Another example of racism that impacted Detroiters occurred on June 6, 1966. James Meredith, who had defied segregation to enter the University of Mississippi four years earlier, was shot in Hernando, Mississippi, during a voting rights march. After he was treated for his wound, he got up and completed the march from Memphis, Tennessee, to Jackson, Mississippi. He was joined by Martin Luther King, Jr. and Floyd McKissick, the new head of the Congress for Racial Equality. As the marchers reached Jackson, Stokely Carmichael, head of the Student Non-Violent Coordinating Committee, uttered the phrase "We shall overrun". He added that because of Meredith's shooting, they now had a new slogan—"Black Power", a phrase which permeated the air in black sections of Detroit. Slogans and posters of "Black Power" and a clenched fist became commonplace in Detroit at this time.

By 1966, it became clear that tourism to Detroit was declining. Robert Cobb, a high school history teacher, thought Detroit needed a tourist attraction and discovered a section of town with old buildings on Plum Street. He slowly began buying buildings for an artists' community. Finally in September 1966, a ceremonial opening of the Plum Street arts district featured Gov. George Romney, Sen. Robert Griffin and Detroit Mayor Jerome Cavanagh. The Mayor promised his support and had the city put in gas lights and trash cans painted bright colors.

Quickly the area was inhabited by loitering college students, drug dealers and motorcycle gangs. From the original 43 shops, three years later in 1969, only 6 to 8 shops remained as customers were scared away by the unruly loiterers. A police presence to prevent crimes did not seem to help.

Prior to 1967, the Detroit Police Department had instituted a policy to man squad cars with four men, and in street language, this was referred to as "the big four". During my time, it would become reorganized into tactical mobile units. And after I left, an extra unit was added called STRESS which became much criticized and will be described later.

Rev. Albert Cleage again created headlines when he launched the Black Christian National Movement in Detroit in 1967. He used a church on Linwood, west of 12th Street, that was apparently a white church earlier, but it changed dramatically in the 1960s.

Sidney Fine wrote that Cleage blamed the NAACP, the Detroit Urban League (DUL) and the Trade Union Leadership Council for not understanding the whole situation or their proper role in the "total struggle". Cleage stressed self-determination and black separatism. He rejected integration, stating that the most important thing happening in Detroit was the shift away from integration to "separatism". He advocated that blacks should think black, vote black, and buy black if they were to be free.

Cleage rejected the civil rights movements and argued that non-violence wasn't working. He rallied against the "social work approach" used by the NAACP and the DUL. Instead, he urged that blacks should defend themselves against brutality and strike back when knocked down.

His movement called for black churches to reinterpret Jesus' teachings to suit the needs of black people. On Easter Sunday of 1967, he unveiled an 18-foot painting of a Black Madonna and renamed his church the Shrine of the Black Madonna.

Cleage was one of many who fomented a rebellious mentality in his followers. According to Mark Chapman in *Christianity on Trial*, Cleage tried to counter Elijah Muhammad's argument. Muhammad said that Christianity was the "white man's religion" to pacify blacks by keeping them focused on heavenly rewards. Cleage wanted Christianity to be valuable to blacks so he blackened Jesus.

After the 1967 riots, he published *The Black Messiah*, which described his version of Jesus as a black revolutionary leader. He claimed that the Scribes and the Pharisees were just like the "establishment Uncle Toms" who profited from the system of oppression. He claimed that "conflict is inevitable unless the white man agrees to transfer power" (Thompson, 85).

I described the riot of July 1967 in the first chapter. Just after the riot, Cleage led a memorial service for those killed. Mayor Cavanagh and Governor Romney were in the audience. Rev. Cleage declared, "We are engaged in a nation-wide rebellion, seeking to become what God intended that we should be—free men with control of our own destiny, the destiny of black men" (Widick, 189).

I believe that Rev. Cleage's theology was too militant and egged on his audiences to increase tensions between blacks and whites, leading to the collapse of Detroit. However, I certainly don't mean to imply that blacks were the only ones who caused problems for Detroit.

I mentioned earlier that hippies and druggies hung around the Plum Street area that had been designated as a historic tourist site. One of the students in the Detroit hippie scene was a white man, John Sinclair, who was working on a Master's degree in American Literature at Wayne State University. My police officers had to handle Sinclair several times, as had the police before I came to Detroit.

Sinclair was arrested for sales and possession of marijuana on November 1, 1964. He dropped out of college in the fall of 1965 to work with hippie artists and rock groups. On February 24, 1966, he was arrested on the same charge, and served six months in the Detroit House of Correction. Following his release, he was arrested a third time on January 24, 1967, along with 55 other people in a drug raid on campus, even though he was no longer a student.

While the trial date languished, he formed a group called TransLove which advocated free love, marijuana decriminalization, and the end of war in Vietnam. Their first major event was promoted as a Love-In on Belle Isle on April 30, 1967, some 2 ½ months before the Detroit riot.

Only a few mounted police were on hand because Sinclair had promised that this would be a peaceful gathering. The crowd of 6,000 became rowdy after imbibing beer, wine and drugs. As some tried to light bonfires with trash, a man drove a motorcycle wildly through the crowd and was arrested by the police. Someone threw a firecracker toward the police horses, and with the resulting disorder, rocks and bottles were thrown as well as more firecrackers.

More police were summoned. Then they formed a line and slowly moved the crowd out onto the bridge and off the island. Windows were smashed, and businesses began to close down in fear of the unruly crowd. Spectators and news photographers trying to cover the melee were attacked when they photographed some beatings.

Next, Sinclair established a "total cooperative tribal living and working commune" called Trans-Love Energies Unlimited for artists and musicians. His commune was fire-bombed twice (in May and June 1968) so he moved it to two large houses near the campus of the University of Michigan in Ann Arbor. Despite the move, he was still active in Detroit by the time I arrived and I will speak of him later.

Another group began to form just before I arrived in Detroit. Some of those who formed the Black Panther Party in 1966 in Chicago came to Detroit to assist the fledgling communist group of blacks called the Revolutionary Action Movement (RAM), a very appropriate set of initials which spelled out their intentions.

The Detroit RAM group was later renamed Detroit Revolutionary Union Movement (DRUM) when blacks took over the organization. That included former Wayne State University students like General Baker, Marion Kramer, Ken Cockrel, Ken Hamblin, Luke Tripp, and Charles Johnson (Kelley, 8).

There is no doubt that the 1960s were really tough times for law enforcement in Detroit. A number of "hate groups" had proliferated and the FBI had initiated a program called COINTELPRO to discredit and disorganize them. The FBI

Special Agent in Charge of Detroit from February 1965 to May 1970 was Paul Stoddard, with whom I had various dealings and communication. Stoddard faced problems with politicians wanting special favors, just as I did.

In Cartha DeLoach's book, *Hoover's FBI: The Inside Story*, he described an interaction with Paul Stoddard. DeLoach was the Assistant Director of the FBI when Michigan Democratic Congressman John Dingell called him one day.

Dingell's life had been threatened by whites because he had supported civil rights legislation. He wanted the FBI to protect him and his family in Dearborn near Detroit. DeLoach had to decline but suggested he call the police to which Dingell responded that he had no confidence in the police.

DeLoach reported this to Stoddard, who responded by saying that the Dearborn police were very good for their size. Stoddard launched an investigation, but never found the people who made the threat to Dingell.

But there is much more to be told about the insidious surveillance and disruption techniques used by the FBI under Hoover's administration. Yes, I must admit that the police used undercover men and surveillance. But I never heard of using the kind of dirty tricks that Hoover pushed his agents to develop. I firmly believe that these dirty tricks played a part in the decline of Detroit as they set groups at war within themselves. But I also firmly believe that armed black nationalist groups operating without surveillance or undercover activities would have resulted in more violence and deaths.

It began with the memo that Director J. Edgar Hoover sent to 23 field offices (including Paul Stoddard in Detroit) on August 25, 1967, a month after the Detroit riot. In it, he described his new program COINTELPRO (short for Counter Intelligence Program).

> Director, FBI
> Personal Attention to All Offices
> Counterintelligence Program
> Black Nationalist Hate Groups
>   Offices receiving copies of this letter are instructed to immediately establish a control file, captioned as above, and to assign responsibility for following and coordinating this new counterintelligence program to an experienced and imaginative Special Agent well versed in investigations relating to black nationalist, hate-type organizations. The field office control file used under this program may be maintained in a pending inactive status until such time as a specific operation or technique is placed under consideration for implementation.
>   The purpose of this new counterintelligence endeavor is to expose, disrupt, misdirect, discredit or otherwise neutralize the activities of black nationalist,

hate-type organizations and groupings, their leadership, spokesmen, membership and supporters, and to counter their propensity for violence and civil disorder. The activities of all such groups of intelligence interest to this Bureau must be followed on a continuous basis so we will be in a position to promptly take advantage of all opportunities for counterintelligence and to inspire action in instances where circumstances warrant.

The pernicious background of such groups, their duplicity, and devious maneuvers must be exposed to public scrutiny where such publicity will have a neutralizing effect. Efforts of the various groups to consolidate their forces or to recruit new or youthful adherents must be frustrated.

No opportunity should be missed to exploit through counterintelligence techniques the organizational and personal conflicts of the leaderships of the groups and where possible an effort should be made to capitalize upon existing conflicts between competing black nationalist organizations. When an opportunity is apparent to disrupt or neutralize black nationalist, hate-type organizations through the cooperation of established local news media contacts or through such contact with sources available to the Seat of Government, in every instance careful attention must be given to the proposal to insure the targeted group is disrupted, ridiculed, or discredited through the publicity and not merely publicized.

Consideration should be given to techniques to preclude violence-prone or rabble-rouser leaders of hate groups from spreading their philosophy publicly or through various mass communication media.

Many individuals currently active in black nationalist organizations have backgrounds of immorality, subversive activity, and criminal records. Through your investigation of key agitators, you should endeavor to establish their unsavory backgrounds.

Be alert to determine evidence of misappropriation of funds or other types of personal misconduct on the part of militant nationalist leaders so any practical or warranted counterintelligence may be instituted.

Intensified attention under this program should be afforded to the activities of such groups as the Student Non-Violent Coordinating Committee, the Southern Christian Leadership Conference, Revolutionary Action Movement, the Deacons for Defense and Justice, Congress of Racial Equality, and the Nation of Islam.

Particular emphasis should be given to extremists who direct the activities and policies of revolutionary or militant groups such as Stokely Carmichael, H. "Rap" Brown, Elijah Muhammad, and Maxwell Stanford.

At this time the Bureau is setting up no requirement for status letters to be periodically submitted under this program. It will be incumbent upon you to insure the program is being afforded necessary and continuing attention and that no opportunities will be overlooked for counterintelligence action.

This program should not be confused with the program entitled "Communist Party, USA, Counterintelligence Program, Internal Security."

I will just add that the groups mentioned in Hoover's memo were attached to the following individuals: Student Non-Violent Coordinating Committee (SNCC)—Stokely Carmichael and H. "Rap" Brown; Southern Christian Leadership Conference (SCLC)—Rev. Martin Luther King, Jr.; Revolutionary Action Movement (RAM)—Maxwell Stanford aka Muhammad Ahmad; Deacons for Defense and Justice (DDJ) begun in Louisiana by Charlie Sims but each chapter had a leader; Congress of Racial Equality (CORE) formed by James Farmer but he resigned in 1966 because of its militancy; Nation of Islam (NOI)—Elijah Muhammad. Every one of these groups was active in Detroit.

By the way, when Director Hoover writes "Seat of Government", he is referring to his own position according to what I've read about the FBI. Rather grandiose, I'd say.

On March 22, 1968, Detroit police officer Lt. William McCoy testified in Washington, D.C., to the Congressional Senate Permanent Subcommittee on Investigations chaired by John McClellan of Arkansas. This subcommittee wanted information about subversive groups and especially about communist groups.

McCoy gave them information on the Revolutionary Action Movement (RAM). For example, he presented the RAM Manifesto, a RAM publication entitled "Black America", another exhibit entitled "Black America, Arm Yourselves for a War of Self Defense and Survival", a publication entitled "The Los Angeles War Cry: Burn, Baby, Burn", and the Black Guard Organizer's Manual. Our intelligence undercover officers had confiscated these documents while posing as RAM members.

On March 30-31, 1968, the Malcolm X Society held a national convention in Detroit to set up a separate black government called the Republic of New Africa. The conference was conducted at the Shrine of the Black Madonna, formerly the Central United Church of Christ, at 7625 Linwood, where Rev. Albert Cleage was pastor.

The Malcolm X Society was an organization used by Milton and Richard Henry whom I described earlier. The Henrys and Rev. Cleage used the meeting to promote various black nationalist activities. They used this name because Malcolm Little, slain leader of the NOI, was known as an advocate of Black Power. After his 1965 assassination, organizations used his name to promote the "martyr" image.

Police Undercover Agents Learned of Revolution

Our Lt. McCoy was undercover at the RNA convention. It was attended by black nationalists who were ready for separation from America, blacks who were interested in separation as a possibility, and technical advisors who had something to offer the new government of the Republic of New Africa such as lawyers, scientists, economists and industrialists. Only delegates were permitted to discuss and vote on issues. The discussion chairman, Raymond Willis, introduced 126 delegates at the opening of the convention.

Approximately 2,000 to 3,000 people registered for the convention which cost attendees $1.00 each. The delegates elected Robert Williams as President (even though he was residing in Red China), Milton Henry or Brother Gaidi Obadele of Detroit as First Vice President, Betty Shabazz (widow of Malcolm X) as Second Vice President, Charles Howard as Minister of State and Foreign Affairs, H. "Rap" Brown as Minister of Defense, Joan Franklin (New York attorney) as Minister of Justice, Queen Mother Moore (Audley Moore of New York) as Minister of Health and Welfare, and Richard Henry or Brother Imari Obadele of Detroit as Minister of Information.

Ambassadors nominated to East Africa were Betty Shabazz, Majile Adefunmi, and George Martin. Ambassadors nominated for the Far East (China) were Robert Williams, Mae Mallory and Henry (Papa) Wells.

The March 30 session at the church adjourned at 5:00 pm and reconvened at 8:00 pm at the Helen Deroy Memorial Auditorium at Wayne State University Campus. Some 500 people attended the 8:00 pm session, according to our undercover officer.

Platform participants were Raymond Willis, Brother Imari, Joan Franklin, Mae Mallory, Lawrence Guyot of Mississippi, Ron Karenga, and Queen Mother Moore.

Attorney Joan Franklin discussed the international law that confronts guerillas as prisoners of war versus prisoners of state.

Mae Mallory stated that the goal was to have a militia of both male and females, to be comprised of "twenty two million" trigger fingers.

Lawrence Guyot spoke of the right to dissent and the role of the black man in his attempt to deal with "the beast" (the United States). He said, "This country must be brought to its knees and it will not be done by hope and sympathy." He further described the financial plight of Mississippi black men who averaged salaries of less than $2,000 a year. A proposal was made to aid blacks by forming black guerillas and the proposal was sent to the committee for study.

Brother Imari moved that the convention and Guyot's Mississippi Freedom Democratic Party affiliate with each other.

A proposal was made and adopted that black draft dodgers or black G.I.s who refused duty in Vietnam or those who opposed "racist wars" should be supported by the group and their attorneys.

On March 31, sessions took place at the Twenty Grand Motel (owned by blacks). Those present signed the Declaration of Independence (in Appendix II). That evening, the meeting returned to meet at 6:00 at Rev. Cleage's church. At 7:50 pm, the meeting was opened by Raymond Willis who announced that the delegates had named their new government the Republic of New Africa (RNA).

Mae Mallory spoke first in defense of Robert Williams who was in exile. She stated that her home was under siege and had been fired upon by North Carolina State Troopers when they attempted to arrest Robert Williams. Williams went first to Cuba but now was in Red China.

She stressed that under the "new government" (RNA) black children would no longer be taught by white teachers and brain-washed with white doctrines. She claimed that the government is planning to get rid of black people, that they are starving Negro babies, drafting husbands and sons, and taking away poverty programs. She pointed out that the Vietnamese lured G.I.s into traps with sniper fire. She revealed that she *had used lure tactics to lead riot control police forces into ambush.*

(It had been suspected that during the 1967 Detroit riot, that blacks lured police and firemen into ambushes so that snipers could fire at them. Such a scenario may have occurred at the Algiers Motel which I discussed elsewhere.)

The next speaker, Brother Baba (Osiejeman Adefunmi) said that the new RNA nation will adopt African attire, African names, have their own holidays and heroes, and their great leaders like Malcolm X will be part of the "Voodoo".

Queen Mother Moore, a long-time card-carrying member of the Communist Party (CPUSA), spoke next and attacked the courts as being biased. She said they railroaded thousands of Negroes to their deaths.

Betty Shabazz, called the "Mother of the Black Nation", advocated using weapons that the whites used such as surgical glue and Stoner rifles. She warned that when the whites get informers, they don't protect the informer once they are through with him.

The final draft of the Declaration of Independence of the RNA was read. The convention ended at 10:00 pm and the next meeting was announced for May 30, 1968, in Chicago.

According to a story by Robert C. Smith called "Imari Obadele: The Father of the Modern Reparations Movement", Richard Henry (Imari) came up with the idea of reparations for the RNA, perhaps getting the idea from Malcolm X.

The RNA manifesto demanded a plebiscite (vote) among African Americans to determine whether they wanted to form an independent nation within the United States, much as Joseph Pogany (John Pepper) had advocated in his communist pamphlet years earlier.

This would be done by the cession by the United States of the states of Louisiana, Mississippi, Alabama, Georgia and South Carolina, and the payment of $400 billion in reparations for the injustices done to black Americans during the slavery and segregation periods.

The idea of reparations was probably due to the success of other groups in obtaining them from the U.S. government; e.g. Japanese Americans interned during WWII, American Indian tribes receiving compensation for their lands stolen by the government, etc. (However, the current reparation movement did not take form until 1988, when Richard Henry/Imari Obadele and his associates formed the National Coalition of Blacks for Reparations in America—N'COBRA.)

The concession of these states would then form an independent black nation of the five contiguous states. The reparation was a popular idea because individual blacks would get part of each government payment and the remainder would go to purchase land for the new republic.

The idea of creating all black states with a plebiscite is the topic of a book written by the spouse of co-author Holloway. *Tragedy in Black and White* by Bob Cheney was published in 2001 but was actually begun in 1970 when the RNA was promoting these ideas. The book describes a fictional story of what might happen if such states were created and reparations demanded.

The RNA had an interesting list of issues they wanted. They advocated community self-sufficiency, political rights, freedom of the press, banning of trade unions, mandatory military service, and the legalization of polygamy which was used by some African tribes.

The FBI considered the militant Republic of New Africa to be dangerous. They conducted raids, covert and overt repressive campaigns, and tried to disrupt them. Of course, we (meaning the Detroit Police Department) used surveillance and undercover officers to track their activities and prevent violence.

After my administration, Richard Henry was arrested and imprisoned in a 1971 raid on the RNA in Jackson, Mississippi, and served five years in prison. Upon his release, he resumed his RNA leadership. He worked for a Ph.D. in political science, taught at universities, and wrote about the RNA. He was recently still employed as a political science instructor at Prairie View A&M University in Texas according to an article in the *Des Moines Register*.

Martin Luther King's Assassination

Shortly after the RNA formation meeting, on April 4, 1968, Rev. Martin Luther King, Jr., was assassinated in Memphis, Tennessee, gunned down by a white man. He was in town to support striking African-American garbage workers. Detroit blacks felt a special closeness since the visit when he had begun his "I Have a Dream" theme there. A walkout of black students at Detroit Cooley High School began walkouts from twenty other Detroit schools as well as black workers at the Chrysler Jefferson Avenue Plant. King was succeeded by Rev. Ralph Abernathy as head of the Southern Christian Leadership Conference.

Activities in the automotive industry made news on May 2, 1968. A walkout of 4,000 workers at the Hamtramck Assembly Plant occurred because workers objected to an exhausting speed up of the production line. This strike gave auto executives the chance to discharge black workers connected with DRUM, whom they perceived as the greatest agitators. Those discharges made news in the third issue of the new revolutionary group's newspaper. That issue of DRUM attacked the UAW for endorsing the annual Detroit Police field day. It also listed a number of deaths attributed to the police department.

The day after the walkout at Hamtramck, on May 3, 1968, Rev. Abernathy led the Poor People's March on Washington, D.C., in an emotional event with over 800,000 marching for Rev. King. King's earlier speech in Detroit made this a tense time for the city. A rally was scheduled to be held at Cobo Hall, Detroit's Convention Center, on this day. The rally and demonstration, which was being telecast over a local channel, was peaceful and orderly until a car stalled. According to Dan Georgakas and Marvin Surkin in *Detroit: I Do Mind Dying,* "At that point, the police suddenly became extremely agitated and, almost without warning, mounted a cavalry-style charge upon the demonstrators. Nineteen people were seriously injured in the action" (158).

Black and liberal spokesmen denounced the actions of the police.

In fact, it was assumed that Robert Kennedy's appearance in downtown Detroit would draw many but without the press coverage, nobody expected 10,000 on May 15, 1968. A newspaper strike kept events in Detroit from drawing large crowds. It lasted from November 16, 1967 until August 8, 1968, just after I arrived to take my job in Detroit.

Kennedy came to Detroit campaigning for the Presidency and speaking about Vietnam. At noon, when he arrived at Kennedy Square named for his brother, the throng was unmanageable. Following his speech, the crowd surged forward, lifted him up and carried him to his car. Fortunately, no unseemly accidents occurred. Sadly, Robert Kennedy was assassinated in California three weeks later.

On May 23, 1968, FBI Director Hoover sent this memo (Welch & Marston, 154-55) about police brutality to all offices including Detroit:

> ...You are instructed to prepare a separate communication to reach the Bureau on or before 6/14/68, to include the following detailed information:
>
> 1. *False Allegations of Police Brutality.* Detailed information is desired to counter the widespread charges of police brutality that invariably arise following student-police encounters...It is anticipated this data can be used through friendly news media to vividly portray the revolutionary-type actions and militant nature of the New Left movement.
>
> 2. *Immorality.* Specific data should be furnished depicting the scurrilous and depraved nature of many of the characters, activities, habits, and living conditions representative of New Left adherents.
>
> 3. *Action by College Administrators.* Set forth information to show the value of college administrators and school officials taking a firm stand in resisting militant minority elements attempting to disrupt or take over college campuses. Specific examples should be given to show the results of being firm, as opposed to a vacillating attitude in considering student demands...

The Republic of New Africa Makes Demands

On May 29, 1968, Milton Henry (Brother Gaidi) as First Vice President of the Republic of New Africa wrote the following letter to Dean Rusk, who was the Secretary of State from 1961-1968. Richard Henry (Brother Imari) drove to Washington, D.C., and delivered it to the Department of State, handing it over to security guards outside the building.

Greetings:

This note is to advise you of the willingness of the Republic of New Africa to enter immediately into negotiations with the United States of America for the purpose of settling the long-standing grievances between our two peoples and correcting long-standing wrongs.

The wrongs to which we refer are those, of course, which attended the slavery of black people in this country and the oppression of black people, since slavery, which continues to our own day. The grievances relate to the failure of the United States to enter into any bilateral agreements with black people, either before or after the Civil War, which reflect free consent and true mutuality. Black people were never accorded the choices of free people once the United States had ceased, theoretically, its enslavement of black people, and this constitutes a fatal defect in the attempt to impose U.S. citizenship upon blacks in America.

The existence of the Republic of New Africa poses a realistic settlement for these grievances and wrongs. We offer new hope for your country as for ours. We wish to see an end to war in the streets. We wish to lift from your country, from your people, the poorest, most depressed segment of the population, and, with them, work out our own destiny, on what has been the poorest states in your union (Mississippi, Louisiana, Alabama, Georgia, and South Carolina), making a separate, free, and independent black nation.

Our discussions should involve land and all those questions connected with the prompt transfer of sovereignty in black areas from the United States to the Republic of New Africa. They must also involve reparations. We suggest that a settlement of not less than $10,000 per black person be accepted as a basis for discussions. We do assure you that the Republic of New Africa remains ready instantly to open good faith negotiations, at a time and under conditions to be mutually agreed. We urge your acceptance of this invitation for talks in the name of peace, justice, and decency.

For the Republic,
Milton Henry

On May 30-June 1, 1968, the RNA met in Chicago with 75 attendees, 55-60 of whom were delegates. The meeting described the "birth" of the RNA, read the letter to Dean Rusk, described the 3% income tax for the new nation of RNA, established the Black Legion (the military arm of the RNA), and set out objectives through October 30, 1968. Those objectives were:

to open a book bindery, record pressing facilities, clothing factory;
to request and collect income tax;
to issue a Brother Malcolm X Certificate of Recognition for $100,000 to buy land in Mississippi and to buy it;
to request and manage a savings stamp program;
to set up social fundraising functions in this country and abroad;
to establish a cultural magazine of fiction and articles;
to establish a theatrical group and promote black playwriting;
to open a government printing office in Los Angeles;

to publish regularly a national news magazine; and
to produce literature to support plebiscites and recruitment of citizens, etc.

Then State Senator Coleman Young told the *Michigan Chronicle* in June, 1968, (the month before I arrived), "If the Mayor is afraid to take on the DPOA (Detroit Police Officers Association) then we will do it for him. Otherwise this city is headed for a bloodbath."

On June 3, Richard and Milton Henry and Mae Mallory left Detroit for Tanzania in Africa to confer with Robert Williams. The purpose of the trip was to secure financial help for the RNA from "Red China" through Robert Williams who was in exile there.

During that meeting, Williams stated that he did not intend to make any statement or do anything on behalf of the RNA. He stated that he had no funds for the RNA and had, in fact, expected the RNA to bring funds to him to help in the establishment of a hospital in Tanzania that he was interested in.

The Henrys returned on June 10, 1968, and held a cabinet meeting on June 16, 1968, at the home of Richard Henry in Detroit. The lack of interest in the RNA and the intentions of Williams were announced to those who attended, which included the Henry brothers, Betty Shabazz, Queen Mother Moore, Obaboa Awolo, Joan Franklin, Ray Willis, Mwesi Chui and various unidentified persons from Detroit, Dayton and Cleveland, Ohio, caucuses. Williams' intentions caused great consternation among the members and they decided that if this were to reach the general membership, the RNA would probably fail.

However, Williams had told the Henrys to push for reparations and to obtain a large number of signatures to show the United States that the RNA had a large following.

On June 29, 1968, Richard Henry announced a petition drive to the members of the Detroit caucus of the RNA. The Detroit caucus was to obtain 30,000 signatures by August 8, 1968, and the petition was then to be presented to the United Nations. The petition insisted that the RNA be recognized as a "free black government" empowered to negotiate for reparations.

A placard pointing out the aims of the RNA and its background was utilized in the petition drive to obtain signatures. In late July, copies of the petition were mailed to RNA consulates in Ohio, New York and California with instructions to obtain 50,000 signatures by August 18, 1968.

The placard had a picture of a smiling black couple and the copy read:

WE ARE ASKING YOU TO VOTE
FOR LAND AND POWER

The Republic of New Africa was established by black people from all over America in convention in Detroit on 31 March 1968. We are working to build a separate free, powerful, rich, humane black nation on land reclaimed by black people in the South. All black people in America are eligible to become citizens and participate in election of officers to be held by January 1970.

We, the black people, in America, insist that the United States government and the world recognize our right to reparations—payment—from the United States government for the labor stolen from our ancestors during a century of slavery and for the damages suffered by all of us since slavery by reason of racial discrimination. We insist that the Republic of New Africa be recognized as the free black government empowered to negotiate for these reparations.

FOR EVERY PERSON: $10,000
$4,000 FOR THE INDIVIDUAL, $6,000 FOR THE REPUBLIC.

The petition asked for signatures and addresses and said the following:

We, the undersigned black people in America, insist that the United States government and the world recognize our right to reparations—payment—from the United States government for the labor stolen from our ancestors during slavery and for the damages suffered by all of us since slavery, by reason of racial discrimination. We insist that the Republic of New Africa be recognized as the free black government empowered to negotiate for these reparations.

On July 8, 1968, DRUM and supporting groups arrived at the gates of Dodge Main. Production was nearly halted as 3,000 black workers stood outside the factory gates. By noon, police arrived, massing across the street from the workers. They began putting on tear gas masks and an officer ordered the workers to disperse. They did, but on the following Monday, July 11, DRUM again demonstrated against the plant. Police proceeded to break up the demonstration.

Since I had accepted the job and would begin July 22, I was glued to newspaper reports of these events.

Thanks to the 1967 riot and DRUM, the UAW and the Big 3 automakers recruited many blacks as supervisors and in-plant managers during the 1970s. "The rebellion {riot of 1967} shook up the status quo in dozens of UAW locals" said General Baker, a former leader of DRUM (*African Americans on Wheels Magazine*, Feb/Mar 2000).

On August 17, 1968, Richard Henry told the Detroit RNA members that the target date of the petitions had been postponed to August 31, 1968, because only

4,500 signatures were obtained of the number required in Detroit. Apparently the RNA petitions felt short of that number and Henry began to develop plans in another direction, but this effort did not go unnoticed by the FBI.

On August 31, 1968, FBI Director Hoover wrote to Paul Stoddard, in charge of the Detroit FBI office, asking that his office create a phony letter with some kind of wording to screw up the RNA and cause dissension within the ranks of the membership.

This is the milieu that I stepped into when I accepted the position of Police Commissioner on June 21, 1968—the longest day of the year in the middle of that hot summer. Mayor Cavanagh was under intense pressure to have a police commissioner who could do miracles immediately.

3

Detroit: A Great City—A Model City

○ ○
"I believe the British government forms the best model the world
ever produced...This government has for its object public
strength and individual security."

—Alexander Hamilton

Detroit: A Great City—A Model City

How did Detroit come to be called "A Model City?" It came about during Mayor Jerome P. Cavanagh's administration. He was elected in a surprising victory over incumbent Louis Miriani in 1961.

During the previous decade, over 100,000 jobs had been lost as auto manufacturers such as Hudson, Studebaker and Packard closed. Other Detroit car manufacturers had been moving operations to areas with cheaper labor, and those workers who could leave moved away.

Cavanagh came into office with an unemployment rate of a staggering 18% in the black community, a huge city deficit, and a nearly all white police force which antagonized and degraded blacks with a constant "stop and frisk" mentality.

Mayor Jerome P. Cavanagh

Mayor Cavanagh served from 1962 to January 6, 1970. He had been politically active as chairman of the Wayne County Young Democrats, served as a deputy sheriff and as administrative assistant for the Michigan State Fair Authority. Cavanagh earned undergraduate and law degrees from the University of Detroit.

He was a young, handsome, bright, charming man as I discovered when I first met him. Dissatisfactions with Mayor Louis Miriani by the black community had contributed to Cavanagh's surprising victory.

The vote was 200,413 for Cavanagh and 158,778 for Mayor Miriani. An aide to the Roman Catholic Cavanagh chuckled and described his first campaign for elective office as "Nickels and Novenas".

The idealistic and uninhibited engaging young man, knowledgeable about the unfortunate ugly and bitter racial riot in June 1943, turned to the black leaders and informed them that he would appoint a police commissioner that they could have confidence in and would "do the right thing" by the city's blacks.

While Cavanagh received 85% of the black vote, many white homeowners were attracted to this gregarious, intelligent new arrival on the political scene. The new mayor started under serious handicaps such as substandard unemployment, migration of the white middle class out of the city, and escalating racial tension. The 1960s were volatile times.

Faced with an approaching deficit of almost $28 million, Cavanagh promised in his inaugural address to make Detroit's economic recovery his "first and greatest concern" along with attention to the problems of Detroit's Negro citizens and all citizens of the city.

Sidney Fine wrote that although Cavanagh had his enemies in Detroit, by the end of 1963 he was reported to be worshipped by the city's press and its civic, business, and labor leaders. Although later as his police commissioner, I had to turn against and refuse his requests that I felt went against proper police professionalism four times, I still felt that he was a man of decency and compassion. So do many of his political admirers and to this day there is a "Cavanagh Clan" that meets monthly despite his death.

In fact, after my term as Commissioner, as sheriff I was invited to attend. I guess they considered me to be one of them, but I wasn't. I was a police professional, but I attended some of those meetings.

During Cavanagh's administration, the economy improved thanks to jobs provided by the big three auto manufacturers. The good years of 1962 to 1967 stimulated employment with the help of business and labor leaders. Detroit had a fairly large and prosperous black middle class. Blacks who worked in the automobile plants were paid 20% more than unskilled workers elsewhere in the nation.

Cavanagh, a likable young Irishman, handled his slate of problems with aplomb. First, he hired a black city comptroller. He appointed Alfred Pelham as Detroit's comptroller. He was the first black to fill an important position in the government. Several blacks were appointed to fill other important city posts.

Next, Cavanagh pushed the state legislature to adopt Detroit's first income tax to provide needed revenue to counter the $28 million deficit left by Miriani.

Then he appointed Michigan Supreme Court Judge George Edwards as police commissioner to reform the 4,000 man police department.

Judge George Edwards Becomes Commissioner

The appointment of George Edwards, Jr., to serve as police commissioner surprised many. When I graduated from John Jay College with my master's degree, the guest speaker at the graduation ceremony was George Edwards. Little did I know that later on I would be Police Commissioner of the same city he served in that role.

Edwards, the son of a lawyer, had grown up in Dallas and attended Southern Methodist University. He then went to Detroit to work as a union organizer with Walter Reuther in his famous UAW Local 174. Edwards was selected to be the Detroit housing commissioner during WWII, but was defeated when he ran for mayor in 1949.

He went on to Harvard for another degree and eventually served as a Michigan Supreme Court Judge until he stepped down at Cavanagh's invitation to be police commissioner. Edwards served nearly two years (1962-63), attempted to increase the number of blacks in the department, and tried to integrate blacks into the police cruisers whose harassment procedures created hostility among blacks.

Cavanagh's first executive order, issued February 22, 1962, stated "City employees were to be recruited, appointed, trained, assigned and promoted without regard to race, color, religion, national origins or ancestry" (Fine, 19).

Cavanagh had designated two agencies to implement the order. He did that because a survey found that while the city was 28% non-white, almost 35% of city employees were non-white. Even as city agencies were prodded to upgrade blacks, because they were disproportionately concentrated among certain agencies, many whites complained.

The quality of black housing was considered better than housing for blacks in other cities. An aide to President Johnson said that although it was bad in some areas that housing was not a terribly serious problem. Indeed the quality of black housing was somewhat above that of other cities—above that of New York, Chicago, Philadelphia, Cleveland, and Gary, Indiana. In those days, the comparisons were not with white housing but with other black housing areas.

The Detroit city government consisted of a strong mayor and a non-partisan nine member city council, all being elected at large rather than representing specific districts. Personally, I believe that council members elected by districts would feel more amenable and responsible to their electorate.

While there was only one black on the Detroit Common Council, there were three black judges in Detroit in 1965, and twelve blacks were members of the Michigan legislature. Sidney Fine in *Violence in the Model City* pointed out that in 1967, Detroit was the only city to have two black Congressmen and they made up half of the black representation in Congress.

Mayor Cavanagh's first action was to improve the poor financial position of Detroit by securing approval of an income tax of one percent for city residents and a half percent for non-residents who worked in the city. This greatly helped to put Detroit's finances in balance. As the astute new mayor and his team strongly pursued federal aid to add to the city's tax base, his administration achieved great success working with a receptive administration in Washington.

Between July 1, 1962 and August 1, 1967, Detroit received $230,422,000 from the federal government for one program or another, according to Sidney Fine.

Cavanagh supported the Detroit NAACP (the largest branch in the nation) goals to ban housing discrimination, with members such as Rev. C. L. Franklin, Rev. Albert Cleage and politician John Conyers, Jr.

Martin Luther King's Appearance in Detroit

When Rev. Martin Luther King came to Detroit on June 23, 1963, Cavanagh was there with 125,000 to greet King and support the black freedom march and civil rights movement. It was the largest civil rights march in the nation up to that time.

King delivered a speech that had some of the same words he would use two months later in Washington, D.C. In Detroit he said,

> I have a dream this afternoon that one day right here in Detroit, Negroes will be able to buy a house or rent a house anywhere that their money will carry them; they will be able to get a job...
>
> I have a dream this evening that one day, we will recognize the words of Jefferson that all men are created equal—that they are endowed by their creator with certain inalienable rights, that among these are life, liberty and the pursuit of happiness...
>
> I have a dream this afternoon that the brotherhood of man will become a reality in this day, with this faith. I will go out and carve a tunnel of hope through the mountain of despair with this faith. I will go out with you and transform dark yesterdays into bright tomorrows. With this faith, we will be able to achieve this new day, when all of God's children, black men and white men, Jews and Gentiles, Protestants and Catholics will be able to join hands and sing with the Negro in the spiritual of old, "Free at last! Free at last! Thank God almighty, we are free at last!"

Cavanagh Got Federal Funds for the Model City

Five months later, after the assassination of Kennedy, President Lyndon Johnson's "War on Poverty" inspired Mayor Cavanagh. He was appointed a member of President Johnson's Task Force on Urban and Metropolitan Problems.

Cavanagh wanted to make Detroit "Model City USA" for federally financed urban programs—a coordinated approach to channel programs and services into the areas of greatest need.

If they could obtain that financing, the city fathers intended to rehabilitate buildings in a nine square mile area in the inner city, create parks and community centers, improve protection by police, and build new schools.

Fine described how Detroit had the ability to secure federal funds, and how most of the money Detroit received from Washington was directed to the inner city. He pointed out that city council members believed there would be a white riot if the white middle class knew how disproportionate the inner city expenditures were.

As time passed and progress was made, despite problems in administration and funding, the Detroit anti-poverty effort drew praise as one of the best programs in the nation. Cavanagh said Detroit's war on poverty was "the country's outstanding success story", lauded the program as "the best in America" and promised residents a "New Detroit". That was less than two weeks before the start of the Detroit riot.

Actually, very little of the money awarded to Detroit arrived because it was drained off to the Vietnam War. White flight accompanied by high unemployment raged on. Edwards had moved on from his post as police commissioner, and his successor, Ray Girardin, had found the white police force and their mentality toward blacks a hard group to control. Less than five per cent of police officers were black despite an intense recruiting procedure to add more.

Cavanagh ran for re-election in 1965 and received almost 70% of the vote. The following year he became the first mayor to head both the United States Conference of Mayors and the National League of Cities at the same time. He was riding high, considered as a presidential possibility, and was pictured on the cover of national magazines. One aide said, "On a clear day, he could see the White House."

Judge Horace Gilmore, a man I came to admire, who headed a Police-Community Relations sub-committee, stated in 1965 that Detroit was "the most sophisticated city in the country on the matter of intergroup relations". The same year, *Fortune Magazine* lauded Detroit for the progress it had made in race relations. The following year, the head of the National Urban League added their accolades for Detroit's race relations and said that the city was on its way to being a "demonstration city" of race relations.

Early in 1967, Cavanagh noted that he was spending three quarters of his daily time dealing with the problems of the inner city. In fact, Nicholas Hood, Detroit's only black councilman, asserted in May, 1967, "With all of its problems, Detroit is far ahead of any major city in America because we have a city administration that will not only listen to the concerns brought to it but will set out to work on those concerns."

Sidney Fine wrote that social scientists visited Detroit in the Cavanagh years to learn how a city could deal successfully with race relations. He noted that admiring articles appeared in *Fortune, Newsweek, Harper's, U.S. News and World Report, Look, Wall Street Journal, Christian Science Monitor, Los Angeles Times,* and the *Cleveland Plain Dealer.*

The Department of Justice called Detroit a "racial model" and the city received various awards and was called the "All-American City."

An aide to Cavanagh remarked that his mayor not only got a great deal of press, he got brilliant press. Cavanagh was described as the "Dynamo in Detroit" who pulled the once dead industrial city out of its physical, economic and cultural doldrums. He was dubbed a hot young mayor of the takeover generation and was named one of the ten outstanding young men of the nation by the United States Junior Chamber of Commerce.

Perhaps Cavanagh was too heady! In the spring of 1967, police officers called in with complaints of "flu" in a strike intended to show the Cavanagh administration and the police commissioner who was boss.

Cavanagh's economic and political team enjoyed great initial success. But when it all blew up, the *New York Times* editorialized on July 23, 1967, that Detroit "probably had more going for it than any other major city in the North".

I understand his favorite song was the "Impossible Dream". At that time, I was still a New Yorker where the *Man from La Mancha* was playing "off Broadway". I saw the musical and that song was one of my favorites, also.

Cavanagh told the populace they didn't need a brick to communicate with City Hall. While racial riots spread across the country, Detroit appeared to stand out as a symbol of hope. Only a month before the riot, Cavanagh had said that Detroit had escaped much of the national civil unrest due to the city's responsiveness to the needs of the streets.

For Jerry Cavanagh, the "Impossible Dream" ended on the day of the riot. It did not bode well for Detroit. Things needed to change—yes! The blacks deserved much better—yes! But evolution rather than revolution would have served the city better as it sat on the threshold of greatness. He did not run again for mayor.

Cavanagh may have committed one political blunder that ended his "impossible dream". The blunder occurred in 1966 when the Mayor challenged the esteemed former Michigan Governor G. Mennen Williams for the Democratic nomination for U.S. Senate. Was it a problem of too much too soon?

The problem that should have been foreseen by Cavanagh and his advisors was the lack of support from the liberals, labor unions and blacks, the same constituency that long had been in Governor Williams' corner.

Cavanagh lost to Williams in the primary because he did not have the expected support from the black community in Detroit. Some results of this political blunder were: a blow to Cavanagh's political invincibility, alienation of some former supporters, and many Democrats blamed Cavanagh's divisive run in the primary for former Gov. Williams defeat for the U. S. Senate. Further, his position against the Vietnam War seemed to dissipate some of President Lyndon Johnson's former ardent support.

Lou Gordon, a Detroit radio and television figure and former supporter, turned against the mayor questioning his integrity and character and his promise to serve out his second term as mayor. I can attest to Lou Gordon's vituperation.

Shortly after being sworn in as Police Commissioner, I was publicly praised by Gordon for stopping a riot on 12th Street. He requested that I appear on his TV show. I wanted to go but many, such as Police Superintendent John Nichols, advised me not to go because of Gordon's feud with Cavanagh, but I had nothing to hide. Being new to Detroit and its politics, I agreed. Soon I felt the sting of Lou Gordon's wrath. He demanded that I investigate the mayor for alleged Mafia connections, of all things. I felt that would be unwise. The alleviation of crime and community tensions with proper and professional policing was my most pressing concern.

La Cosa Nostra

There were concerns about the Mafia in Detroit. During the Prohibition Era, syndicated gangs including the infamous "Purple Gang" set up in Detroit to smuggle whiskey from Canada across the Detroit River. But by the time I came to town, I thought there were only a few aging Mafia members left in town and most operations had moved on to other towns.

But, of course, I was not privy to FBI insider information. For example, on July 21, 1968, only a day before I began my job, a bomb exploded at Grace Ranch in Tucson, Arizona, owned by Peter J. Licavoli, Sr. He had been linked in congressional investigations to the Detroit mob. The FBI was asked to send agents out to Licavoli's house in Grosse Pointe Park, Michigan, a posh Detroit suburb, to investigate.

On October 8, 1968, they filed a report that is now available under the Freedom of Information Act.

> Peter Licavoli, 1154 Balfour, Grosse Pointe Park, Michigan, was interviewed at his Michigan residence during which interview Licavoli advised that he has no information as to who did the recent bombings in the Tucson, Arizona, area or why. He advised that in his opinion, the bombings were harassments, and he offered conjecture that they could have been done by "the newspapers" so that they would get big headlines and sell more newspapers or by some "vigilantes" trying to get him and Joe Bonanno to move out of the Tucson area. He also indicated that the bombing at his Tucson, Arizona, ranch on

July 21, 1968, could have been done by some disgruntled former tenant; however, he advised that he did not know the identity of any such tenant.

He remarked that he considers these incidents as being harassments inasmuch as if anyone wanted to kill him or Joe Bonanno they would direct their attacks against them and not their property. He advised that he has known Bonanno for years and that there is no hard feelings or disagreements between them; that he has been in Tucson, Arizona, for 24 years; and that Bonanno was there before him.

Licavoli denied knowing the identity of anyone who took over the New York interests of Joe Bonanno. Licavoli stated that in years past he has been involved in gambling, but that now he is a legitimate businessman in the real estate business. He also advised that he was returning to Tucson, Arizona, on October 15 or 16, 1968.

There had been a grand jury investigation of the Detroit Police Department and a restaurant in the Detroit's Greektown that generated rumors about the Mayor and his office.

Councilwoman Mary Beck started a recall campaign against the Mayor. I, too, later became victimized in this feud between political figures. Rumors floated about the Mayor and his family. That there were marital difficulties was corroborated when Helen Cavanagh, the mother of their eight children, filed for separate maintenance on July 18, 1967. That was five days before the riot.

On June 21st, the day I was brought into the mayor's office to discuss being the new police commissioner, I saw the picture on the wall of the mayor, his most beautiful wife, and eight fine-looking children, six boys and two girls. I remarked to the mayor, "My mayor, you have a most beautiful family", not knowing anything about their marital problem.

Later I was shocked to learn that the family had indeed broken up. The Catholic Church granted an annulment—amazing to me after eight kids!

The only other intimations I heard about the Mafia during my time as Commish was in January, 1969, after seven months on the job. I heard that William Ellenburg, Police Chief of Grosse Pointe Park, had been selected by Carl Stokes, black mayor of Cleveland, to replace his police chief. However, Ellenburg was exposed by the *Detroit Free Press* to have been accused by a Detroit lawyer as being on the payroll of the Mafia. Stokes came to Detroit to defend his choice. He found that he had not checked with the Michigan state police, FBI, or International Association of Chiefs of Police (IACP) who all had qualms about Ellenburg.

Stokes lost his poise during a TV interview and criticized Detroit reporters. In the end, Ellenburg resigned and Stokes found another chief.

I never knew of any link between Cavanagh and the Mafia or any other illicit group. I had nothing but respect for Cavanagh. It was a sad occasion when I paid my respects at Holy Trinity Church when Mayor Cavanagh died. His six boys were pallbearers. I was told that he died of a heart attack in a hotel room in Lexington, Kentucky, on 11/27/1979 at age 51.

How People Become Criminals

I think I'll add a little bit about how Detroit or any "model city" could become filled with criminals, whether or not there were other influences present. I think all good cops know what makes people commit crime, whether it be the Mafia, politicians, employees, executives, police officers, or common criminals. In fact, I guess we've all known it for hundreds and even thousands of years.

Sigmund Freud said that people are born selfish with the goal: I want what I want when I want it! As parents teach children the difference between right and wrong, a child accumulates "learnings" that lead to the development of a conscience and patience. Once children become adults, they make choices about whether to be selfish or follow their conscience and think of others.

Moral theoreticians came up with stages that children go through in the development of a conscience. They say that in the beginning, all children are hedonists. Next they learn to do things to avoid punishment and pain from parents and adults, and instead do things that bring love and pleasure. As they begin to interact with other older children, they learn to share, give and take, and follow rules so they can maintain friendships and avoid embarrassment and penalties. Next comes a realization that law and order in their community, school, workplace and society requires that everyone follow rules or they will run into trouble with authorities. Most youth finally accept the social contract to "do unto others as you would have them do unto you."

Omar Khayyam realized that once people have a conscience, they may regret their actions, apologize, and wish they could take it all back. But, of course, it is too late once an act is done.

> "The moving finger writes; and having writ,
> Moves on: nor all your piety nor wit
> Shall lure it back to cancel half a line,
> Nor all your tears wash out a word of it."

Those who have reached at least the rule-following stage of moral development are less likely to return to their earlier selfish outlook. Those who, for a vari-

ety of reasons, do not develop a conscience, tend to be repeat offenders or recidivists. Police have long known that a large proportion of crimes are committed by a small number of criminals. If they are taken out of circulation, the crime rate is reduced.

There are other influences besides morals that persuade people to make criminal choices. Criminologists believe that crime occurs depending on conditions where people are, such as the likelihood of getting caught in a particular area. For example, some suggest that a would-be burglar examines a house thusly. If the house has a less visible entryway, if there are few who could see the criminal, if there is no visible alarm, if there is no barking dog, he is more likely to run the risk. He therefore chooses to avoid pain and gain pleasure/profit.

Criminals begin early to choose how they would spend time, who they would spend it with, what they would do for pleasure, what they would use as excuses, who they would choose as victims, and what they would tolerate in the way of pain or punishment. There are no experts today who think, like some in the days of old, that criminals are born. They are made, according to FBI profilers and psychologists. Criminals make choices about what they are going to do. Things that influence a criminal as he decides whether to risk getting caught include whether the community looks disorderly, whether residents are less vigilant and whether police presence is quick and responsive.

But, just as the criminal considers his options, so do potential victims. People choose where they will go and when, whether there are risks in the environment, how much they care to protect their living space such as their house or car, and how prepared they are physically (strength, self-defense training, etc.) and with safety items (pepper spray, cell phone, weapon, siren, etc.) to encounter a criminal. So it takes the criminal and the victim to make a model city fall apart.

4

Detroit 1968–1970: My Tenure as Police Commissioner

○ ○

"Of all the tasks of government, the most basic is to protect its citizens against violence."

—*Secretary of State John Foster Dulles*

Detroit 1968-1970:
My Tenure as Police Commissioner

When Mayor Cavanagh invited me to discuss the position of Police Commissioner of Detroit, he treated me to a nice lunch on a yacht. As we sipped drinks and ate cold-cuts, he described the city, its people and government, and outlined the problems and needs of the police department. He spoke frankly about the 1967 riot and about a two-year-old scandal that had involved some police officers of rank with the proprietor of a restaurant in Detroit's Greektown.

I asked him what he personally wanted from the police department, and he told me simply, "a fair, effective and efficient department". I questioned whether he believed the police commissioner should run the department free from political influence or interference from other city officials.

I was concerned because I retired from the New York Police Department as Inspector and in command of Operations due to my observation of the influence of politics on the New York police executives. I wanted my administrative responsibility to stand or fall on the performance or lack of performance of police responsibilities, not political responsibilities.

I told Mayor Cavanagh that I shared his beliefs as to police policy and objectives, and that I thought with his backing I could make a contribution to solving Detroit's problems. He stuck out his hand, and I shook it. As of then, I was Detroit's police commissioner, although the people of Detroit didn't know it.

I suppose I ought to explain why I was being considered for the position of Police Commissioner for Detroit. When a city is being criticized for "police brutality" as Detroit was, citizens recommend things such as "put more blacks on the police force", "serve all citizens, not just the whites" and "build rapport and trust by getting closer to those you serve". I was known for doing those things in the New York City Police Department, and teaching about them in my law enforcement courses at John Jay College.

New York Scooter Experience

In the spring of 1964, I put nine scooters into service on an experimental basis in Central Park in Manhattan, and Prospect Park in Brooklyn. Robbery and other crimes dropped significantly in the two parks during a four-month trial period. The program continued until September 1, 1965, when 50 more scooters were put into service in 17 precincts, still primarily for park patrol. Each of the 17 precinct commanders evaluated the experiment, reported favorably, and requested that the program be continued.

Beginning October 20, 1965, the program was tested for general street patrol in 15 selected precincts, and again was received favorably.

Scooters were in constant demand because they could cut through traffic blockages, even riding on sidewalks when necessary. Besides quickly unlocking vehicular congestion, they could survey problem areas and report to precinct commanders. In the vicinity of bridges and tunnels, when traffic lanes were reversed to expedite the flow of vehicles from major roadway approaches, the scooter men were utilized most effectively. They also delivered messages and supplies through otherwise impassable locations.

The Tactical Scooter Unit became a team patrol because they could keep in touch by radio. They operated either as partners or as a group according to the need. From this point on, the use of scooters became an accepted part of New York police operations, some 700 being acquired and put into operation by the time I decided to retire from the Department in 1966.

The scooter patrolmen improvised on and changed their patterns of street patrol much as baseball or football players adapt set plays to meet rapidly changing conditions. Within a precinct, teams were organized for group operations; precinct units could quickly be welded into a swift, highly maneuverable and unpredictable crime fighting force.

The advantages of scooters was that they greatly extended patrol coverage, permitted better police observation, could move easily in congested areas, freed radio patrol cars for response to major incidents, were economical, could be quickly mobilized, reduced the fatigue of foot patrol, increased the morale of and stimulated recruitment, provided a visible crime deterrent, established rapport with juveniles, and were well received by the community.

In the 1950s and 60s as police became more modernized and motorized, crime still increased, community tensions exacerbated, and youth hostility rose. The police officer was set apart in his police car, dealing impersonally with the public and he was less responsive for the enforcement of community standards and neighborhood interactions. No wonder he did not garner the respect of the citizens when it appeared as if he wanted to avoid dealing or talking with them.

We lose respect for our physicians when they don't want to talk with us about our problems but simply write prescriptions and order things that affect our very lives.

The good, trusted police officer of yesterday, the policeman on post has now given way to the "law enforcement officer" which implies a punitive or repressive role. I thought it was time to return to some of the values and respect of yesterday. The bicycle, Segway or scooter can literally bring back the beat or foot patrol officer who interacts with the public. A willingness to interact with citizens is the only way that American law enforcement will regain respect from citizens.

The origins and success of the motor scooters as I developed them in New York City was astounding, even after much derision. "Macho" cops looked with disdain at this small two-wheeled vehicle. They would prefer motorcycles. They did not understand. The motorcycle, which is good for escorts and chasing speeders, is a two-wheeled "pursuit and punitive" machine. The motor scooter is a "protective patrol vehicle."

The physical difference is that a rider straddles a motorcycle like a cowboy on a horse, but a rider sits in a motor scooter and puts his legs in front of his seat as he wheels about the city.

Police executives generally viewed motor scooters askance. Police departments in the United States had mostly followed along with August Vollmer's dictum regarding how the automobile made foot patrol obsolete. But my experiment showed that the scooter could and did extend the range of delivery of available police personnel at minimum expense.

The history and results of scooters in the City of New York, first for parks and then for city street patrols, is covered in a 1966 article I wrote for the *Journal of Criminal Law, Criminology and Police Science* published by the Northwestern University School of Law. The article was entitled "The Motor Scooter—An Answer to a Police Problem".

There were many advantages to scooter patrol, especially in densely populated areas. In fact, I had some suggestions from the School of Hard Knocks for visionaries.

1. Police officers selected for scooter team operation should *only* be volunteers. Forcing someone to ride a scooter when he or she wants a car or motorcycle can ruin the program.

2. Careful training must be given with emphasis that the scooter's function is as a slow-moving *protective* patrol device, although speedy response as a team is available.

3. There should be no stunt riding or cowboying with scooters. Scooters do not chase cars. (I removed one officer who pursued a wanted car in Central Park even though he made a good arrest.)

4. Officers for team scooter patrol should be intelligent, educated, sensitive to cultural differences, and adept at good community relations since they are selling good police services that *serve and protect* the public.

5. Such officers should be considered generalists, knowledgeable in all aspects of good police work, and should be just as important as specialists, investigators or detectives, and should have opportunities for promotion and pay advancement within the patrol division.

6. Motor scooter teams should not be deployed after 10 or 11 p.m. and certainly not after midnight. Those hours are for automobile response units when most good people are home in bed. Better hours encourage volunteers for scooters.

7. Scooter patrols, especially in scooter team configurations, have great potential not only for crime reduction and traffic alleviation but can be quickly mobilized as a "task force" when necessary.

With proper leadership and deployment during hours when the "good people" are around, a resurgence of public confidence will take place. The scooter patrol officer can answer today's plaintive cry: "Where is the cop on the beat? Why isn't he around when we need him?"

The old-time foot patrol in various new forms brought back to the people truly Community Oriented Police Services to restore the comfort, health, morals, safety and prosperity to American cities. This enabled law enforcement officers to regain respect because they earned it as they served and protected citizens.

Policing would, of course, include law enforcement and also protection, so it was, in effect Dual Purpose Policing. This policing defines proper roles and responsibilities for each: the law enforcement and response part and the proactive prevention and protection part. It provides for communication and trust for the people of the community.

Dual Purpose Policing offers service and protection on the one hand, as well as responding to crimes already committed and enforcing laws. Patrol cars are mostly for response and enforcement. Scooters are mostly for service and protection. Both must work together in a designated area of patrol responsibility. Cars can do what scooters cannot do and scooters can do what cars cannot do. In essence, both present a teamwork concept of good policing.

I always believed that the test of a good police officer was not his record of arrests or citations, but rather the absence of crimes and disturbances in the area he patrols. The police officer is unique. He can be a dynamic force in the community for better or worse. He speaks to the public for the establishment with authority, and there is no reason why a police officer should not possess social graces.

Tact is often more important than technique at times. In Dual Policing, we can bring the functions of police into proper perspective. Both types of officers, the enforcer and the protector, work on a team to prevent crime, reduce community tension, and bring peace and order to the community entrusted to their charge.

To achieve Dual Purpose policing, I intended to change policing methods, diversify forces, use mobile foot patrols, include more minorities and women in policing, use more non-deadly weapons, and have educated police who could speak with and relate to the public.

Here is what I believed was the crux of the matter! In our movement toward professionalism, we emphasized Law Enforcement and lost sight of good protective policing. We put cops in cars, sent them out in response to calls for service or help, *mostly after the fact*. That is Law Enforcement. Certainly we need it! Crime continues—vicious and horrifying crime at times.

We need such police officers in police cars to respond as quickly as possible. But what about the Protective and Preventive part? The only way to serve and protect as well as enforcing laws is by putting them where people can see them, talk to them, get to know them, confide in them, on visible and accessibly simple two-wheeled scooters.

Many placed great emphasis on police power and penal severity. Our jails and prisons were bursting. Not the answer! Rather the prevention of crime, prevention of vandalism, and prevention of disorder were and are the answers. Crime and disorder disintegrate a neighborhood, driving down property values and tearing at the very soul of a city or community. I suggested that we change because police practices had been a major reason for riots, insurrections, demonstrations, and community tensions.

Police in cars are isolated from the good people, responding primarily to the bad people, becoming cynical, frustrated, and unable to do a good acceptable job, in effect handcuffed by the police system. This makes them impersonal to good citizens, hardly known as humane beings. This philosophy of policing is why I was interviewed.

I Accepted the Job

Well, to go back to my interview, I had anticipated an in-and-out visit with no overnight stop, so I had brought no additional gear with me. When I accepted, the Mayor's aide picked up some toilet articles. The Mayor and I checked our waistlines and he provided an additional accommodation. When I appeared at the press conference the following day, I was wearing his underwear, his shirt and his tie!

I had a steak dinner that evening with Cliff Owens, a police aide to the Mayor, and went out to call upon the retiring Detroit Police Commissioner, Ray Girardin, at his home. The one-time career newspaperman was most generous with information about the commissioner's job, and particularly about relations with the local press. He seemed genuinely relieved that someone had finally appeared to assume the burdens of the commissioner's responsibilities.

Back at the hotel, when I called my wife, I told her I was impressed with Detroit as a city, the Detroit police as a department and Mayor Cavanagh as a charismatic city official. I reminded her of something we'd talked about many times before. I was concerned that policing in America was in trouble, importantly because too much of what police did was not acceptable to the American public.

I felt I could make policing acceptable to those who needed its services. I thought I could do something to improve community relations, and help remove the problem of policing as a thorny issue in American society. Additionally, I felt I had an unprecedented opportunity to put into practice the things I myself had theorized about for so long in New York, and preached in my classes at the New York City Police Academy and John Jay College for Criminal Justice.

The next morning, I was taken to the City-County Building for a press conference to announce my appointment. June 21st, the longest day of the year, began as reporters and news magazine writers crowded into the room. The Mayor opened the conference by saying he had scouted the entire country, and had found the best man. I stated, "I want police to think of themselves as protectors of liberty. Protecting the rights of the individual is their function."

Then I added, "There will be no room for bias, bigotry or brutality!" I went on to promise that I would do my best to maintain a high level of crime fighting, raise the level of police performance especially in the area of professionalism, and to stem the rift between police and the community and improve the relationship.

When I returned to New York, the news was out and most of my friends and work associates had the same reaction: "Not Detroit!"

I tried to bone up on information about Detroit, of course. As far as segregation, it appeared to me that Detroit was a little less segregated than other large cities I had seen. I thought its school systems were better than other large Midwestern cities. The *Washington Post* described Detroit as one of the country's leading examples of forceful reform in education. I had checked into this because of my daughter, Betty.

Also the *Post* described the city's poverty program as the most effective in the United States. I thought that all in all, Detroit was moving along very well in facing its problems.

Detroit was fifth in population, fourth in reported crimes, third in serious crimes, and the inner city had begun to shrink as the suburbs grew dramatically. Within the city proper, black citizens accounted for more than one-third of the total population. Black pupils made up more than one-half of the public school population. But black officers accounted for only about six per cent of the police force.

As far as the racial pulse of the city was concerned, while more blacks than whites were disadvantaged economically, most blacks as well as whites were enjoying a generally high level of economic prosperity.

The memory of the 1967 riot overshadowed all approaches to crime control. A concerted civic effort to unravel the causes of the riot and deal with them had already produced some healthy results and had created an ongoing mechanism aimed at keeping channels of communication open between all segments of the community.

New Detroit: The Answer to the Riot of 1967?

This mechanism was an unusual organization called New Detroit, Inc., which began as a temporary committee of concerned citizens. Let me describe more about the peculiar nature of New Detroit.

As I took office as commissioner, New Detroit was pointed out to me, and accepted by me, as a significant civic resource and a remarkable indicator of the city's capacity to develop its own means for bettering communication between citizens and stimulating self help.

It was a tremendous idea and an exceptional organization. Much to my regret and to the detriment of the police department and the city, I eventually ended up in public disagreement with some of the leadership of New Detroit over the organization's approach to helping the police.

In the aftermath of the July 1967 riot, a telegram from Gov. George Romney and Mayor Cavanagh called 150 local leaders to take some responsibility in returning calm to the city. They were asked to donate the services of several high-ranking managers and specialists. The heads of Ford, General Motors and Chrysler, the UAW, three major banks and three utilities met with community leaders and activists to discuss Detroit's problems. A coalition with a pledged budget of $3.5 million called New Detroit, Inc. emerged.

An established civic assistance organization financed by private funds, the Metropolitan Fund of Detroit, provided an initial staff structure and housing. Eventually New Detroit incorporated, expanded, and developed the capacity to obtain as much as $10 million a year from major business donors in Detroit. They invested the money in projects principally designed to help disadvantaged and minority groups in a variety of areas such as housing, education, employment, community services, recreation and others. I was soon to learn much more about New Detroit first hand.

I determined to learn more about New Detroit by talking to the Mayor and many others after I arrived. New Detroit came to be operated by a cadre of paid staff, a substantial number of volunteers from private industry who served a fixed period (six months) and were paid by their normal employers for their time. They had a board of trustees of such breadth that it permitted ADC mothers, black ghetto militants, and neighborhood improvement leaders to discuss problems and issues face to face with the established political and economic leadership of the city, including the heads of the major auto companies.

In August of 1967, the first president of the New Detroit Committee was William Patricks, followed by Lawrence Doss, Walter Douglas, S. Martin Taylor, Paul Hubbard, Charlie Williams, William Beckham and the current president is Shirley Stancato. The first chairman was Joseph Hudson of Hudson Department Stores, who began with 39 members and grew to a 100-members board of directors.

New Detroit, Inc. worked hard to understand the problems that caused people to riot. One of the earliest findings was that at least 100,000 housing units available in Detroit in 1968 were substandard. Many apartment buildings affordable by blacks had poor plumbing, no locks, cracked windows, peeling paint and unsafe stairways. With rampant unemployment, poverty and crime, New Detroit operated much like a social agency.

Meetings were long and emotional. Hard as they worked, New Detroit was unable to keep whites from leaving and to keep jobs from vanishing (McDonald).

Problems that contributed to racial unrest in 1967 were identified in the group's first progress report. Interestingly, New Detroit leaders recently agreed that most of those same problems still remain after some 30 years.

Joe Hudson, whose family was intertwined with the Hudson Motor Car Company, was a good example of the problem affecting Detroit. Hudson's corporate policy was to open additional department stores in the suburbs, pulling residents out of the city to shop. Thus Hudson and businessmen like him had contributed to the economic decline of the inner city since the early 1950s. His department stores finally merged with Fields and in 1983, the downtown Hudson's store closed (McGraw, June 26, 2001).

Another person who was one of the first heads of New Detroit, Inc. was Max Fisher who died March 3, 2005. The son of poor Russian Jewish immigrants, he got his start in the oil business and spread out with investments, including malls on the outskirts of Detroit. Beginning in the 1950s, his wealth and sentiments caused him to become a go-between the White House and Israel, to ensure that Israel received all help possible from the U.S. He was a financial supporter and close friend of Richard Nixon and Gerald Ford.

He was all over the place with shrewd advice to presidents, Israeli prime ministers, businessmen and companies and brought much to Detroit.

In the mid-1970s he helped build the Renaissance Center, and helped make Detroit's United Fund drive and the Detroit Symphony expansion of Orchestra Hall successful.

Of course, by the time I came on the scene in Detroit, Max Fisher was 60 years old, and thought of himself as a mover and shaker, especially in the 1968 campaign for Richard Nixon. He was no longer the modest man that I had heard about (McGraw, March 4, 2005).

Another founding member of New Detroit was Damon Keith. He is a man I much admire and I will tell more about him later.

These and other powerful personalities felt they knew best what Detroit needed as they pulled the strings of New Detroit, Inc. In my opinion, however, they played some role in creating the decline of the inner city. I know that they wanted to play a major part in the recovery of the city but I often found them working against the good of the city and favoring the vociferous voices that appeared before them—but not mine.

A good example of those eager to speak to New Detroit was a black militant named Frank Ditto. Despite the fact that this street gang leader wrote newsletters urging that police officers be killed, he got $250,000 from New Detroit for bogus reasons. Some have accused New Detroit of giving money to groups and individuals for "thinly disguised riot insurance" without helping worthy people and groups (Jacoby).

Detroit businessmen visited Ditto's "Voice of Independence" headquarters shortly after the riots. Ditto said the government couldn't lick this problem so businesses have to. He said, "If you cats can't do it, it's never going to get done" (*Business Week*, Feb. 3, 1968).

These confrontations and ventilations by radicals who had no platform or good works to propose sopped up much of the money of New Detroit before I arrived and continued during my term.

What I Found When I Arrived

The day of July 22, 1968, arrived and I was to begin my job. Johannes F. Spreen, once a little immigrant lad landing at Ellis Island from Germany, who later joined and served as a cop in the New York City Police Department, would today take the helm as Police Commissioner of the fifth largest city in America.

After I was sworn in as Detroit Police Commissioner on July 22, 1968, on my desk I found two things which I still remember clearly. One was a copy of John Hersey's book *The Algiers Motel Incident* which had come out the month before. This Pulitzer Prize novelist captured the nation's attention with his slanted depiction of the beating and killing of three young blacks on July 26, 1967, during the four days of riots in Detroit. The book became a best-seller and added to negative views of Detroit police and "Motown justice". When I arrived at my post, the Detroit police officers charged with the killings were still on trial.

The other item I found on my desk was a letter about the Poor Peoples Campaign (resulting from the Poor Peoples March on May 3rd which erupted into an assault on demonstrators by the Detroit Police at Cobo Hall as I described earlier). The State Civil Rights Commission wanted to know what I was going to do about it. Tough beginning!

The next day Mayor Cavanagh and I walked 12th Street—the scene of the triggering event of the riot the year before. Reporters were in tow. Being questioned, I did remark, "Where is the ghetto here? I see lawns. I see people raking and mowing. Hey, there are houses along 12th Street. New York in the Harlem and other areas had three, four and five-story tenement buildings. That's a ghetto."

Mayor Cavanagh and I together dedicated a mobile recreation facility for the neighborhood kids, a huge truck trailer filled with water as a "swim-mobile," sponsored by one of the local television stations.

The day was sunny, and the kids were happy, splashing in the water. That night, it was a different story.

My second night in Detroit was not many hours old when I was down on Twelfth Street again, this time in the darkness of the summer night, inside a scout car full of concerned police top command officers. We cruised slowly up the six-lane-wide street following a sweep of police cars, each with four heavily armed officers.

Even I, who had not seen the riot of 1967, could feel the tension in the air, in the eeriness of the too-empty streets, the rows of storefronts, the expressions on the faces of the Superintendent and the precinct commander riding with me, and the rigidity of their bodies as they stared out the windows.

The few people on the streets dispersed, as the loudspeakers on the scout cars asked them to. Trouble that night was limited to some isolated fire bombings and reports of looting. Here and there a few scampering packs of youngsters were sighted, who disappeared before the police patrols.

Our command car halted, and we had a standup staff conference on the pavement in the middle of Twelfth Street before returning to headquarters. I got to know a lot of the ranking officers in the department in a hurry that night.

The police alert lasted four days, and there were a number of arrests, but there was no repetition of the disaster of 1967. That event was covered by the *Detroit Scope Magazine* in an article called "He Walked Down 12th Street to Stifle a Riot." I'll include an excerpt.

> Caught in the delicate balance between sufficient force and restraint, Police Commissioner Johannes Spreen gave a commendable performance of agility last Thursday morning, during the 12th Street incident. Beginning about 12 p.m., with a group of youths breaking windows and setting two cars on fire, the activity slowly mushroomed until a tactical alert was ordered at 2:30 a.m.
>
> Commissioner Spreen, Superintendent John Nichols, Deputy Superintendent Charles Gentry and Sgt. Harold Liggett, aide to the commissioner, arrived on the scene at 2:45 a.m. By then there were seven fires—two suspected arsons and three started by Molotov cocktails.
>
> Bullhorn in hand, Spreen walked the uneasy streets urging residents to return to their homes. He remained upon the scene until the tactical alert ended at 6:43 a.m.
>
> In all, there were 16 arrests, mostly for breaking and entering and one for assault on a Tactical Mobile Unit officer. The officer, uninjured, managed to seize his assailant inflicting only a minor abrasion on his forehead.
>
> Peace returned with the dawn and the weary commissioner departed 12th Street where the riot seeds were planted last July. Spreen has probably not seen the last of 12th Street, a place where scattered minor incidents mark a return to normalcy. Let's hope that when necessary, he can match the way he gently nipped last week's riot.

Thus my first press release was positive but I knew trouble lay ahead. Sergeant Edward Wolski, Jr., was killed on Monday, August 5, 1968, and had served for 18 years. He was shot and killed after responding to a "family trouble" call and locating a man who had been firing a handgun. He saw the suspect flee into an apartment at Jeffries Housing Center. He radioed his location in, and then approached the building. The suspect opened fire striking Wolski, but the sergeant was able to return fire before he died. He was struck by the suspect three times. Sgt. Wolski was survived by his wife and two children and had received 40 meritorious citations.

A sergeant was dead and two patrolmen were injured by the time the suspect was subdued. The police were white and the family of the suspect was black. I was quickly on the scene but by the time I got back to my office, a story was bouncing around the newswires that Detroit was up in arms about another racial confrontation. It was actually a domestic disturbance and I had to call a press conference in the middle of the night to get the matter straight.

After I arrived in Detroit, I realized that training in the ABCs was sorely needed—training in attitude, behavior and conduct—if they were to become more professional and less brutish. Common Council did not provide training after policemen graduated from the academy, so I started "Seven Minute Seminars" using videos provided through private funding.

I had arrived in Detroit with no illusions about my position as a commissioner with a probable time limit of 17 months (the time left before the end of Mayor Cavanagh's term) to get things turned around. The tension between the police and the black community was more serious than crime itself. Many things played a part in the problems of Detroit, but I recognized the need to develop a new role model for the police.

I decided on a "wild idea" which was principally to get the cop out of the car and back face to face with the public. I couldn't leave him on foot so I put him on a scooter. It had worked in New York City. Why not here? I wanted to have a scooter patrol contingent ready for the World Series in October, since crowds would be on hand to see the Detroit Tigers play the St. Louis Cardinals from October 2-10.

The atmosphere in Detroit was very tense. Only two weeks after Sgt. Wolski was killed, I lost my second police officer on Thursday, August 15, 1968. Officer Riktor Gutowsky, age 28, was killed when his patrol vehicle struck a bus while involved in a high speed pursuit. This young man was survived by his wife and three children and had received seven citations for meritorious police work.

Radical Groups Operated in Detroit

During the first week of September, bombings shattered the cars of two Detroit policemen. The first explosion struck a car in Detroit's Woodward Precinct, and the second not only demolished Patrolman Richard Lloyd's car but several nearby cars. I ordered all-night guard on parking lots at all precinct station houses. The explosions were caused by 10 to 12 fuse-lit sticks of dynamite, said investigators.

On September 29, 1968, a bomb exploded at the recruiting office of the CIA in Ann Arbor, Michigan, near the campus of the University of Michigan. No one was injured but a crater 7" to 12" wide and 6" deep was caused by "straight dynamite". The bombing was one of eight anti-establishment bombings in the Detroit area at the time. The White Panther Party and its founders, John Sinclair and Lawrence Robert "Pun" Plamondon and member John Forest, were the prime suspects by the FBI because they were located in Ann Arbor (Damren).

On October 4, 1968, Richard Henry (Imari), absorbed with the RNA and preparing to go to New York, resigned from his position as technical manuals editor at the U.S. Army Tank Auto Command in Warren, Michigan.

On October 8, 1968, a delegation of RNA members left Detroit for New York. Their purpose was to assist the militant teachers' strike in the Oceanhill-Brownsville School District and to distribute the pamphlet "Now We Have a New Nation." On that day, the New York State Police stopped them for speeding in Oneida, New York. Those in the car were Leroy Wilds (20), Warren Galloway (26), Dorothy Sanders (40) and Salena McCutcheon Howard (28), all from Detroit.

Wilds had a .38 caliber five shot Smith and Wesson revolver. In the trunk, police found a .30 caliber M-1 carbine; 160 rounds of .30 caliber ammunition; and other assorted ammunition.

The four subjects were arraigned and placed under $10,000 bond. Charges against all but Wilds were later dropped. (On October 29, 1968, Wilds pled guilty to illegal possession of firearms. He was given an unconditional discharge on December 9, 1968.)

In 1968 when the Tigers beat the Cardinals for the world championship, I had been commissioner for only a little more than two months. Detroit, an underdog team pulling a big surprise, had the whole city looking for something to cheer about after the trauma of the 1967 riot, and everyone was out in the streets downtown.

It was the year of the Tigers. We set a home attendance record and Detroit was called Tigertown, U.S.A. The Cardinals had led the series until the final game, which was played in St. Louis. The "City on Fire" shut down to watch the game. The stadium was filled to capacity. The Tigers finally won their first series since 1945.

On October 6, Hubert Humphrey had come to town to attend the 4th game of the World Series and greet supporters. We managed to handle the crowds well.

Mayor Cavanagh, using the V for Victory, said the win saved the city. When the Tigers won it, black and white fans gathered at the airport to greet the winners. It seemed like life was back to normal again. I knew better. It was almost like a riot, but everyone was laughing. I called it the "Happy Riot."

For about six hours after the final out, Detroit enjoyed itself. After dark, however, a few individuals who hoped to escape attention in the crowds broke some store windows and some pilfering occurred.

Superintendent John F. Nichols had all police units deployed for the crowd-control mission. All precautions were taken to exercise restraint, to allow for the normal human exuberance, but to keep alert for those seeking to capitalize on the crowds and merriment to commit crimes.

In addition, with the cooperation of the news media, I was able to present a public appeal to all citizens of Detroit to keep their celebrating within bounds, and live up to the city's proud slogan, "City of Champions."

Just before the games, Detroit had a new secret weapon in its emergency police preparations. Thanks to the Greater Detroit Chamber of Commerce, which came up with the funds in the nick of time, the first motor scooters for the newly formed community-oriented patrol were delivered less than two weeks before the Series started.

A team of 30 patrolmen and sergeants was quickly organized, and the first big assignment was series crowd control downtown.

When the "happy riot" was at its height, of course, the streets were jammed, and traffic was at a standstill. Police on foot were virtually limited to stationary observation. The patrol cars, symbol of modern police department mobility, were immobilized.

At the first signs of unlawful disturbances, the scooter patrolmen were the only police able to move around, and to respond.

As a result, the scooter patrols made most of the arrests, and to my mind, may have made the difference between a celebration that was contained before lawless elements could get out of hand, and something much worse.

As far as I and others in Detroit were concerned, the scooter patrol won its spurs that night.

The *Michigan Chronicle,* (Detroit's Negro newspaper) which is usually very critical of police operations, used a front-page photo of a Detroit scooter officer overcoming a gunman in the street, as an example of effective police service during the World Series aftermath. Alas, scooters didn't help us with the RNA activities.

On October 13, 1968, an RNA meeting was held in the New York apartment of Charles Moore and of the 18 who attended, most were from Detroit like the Henry brothers, and the three who had driven to New York but had charges dropped. When Attorney Charles Howard died, he was replaced by Wilbur Grattan as the new Minister of State and Foreign Affairs.

Richard Henry (Brother Imari) discussed "Open Conflict with the Police" and "Open Guerrilla Warfare and Attacking Police Stations". He also discussed meeting within two weeks with all militant groups including the Revolutionary Action Movement (RAM) and the Black Panther Party (BPP). I have those documents because our undercover police officers confiscated them from meetings.

Milton and Richard Henry began to argue, accusing Richard of exercising "dictatorial powers" by involving the RNA in matters that would harm the organization. For example, Richard tried to get the RNA involved in the Ocean Hill-Brownsville School District strike (in Brooklyn) without even consulting the RNA's New York branch. Apparently, Richard won out because of what happened the next day.

On October 14, Richard Henry held a public meeting at a Brooklyn church of some 75 persons, including Robert (Sonny) Carson of the Brooklyn Congress of Racial Equality (CORE). He announced that the RNA was abandoning efforts to obtain five states for at least three years while they concentrated on establishing an enclave in Brooklyn.

An article came out in *The Nation* on October 14, 1968, with the title "Detroit's Year Without News". The gist of the article by Jerome Aumente was that Detroit was slowly groping back to normal after one of the most destructive riots in the nation's memory and a newspaper strike of 267 days (from November, 1967 to July, 1968).

There were certainly days when I wished the *Detroit News* and the *Detroit Free Press* would go on strike again, but there is no doubt that a city that could only see its happenings in short TV sound bites devoid of details was left guessing with little peace of mind. There was simply too much happening in Detroit and too little information exchange to make decisions and bring about political and social change.

On October 23, 1968, at the regular weekly meeting of the Detroit RNA, Richard Henry (brother Imari Obadele) stated that the RNA had opened a New York office to take advantage of the unrest in the area due to the teachers' strike. He requested that the RNA Detroit Consul furnish him with $250 a month for office space in Brooklyn. He told the Detroit group the same thing he said earlier in New York, that the RNA would wait three years to obtain the five southeastern states and concentrate on New York. He distributed a pamphlet entitled, "The Black Institution's Role in the Black Revolution for Land and Power in America" which he had written.

In the following weeks, four other policemen were wounded in gun battles. Then an incident occurred in which dissidents threw a lye-like material in the face of one policeman, marched against a political crowd and injured a dozen or so persons.

On October 29, 1968, Governor George Wallace came to speak at Cobo Hall in Detroit. We worried that the appearance of this racist man would foment all kinds of problems with dissident crowds. Security had to be very tight. A crowd of 9,000 showed up to hear Wallace—about 8,000 supporters and 1,000 hecklers. At the end of his speech, Wallace told the hecklers—mainly blacks, "You better have your day now because after November 5, you're through in this country". That set the crowd going.

Another police-black confrontation seemed about to occur. A large crowd of several thousand milled around outside of Cobo Hall, the convention center, heckling the police and Wallace supporters and setting fire to a Wallace poster.

After the crowd failed to heed an order to disperse, the police attempted to clear the area. A Tactical Mobile Unit (TMU) officer was blinded by mace thrown by someone in the crowd. Even though 800 demonstrators battled 350 police, somehow, no serious injuries occurred. The police officers attempted to be impartial and tried to take only the action necessary to insure the protection of people at the Cobo Hall site.

Sheila Murphy, then 20 and a white organizer for Ad Hoc, which had raised money to assist Detroiters involved in earlier conflicts with police, spoke to news reporters and claimed that a police officer said to her, "We'd kill you if we thought we could get away with it."

Murphy was quite an activist against the police. She came to my office twice. I felt she was very anti-police. Sheila Murphy, now Sheila Cockrel, married Ken Cockrel, the black lawyer who defended the killers in the New Bethel incident of March, 1969, to be described later.

Also Sheila was apparently active with the Catholic Archdiocese. She received money from them to purchase video cameras to photograph "bad" police actions. I later wrote a column for the *Detroit News* that the Archdiocese should have provided video cameras to the police also to photograph the rebellious demonstrators who threw offal, wine, red paint, stones, etc., at police lines.

And if I had stayed as Police Commissioner, I would have probably done as I had remarked to some of our officers, put more women police in the front lines so the news photographers could see really what was being done. Unfortunately at that time, we did not have that many police women in uniform and on patrol to so use.

They say that a new police chief usually has a honeymoon period of around 100 days. So much for honeymoons! The first week of November 1968 was hell.

Veterans Memorial Hall Incident

A real ugly incident occurred on the night of November 1st. This was three days after the Cobo Hall incident where police had charged demonstrators at the George Wallace appearance. The Detroit Police Officers Wives Association was holding a dance on the first floor ballroom and over 100 couples were in attendance.

This night I had just come out of the hospital for surgery to remove a large (I later learned it was benign) tumor from my right side. I had also invited the President of John Jay College to Detroit to speak to a club. After his speech, my wife, Elinor, and I took him to the airport. I wanted to walk him down to the plane but Elinor said, "No way, you're as white as a ghost. We must go home."

But I protested. I said, "Honey, we must go to the Detroit Police Officers Wives Association Dinner Dance." Elinor again said, "No way. You've just been operated on. We're going home."

I often wondered would that ugly incident that followed have been averted if we had appeared at that function.

But it did happen and caused me and the department a lot of grief. I had the police brutality at the Cobo Hall Poor Peoples March to deal with even though I was not yet commissioner, the Algiers Motel book, police overreaction to the crowd at the George Wallace rally, plus a few other interesting things. All these were in the first 100 days—no honeymoon.

The Veterans Memorial incident occurred on about the 100th day, I believe. This incident occurred inside and outside the Veterans Memorial Hall on the night and early morning of November 1-2, 1968.

The Ebeneezer AME Church was sponsoring a high school dance on the sixth floor attended by a black audience. On the first floor, off-duty police officers and their wives were at the Detroit Police Officers Wives Association dinner-dance.

There were charges and counter charges. The police wives alleged that some black youths from the dance had abused and/or insulted them. The interaction between police officers, wives and the youths occurred because there were insufficient toilets on the ballroom floor, necessitating people to take elevators up to floors where there were toilets.

Word circulated that black hooligans were causing trouble on the elevators. Women complained of obscene gestures and sexual threats.

The result was that some teenagers were beaten and kicked, including some of Detroit's black elite. One teenager, Derrick Tabor, 17, son of the Rev. Willis Tabor, was hospitalized. Derrick Tabor was able to call his father who got to the scene while the beatings were still in progress. The 15 year old son of Rev. Nicholas Hood, Detroit's only black councilman at the time, while not personally injured, was an eyewitness to the whole affair.

A security guard reported that there were black teenage stragglers in the elevator who left after he confronted them. A James Heaney, 60, attorney and realtor, backed up the police and the security guard.

In addition to the beatings and kickings, a car belonging to a black had been hauled away. When it was returned, it was plastered with George Wallace stickers.

Meanwhile I was home in bed recovering from the tumor operation the day before. I did not learn of this ugly travesty till the next morning. In the meantime the press, radio and TV had a field day. The Mayor made comments regarding the "blue curtain of secrecy" asserting it was hampering an investigation.

The next morning I woke up and found out about the incident at the dinner dance, I was enraged at the actions and stupidity of those unprofessional police officers and that "blue curtain" and that these police left the scene that night without taking proper police action.

On Sunday I called Carl Parcell, President of the DPOA, to meet with me without the press. He brought along his Vice President Chuck Withers. I then really laid into them. I was indignant. I was fuming.

I excoriated them that morning unmercifully. I demanded that they rend that "blue curtain" asunder. I said those "police wrongdoers" have given much ammunition to the liberals and agitators against the Detroit police, and have cut the legs off their Commissioner. I also quite scathingly told them, "You and those reprehensible, unlawful lawmen couldn't even be a patch on a New York City police officer's ass. You tell me that some of the wives were groped, and grabbed by their breasts and rear ends, etc. Well, then, arrests should have been made and force used only as necessary. But you guys just beat them up and left the scene and smirked, and so left this fine city again on tenderhooks!"

Well, within hours some movement to split that blue curtain appeared.

The City Council Was Surprisingly Negative

However, the Common Council quickly grabbed the headlines with denunciation of the police at the Memorial Hall with comments that the FBI or State Police should be called in to investigate the Detroit Police Department. They demanded the appearance of the Commissioner—me.

I did appear on November 7, 1968, and before answering their "eager" questions I demanded the right to make a statement first. I still have that document.

If the facts as alleged are true then I can only express abhorrence and dismay at the actions of a handful of officers. I am further saddened by the knowledge that if this matter is not resolved quickly, fairly, equitably (with the principle of equal justice firmly in mind) that this can seriously reflect on 4,700 other police officers who were not there, were not on the scene, and I am certain are not in sympathy with such actions.

The point that is missed by some police officers is that they occupy a unique position in society, because they are sworn to uphold the law, to provide protection of life and property, and to protect the human and civil rights we enjoy in a land of liberty, therefore, they certainly cannot be above the law.

The police officer has taken an oath to uphold the laws of the land. When such a man, selected by society to represent them, violates the rights of others, he in effect violates our trust in him and also our rights. It diminishes all of us, and certainly public confidence in law is seriously weakened. We must have the confidence of the public in the just and orderly processes of law or else respect for authority will become an illusion never to be grasped.

Not only can we not break the law but also there is accountability to our fellow members of the police profession, not only in this city but all throughout America.

If the facts as alleged are true, then some off-duty police officers engaged in unlawful and improper conduct and actions.

The Detroit Police Department cannot and will not tolerate any unlawful actions on the part of individual officers (whether on or off duty)!

A crime committed by anyone is reprehensible, certainly the more so when committed by someone sworn to prevent crime and to protect his neighbor and fellow citizens.

The constitution of the United States and the State of Michigan and laws duly adopted guarantee to everyone equal protection under those laws.

None of us want an officer or officers who could have committed such acts as alleged.

There is no room in this department for such a man, no department can possibly rise above him if his actions are condoned and allowed. I have the utmost faith in the overwhelming preponderance of the men and women in this department, in their high caliber and their excellence. This department must be maintained so that we can continue to strive for a profession with pride.

I ask that any member of this department or anyone that was at the affair to come forward and bring it to the attention of District Inspector James Bannon. I have issued an administrative directive to all members of the department to this effect.

This department, including the leaders of the various department organizations and I, are as anxious as anyone else to find the truth and deal with it as quickly as possible.

I feel that this department can and will conduct a full, fair, complete and impartial investigation and I want that opportunity.

I then demanded from the City Council the right to investigate my own department, and that I did.

The newspapers wrote about the incident November 8 and noted that the Wayne County prosecutor's office suggested awaiting my internal investigation.

State Senator Coleman Young told reporters that some of the children had already requested that Wayne County's new 23-member grand jury investigate the incident without waiting. Young transformed the incident into a *cause celebre.*

According to Mayor Cavanagh's earlier comments, a "blue curtain" of police secrecy (Cavanagh meant the police union) hampered the investigation. But we had to sift statements for the truth. He trusted that I would manage things properly.

I was able to announce the results of our investigation within a few days. I suspended nine officers and fired three, and gained a little peace for the city. However, police morale dipped to a new low when the suspensions and firings were announced. Crime figures started to rise after a brief lull.

The rush to judgment brought out an article on November 10, 1968, on who runs the police department. How can one person please the police union, the press, the politicians, the people and the police all at the same time? I will excerpt the article by David Cooper in the *Detroit Free Press* which displayed the problems a police commissioner had in Detroit. Here are some excerpts.

> Detroit faces a growing crisis over control of its police department and policemen...
>
> Mayor Cavanagh concedes the crisis exists. So do Negro leaders, but they are not certain Cavanagh will exercise enough authority to cope with it.
>
> The announcement late Saturday by Police Commissioner Johannes Spreen that department investigators have identified the off-duty police who beat Negro youths after a police dance at the Veterans Memorial last Saturday may alleviate some of their fears.

But the broad question remains: Who runs the department? The police themselves or the City of Detroit? The City Charter makes it clear who is supposed to run the Police Department: The civilian authority of the City of Detroit.

Recent events, however, have shown that Mayor Cavanagh and his new police commissioner, Johannes Spreen, are having difficulty asserting their authority.

Item: Private directives from Cavanagh to Spreen in August about the police recruiting of Negroes turns up mysteriously in the hands of a hostile city councilman, Philip Van Antwerp, who uses them to criticize the mayor for causing "low morale" among police.

Item: As high-level police officials try to investigate the alleged beating of Negro teenagers by off-duty policemen, Cavanagh complains that the police are not cooperating with the probe. Again, Spreen had to issue a formal order to policemen requiring them to step forward with the information.

Item: The police union becomes more bumptious and demanding. The police longed to defeat the pension change at the polls Nov. 5. The union lost narrowly in the election; the pension change was approved by voters. City officials heaved sighs of relief, mainly because the union's political muscle had been weakened somewhat...

Sources close to the new commissioner say Spreen, since taking office last summer, has tried not to ruffle the feathers of the department's rank and file. Rather he has attempted to gain the confidence of his men...

The commissioner showed Saturday he wants to command the department. The question now is whether the police rank and file will let him.

It was not entirely over, however, because James Evans, father of a 17-year-old hospitalized overnight after the incident, filed a $140,000 lawsuit against 10 policemen, five officials of the Detroit Police Officers Wives Association, and Carl Parsell, president of the DPOA.

Meanwhile other issues were bubbling to the surface in Detroit. With the help of black clergy, the Detroit Revolutionary Union Movement (DRUM) secured a church to hold a mass rally on November 17th with a large community turnout. DRUM sold raffle tickets prior to the rally which served to raise funds and publicize the group. First prize was an M-1 rifle and second prize was a shotgun. Inspired by DRUM, additional groups were formed such as the FRUM (Ford RUM) ELRUM (Eldon Avenue RUM), etc.

Needless to say, law enforcement officials were watching DRUM closely, but from a distance.

Before I arrived in 1968, the Detroit Free Press had conducted a survey of residents and had determined that the number one problem Detroit's black residents faced in the period leading up to the riot was "police harassment and police brutality." Many suggested that police might not have been so brutal had they been more racially representative of the communities they served.

There were 437 Negroes in the survey and they were read a list of 23 possible grievances which they ranked. The results were published by the *Detroit Free Press* on August 27, 1967. By each item, responders answered, "How much did each of these grievances have to do with the riot?" Answers could be "a great deal" or "something" or "nothing". Here are the *percentages* of the 437 responses under the category of "a great deal". For example, just over half thought police brutality had a great deal to do with the riot:

Police brutality	57
Overcrowded living conditions	55
Poor housing	54
Lack of jobs	45
Poverty	44
Anger with local business people	43
Dirty neighborhoods	42
Too much drinking	40
Broken political promises	39
Failure of parents to control children	39
White public officials	32
Teenagers	32
Hatred of whites	29
Lack of strong Negro leaders	29
Black nationalism	26
Anger with politicians	22
Failure of schools	22
Not enough integration	21
Negro public officials	18
Not enough welfare services	17
Middle class Negro frustration	14

Poor transportation	7
Anger with fire department	2

The survey had no question about the race of police and just mentioned "police brutality". However, blacks constituted only 5% of the overall police force in 1967, and only one out of every eight black officers held a rank higher than that of patrolman. (Fine 1989:109) So it was assumed that white officers were brutal to black citizens but that was not always the case. In the Algiers Motel incident, a black security guard rushed in with the National Guardsmen and Detroit policemen and was described by witnesses as beating and wounding them.

I knew that relations between black citizens and white police in Detroit required a major overhaul. Even though I intended to recruit more blacks into the police force, I knew that would take some time. We needed to change the perception of police to show them as protectors instead of enforcers.

I believed that the police had become isolated from those they served due mainly to being sealed inside an impersonal vehicle with flashing lights and screeching sirens, and I was worried. When such a patrol officer has contact with people, he acts as a controller of a situation that has already occurred. I thought that a more appropriate vehicle was a scooter which, like a cop on a bicycle, allows the policeman to be talked to and to be more a part of the community.

The press made a point about my emphasis on rapport and love. But obviously something different needed to be tried. Here is an excerpt of one editorial in the *Detroit Free Press* called "Rapport Is the Key".

> Johannes Spreen is an exceedingly vulnerable guy. Anyone in his position who talks about things like "rapport" and "love" as the key to police work in Detroit puts his neck on the block.
>
> It is so easy to characterize him as offering simplistic answers to complicated problems. But we really are talking about something just that basic.
>
> The black man who complains that the cops are giving him a hard time doesn't want some high-powered formula for having X number of policemen at such-and-such a spot at certain times. What he wants is for the policeman to look at him without curling a lip and to give him a citation or make an arrest without insulting his manhood...
>
> Or to turn it around, the policeman who wants "community support" really wants to be able to make an arrest without having his every move questioned.
>
> In a word, rapport.

What makes this "simplistic" under some circumstances is that this is easy for the commissioner to say, either in his office or on the green pea circuit, but his word is not the law. He has trouble getting the command down to the line officer. The boys on the beat find it a terrible temptation just to laugh when the "old man" starts talking about love again…

The test of Commissioner Spreen's stewardship will not be his goals—they are good, and he is painfully earnest about pursuing them—but whether he can make them the goals of men on the line.

Commissioner Spreen's scooter patrol has enormous potential for breaking down the hostility that exists. An arch-critic of the Police Department confessed to us a few days ago that the scooter patrol is working, that even his own attitudes are being softened up.

But the officer out on the street still holds the key. He has encountered hostility so long that he expects it, and he is not likely to make the first gesture. Yet, if he can, in small ways, begin to break through the wall of prejudice, then he can build the rapport the commissioner is talking about.

And the trouble—the reason so many police officers don't cooperate—is that it is so easy to mistake being considerate for being soft. We can't afford softness on the part of our police, but neither can we afford the kind of blind faith in overwhelming force that the Detroit Police Officers Association (union) so often seems to manifest.

Somewhere in between there is a better way. Commissioner Spreen calls it rapport, and that's as good a word as any.

The FBI Had Its Own Agenda

I thought Paul Stoddard and the FBI were doing a fine job. Of course, I never saw the actual communications between Stoddard and Director J. Edgar Hoover until the Freedom of Information Act permitted me to see their memos recently.

I had been on the job as Detroit Police Commissioner no longer than four months when Stoddard wrote this memo to Hoover on 11/22/1968. The FBI and the police, of course, were in frequent contact as we shared information learned from undercover officers at meetings of various groups such as the RNA.

Stoddard had followed Hoover's directions in a memo of 10/31/1968 to create a phony letter to create problems within the RNA membership.

To: Director, FBI
From: SAC, Detroit
Subject: Counterintelligence Program
Black Nationalist Hate Groups

Racial Intelligence
(Republic of New Africa)

Re: Bureau airtel to Detroit, dated 10/31/68

Per suggestion set forth in re: Bureau airtel, Detroit requests mailing letters prepared on commercially purchased paper to various members of the Republic of New Africa (RNA) with the exception of Richard Henry, signed by a concerned RNA brother.

This letter will read as follows:

Dear Brother and Sister:

Lately I have been concerned about the lack of funds of the RNA. I know that many brothers and sisters have paid taxes and have donated on various occasions to the Republic. Where has the money gone, and why haven't we purchased our land with it?

I do not make any direct accusation at any brother or sister but I would like to know how Brother Imari owns a house, supports a family, and travels all over the country when he is not even working. I think we all deserve an explanation of the use of the RNA money, and I think we are foolish to donate and pay taxes to support one man, when the Republic is in such dire need of money. I think this question should be raised at the next Wednesday meeting. I'm not signing my name because I do not want to create a personal conflict among us.

A concerned brother.

This letter will be mailed to Detroit members of the RNA only and if a favorable response is received, a similar letter will be prepared for nationwide RNA member circulation.

Detroit requests Bureau approval.

Hoover responded to Stoddard, but not until December 3rd, with the following memo:

Detroit is authorized to send the anonymous letter set out in your letter to the bureau to selected members of the Republic of New Africa (RNA) using commercially purchased stationery.

Insure this mailing cannot be traced to the Bureau and advise of results. If results are favorable, consider submitting a recommendation for circulating this letter to other RNA members in other cities.

Note: This anonymous letter criticizes Richard Henry (brother Imari), an RNA officer who allegedly is using RNA funds for personal expenses. This has been a matter of discussion with enough RNA members so as to protect our sources. Criticism of leaders of black nationalist extremist groups, such as the RNA, for misusing funds, is an effective method of neutralizing these leaders. Since this is an anonymous letter, there is no possibility of embarrassment to the Bureau.

We, as law enforcement officers, were never told to create such materials but I can't say that we were against disabling groups that perpetrated chaos, violence or harm to citizens.

The Republic of New Africa Was Becoming a Threat

Meanwhile, the RNA held a meeting in Brooklyn on December 7-8. They formulated plans for conducting a plebiscite vote in the Ocean Hill-Brownsville District to declare Ocean Hill-Brownsville as an "independent state". Our undercover officer brought back documents, some of which are still in my possession, from the RNA meetings. There were moments when I thought I should not publish them because someone might come after me, even after all these years. But I decided to describe them so that the public would know why the police had to control these revolutionaries.

The working strategy for that meeting as proposed by Richard Henry (Imari) included obtaining a vote of the Ocean Hill-Brownsville area to become an independent state (he compared it to West Berlin) so that the U.S. and U.N. would be impressed. Brother Imari added that the RNA must restrain themselves from immediately opening a military campaign to get rid of the occupation force of police the moment they won the vote.

He had prepared a list of possible obstructions that might be created by police or government such as terminating water supply, phone service, trash collections, mail delivery, ADC and/or relief payments, barring of school buildings, etc. He also prepared solutions to those problems short of military responses. But he did propose the institution of a uniformed unarmed "Domestic Tranquility Patrol", announcement of all promises of military support received from groups like the black underground army in America, and instituting a "top-rate counter-espionage section".

Among those at the meeting were a large component from Detroit, the Henry brothers, Wilbur Grattan, Joan Franklin, Mwesi Chui (John Taylor), Obaboa Awolo, Leroi Jones, Herman Ferguson and Baba Oseijeman Adefunmi.

One of the results of that meeting was the creation of a "Freedom Corps". A Steering Committee composed of RNA members from 33 college campuses was created to develop the Freedom Corps. The next meeting of the RNA was set for January in Detroit.

In December, 1968, the trial of the officers and a security guard who were charged with killing three black men and beating others at the Algiers Hotel in 1967 finally concluded. The officers who had been suspended were fired even though they were not found guilty.

Widick wrote about the results of that trial. He said that one and a half years later, three suspended Detroit policemen, Ronald August, David Senak, and Robert Paille, and a private guard, Melvin Dismukes, a Negro, were tried on charges of conspiracy against the civil rights of the three dead men and seven other individuals. An all-white jury found them not guilty. He added that Detroit's black middle class and labor moderates found themselves scorned by the new generation of young militants as "Uncle Toms".

After the suspension and firing of the officers, Carl Parsell, President of the Detroit Police Officers Association, issued this statement in December.

> The DPOA believes…the charges of police brutality are part of a nefarious plot by those who would like our form of government overthrown. The blueprint for anarchy calls for the destruction of the effectiveness of the police. Certainly, it must be obvious that every incident is magnified and exploited with only one purpose. A lot of well-meaning people, without realizing their real role, are doing the job for the anarchists.

The criticisms of the Detroit police officers had been stirred up again in light of the results of the trial. I knew the morale of the troops was sagging badly. As Christmas neared, I sent a message to all members of the Detroit Police Department which I've excerpted here:

> This is Commissioner Spreen wishing all of you the happiest holiday season ever. In sending this Christmas message, I have an opportunity which doesn't come often enough—that is, an opportunity to say "Thank you" for your fine and dedicated performance every day of the year.

I know from my own experience in the various ranks that policemen often feel that they have been forgotten—forsaken by the department executives and forsaken by the people they strive to serve. This will not be so in Detroit. It is my firm belief that good internal relations within the department are just as important as good external relations with the community, and I will dedicate myself to the improvement of both.

I wish that I could thank each of you personally and tell you how very proud I am of you. Your excellent performance since I have been commissioner—a performance which is reflected in Detroit's remarkably low crime figures—shows that you understand and that I am 100% behind your professional performance.

Although my job doesn't permit me to get to know each and every one of you, I'd like it better if it did. Nevertheless, even though I don't know all of you, I am proud to be working with a department team of fine men and women who serve the people of this city so well.

In this service, the hours and hardships of a police officer are perhaps felt more by our patient and understanding wives and families who sit at home and worry and wait...

Please allow me to extend my best and most sincere good wishes to you and your devoted families for a very merry Christmas. And my hope is that in the New Year, our efforts may continue to yield a reduction in crime and community tension in Detroit.

I lost my third police officer on Friday, January 10, 1969. Officer Stanley Rapaski was shot and killed when he was identified as a police officer during a robbery at a bar while he was off duty. During the robbery, the bar owner told the two suspects to leave because Officer Rapaski was a policeman. The suspects instead went to Officer Rapaski, disarmed him, and then shot him as he lay on the floor. The suspects fled the scene.

One was later shot and killed by other officers and the second suspect turned himself in.

Someday I ought to write about how difficult it is to tell an officer's widow and family about his death. It is one of the hardest things we have to do. There is nothing like personal experience to show how complex the relationship is between law enforcement executives and officers.

When I became the Detroit Police Commissioner, I walked into a hornet's nest from every direction, including the police force. The press had many articles about my handling of the force I inherited and I'll quote from some of them.

William Serrin, *Detroit Free Press* reporter, wrote an article called "Spreen: Six Months of Crises" which I'll excerpt here.

When Detroit Police Commissioner Johannes F. Spreen took office in July, the 6-foot-5, 235-pounder was wished good luck. In his six months, Spreen has seen his 4,706—man department hit with three incidents in which police were accused of excess force against citizens. And at least 125 allegations of police misconduct, some of them substantiated, some not, lie on Spreen's desk from his Citizens Complaint Bureau, the quasi police review board.

Police morale sags badly and some say the frustrated and embittered policemen are nearing open revolt. This is probably overstating the case, but many are convinced that an ill-timed clash of antagonisms on the part of both Negroes and police could bring an eruption of major violence at any time.

Whatever action Negroes take is almost certain to bring repressive police response. And that response is certain to bring strident demands from Detroit's Negro leaders. The lines of combat are drawn...

Spreen clearly is on the hot seat. Liberals, Negro politicians—some sincere, some intent on grabbing headlines—say he doesn't go far enough to curb the racism that, in some degree, certainly exists in the Detroit department.

Police are angry with him for the 12 officers he has suspended so far. Even Spreen admits: "I've got a lot of policemen mad at me."

The problems have dogged Spreen from the day he took office—July 22, 1968. The next day was the first anniversary of the beginning of the Detroit riot, and for the next five days, Spreen didn't even go home. He camped on a cot in a conference room next to his third-floor office....

In an almost united front, Detroit's Negro politicians demanded that Cavanagh personally condemn the police department for racism. They further demanded that the department give psychiatric tests to find racists on the force and called for a federal investigation, if necessary, into the youth's charges...

Spreen says unexpected incidents between police and Negroes have kept him from establishing the rapport he'd like to have with his men...

Says one top observer: "There's always been a saying among cops in Detroit. "We don't give a damn who's commissioner: We'll make him do things our way or we'll break him."

Tom Johnson, an official of the Civil Rights Commission who is knowledgeable concerning police, says: "When it gets down to actually who runs the Detroit Police Department, I'm afraid you have to say the D.P.O.A. (union) runs it...the decisions the commissioner and superintendent make are influenced by what the D.P.O.A. will do."

The police reforms that are needed in Detroit are obvious. First most observers say, "Detroit must increase the number of Negro officers and insure that the old-line commanders do not thwart this goal."

I struggled to demonstrate fair play and community concern by holding a recruiting drive aimed especially at blacks. It paid good dividends but just as I was about to announce a new budget, black politicos escalated a minor flap over a black teenager resisting arrest into a charge of "police brutality." This was coupled with off-duty Officer Rapaski's murder during a robbery.

I tried to decide what to do. I issued a document unique in police annals, an almost poetic dissertation on "love and crime." It called for a 100 day "love in" to unite the community and establish a moratorium on criticism of police until reforms could take effect. While I worked on that, the RNA was at work again according to our undercover intelligence unit.

On January 18-19, 1969, the Republic of New Africa met at the Twenty Grand Motel at 14th and Warren Streets in Detroit. Our undercover officer brought back several documents that were distributed at that meeting. They included a handbill urging the "brothers and sisters" to serve in the Freedom Corps, and pamphlets entitled, "To Build a Nation, the Freedom Corps Working Papers", "The Freedom Corps".

The *Esquire Magazine* published an article regarding the Republic of New Africa in January, 1969, written by Robert Sherrill. It was entitled, "We Want Georgia, South Carolina, Louisiana, Mississippi and Alabama Right Now." Some highlights from that article follow.

In the interview of Milton Henry by Sherrill, Henry stated that the RNA has 100 acres in Mississippi, that the method to take over Mississippi would be by electing sheriffs in counties with a black majority, that "having a majority isn't meaningful until the day comes when we have enough people standing at the polls with guns to protect our vote. The reason we are setting up a black legion is so we will get our votes counted." Henry stated, "If we had only four sheriffs down there, with all that can be done with deputizing, we could change the state of Mississippi."

He continued, "In terms of real control of the land and real confrontation, there will be other things going on in this country. It could be burned to the ground while U.S. officials are playing games with us. They could be engaged in very costly guerrilla activities." He went on to say that they could beat the U.S. Army with the aid of nuclear weapons from their allies, such as China.

Henry said, "We've got a second strike power right now in our guerrillas within the metropolitan areas—black men armed. Say we started taking over Mississippi—which we are capable of doing right now—and the U.S. started to interfere. Well, our guerrillas all over the country would strike. Our second strike force capability would be to prevent the United States Armed Forces from working us over, not the local forces. The local forces could compete with our forces."

Henry went on to say, "If the whites defeat our objectives, the country will be ruined in the process...They aren't going to win in Vietnam and they can't win in the United States. We can fight from within…The United States can be destroyed…This country will either talk to the separatists today or will talk to them later, at which time perhaps this country will have lost a great deal in terms of lives and property."

Henry showed reporter Sherrill two AR-15 rifles and stated, "We train regularly."

Obviously the Republic of New Africa had been posing a more serious problem than the public knew before that article was published. But the article also brought publicity and more recruits to the RNA.

My New Approaches to Calm Detroit: The Love In

Meanwhile, I had come up with a program to try to calm things in Detroit. I initiated a "Love In" on Valentine's Day to run for 100 days. Bob Talbert of the *Detroit Free Press* wrote on February 21, 1969, "Spreen's Love-In: Here's Why We Can't Afford Not to Join."

> Spreen's intention is to humanize the cop. He's taken some imaginative steps in this direction by demilitarizing the prowl car with his scooter-patrol Rangers, men with first names and faces that smile, who laugh with the man and woman on the street…
>
> On July 22 Spreen took office, inheriting a department's troubled past, and an immediate riot anniversary confrontation the next day…
>
> So Big John Spreen has now asked us for love.
>
> He deserves this much at the very least. The man has some dramatic, innovative things to show us about what can happen when policing really works. But he didn't have them yesterday because he wasn't here yesterday. If we give him the time today to show us, he will give us a tomorrow that works.
>
> During this "Love-In" period the best thing we can do is get to know our policemen. Invite them into your homes, your offices. Get to know them socially as people with first names and faces.
>
> So what is this love that Johannes Spreen is talking about? He says:
>
> "It's caring about your neighbor so you report an assault you witness upon him or his home. It's caring about your city so that you don't want to see it suffer. It's doing your thing well within the law and within the bounds of propriety. It's putting your personal desires and politics second to your concern for your city.
>
> "It's helping to professionalize your police rather than policing your police. It's your never getting tired of asking what can we do to help. It's wanting to change things with calm, cool reason and considered judgments, not with destructive 'to hell with it' attitudes. It's having faith in people and police

officers and the hope we can all live together in a better Detroit. It's making the policeman 'my man' not 'the man.'

"It's believing that a miracle can work in this city. The miracle of those silent, uncommitted citizens of our city speaking out and committing themselves. That's what love is. That's what it can be. That's what it must be."

Spreen has laid it on the line. You and I can't afford not to join his "Love-In."

The media helped get the idea out to Detroit that love could be the new basic ingredient of peace and could counteract violence. I was showing Detroit a role model of a man who talked about love and care. I thought that was important then but I really know it's important now. I'll go ahead and give the full declaration from my Valentine's Day speech in 1969 at the 12th precinct. It was called "Love and Crime" and it shows where the community individually and respectively can help.

The problem of crime is complex and difficult and requires competent, well-trained, acceptable, professional police and sheriff's departments to cope with it. But, if I had to pick one thing that could really do the job and solve the problem, it would be love.

Love! What is it? It can be called a hundred different things, and the young don't have a monopoly on it. We seniors over 30 know about love also, and we are, hopefully, balanced by our experience. Maybe we can teach the younger generation a few things about love and work together for a pleasant and peaceful future.

What is this love that can cut down crime and cancel community tensions? What is this love that can do more about crime than all your law enforcement agencies, vigilantes, guns and tanks? Let's try to define it:

- If it's caring about your neighbor so you report an assault you witness upon him or his home, that's love.

- If it's caring about your community so that you don't want to see if suffer, that's love.

- If you care about your fellow citizens no matter what their hue, that's love.

- If you care enough to willingly serve your country and your community, that's love.

- If you are concerned about the conditions that can tempt man to harm his neighbor, and you want to see them alleviated, that's love.

- If you get concerned about crime and do something constructive about it, that's love.

- If you feel that there are things wrong, injustices, evils in this world, and you earnestly wish to do something about them, that's love.

- If you want to change things that do not seem right to you, calmly, coolly, with considered judgment, rather than with a destructive "to hell with it all" attitude, that's love.

- If you do your thing well, within the law and within the bounds of propriety, that's love.

- If you put your personal desires and politics second to your concern for your community, that's love.

- If you concentrate more on helping to professionalize your police than to complain about or ignore your police, that's love.

- If you can take a negative and help turn it into a positive, that's love.

- If you follow the principles of honesty, truthfulness and fairness, that's love.

- If you use consideration, care, courtesy and compassion in your dealings with all you meet, that's love.

- If you live according to the Golden Rule, the Ten Commandments, or your moral, ethical or religious beliefs, that's love.

- If you consider the feelings of the other person as an individual who is with you on this small spinning speck of dust called earth, that's love.

- If you have faith in people and in your police, that's love.

- If you have hope that we can all live together in a better world, that's love.

- If you offer charity to all your fellow men, that's love.

- If you believe there may be a spot in heaven for all, regardless of their race, color or creed, that's not only love but heaven on earth.

Well, I could talk the talk, but could I and the cops walk the walk?

The day that Talbert's article about the Love-In came out was February 21, 1969. That was also the anniversary of Malcolm X's assassination. A rally was held at Northwestern High School in Detroit. The rally was to lower the flag of the U.S., to raise the separatist flag used by the RNA, and to rename the high school the Malcolm X High School. At approximately 4:00 pm, 250 people assembled, including members of the RNA. The green, red and black separatist flag was raised. The U.S. flag had been lowered earlier by school officials. Fortunately no incident developed.

On February 28, 1969, I prepared a statement of community relations needs, general operations and managements needs, as well as training equipment and program needs including the cost of needed equipment.

The scooter officers had begun operations in November and were encouraged to be proactive, not just reactive, to win friends for the Detroit Police Department. Our "Buck Up Your Police" fund began on March 1, 1969, and realized $50,000 in single dollar contributions for scooters, police, books and bookshelves in all 13 precincts. It created a bond, a partnership with police, of old, young, black and white.

On March 7, Common Council member Nicholas Hood, a black man whose son had been present at the dance incident back in November, wrote this to me:

Dear Commissioner:

I want to congratulate you on the forthright disciplinary steps which you have taken in regard to the teenage dance incident at the Veterans Memorial Building, and the Christmas Day Curry case.

It is such difficult and forthright action on the part of the police which will also give them the kind of image which is necessary for commanding the support of the community.

Most sincerely yours.

It was nice to have such a letter but the Common Council was not ready to help the police department in any substantial way, nor was New Detroit.

I was shocked to learn that on March 11, New Detroit wanted $300,000 set aside for a study of police attitudes. I said that took much time and I asked for $150,000 and support for increased police supervisors. They described a 24-member Advisory Committee to set up the study which included eight members recommended by me, eight persons representing the concerns of black citizens, and eight persons representing the city administration, New Detroit and other community interests.

On March 20, 1969, Governor William Milliken toured police headquarters with me. It was a good opportunity to show him the facilities. He got on one of our motor scooters to have his picture taken and it made rather nice publicity for our innovations.

The New Bethel Church Shoot-out

The RNA had written a letter on March 3rd inviting blacks to the new RNA meeting on March 28-29 and it would lead to the worst incident during my term of office.

The RNA now had a new stationery and letter head. At the top was "Republic of New Africa, An African Nation in the Western Hemisphere Struggling for Complete Independence".

Robert Williams was still listed as the President. Milton Henry, Esq. was still the first vice president and his office address was listed in Pontiac, Michigan. The rest of the officers were listed thusly: Second Vice President: Betty Shabazz; Treasurer: Obaboa Olowo; Minister of the Interior: Imari Obadele; Ministers of Culture: Oserjeman Adefunmi, Leroi Jones, Ron Karenga; Minister of Education: Herman Ferguson; Minister of State & Foreign Affairs: Wilbur Grattan; Minister of Justice: John Franklin, Esq.; Minister of Health and Welfare: Queen Mother Moore; Minister of Finance: Raymond Willis; Minister of Information: Charles Enoch, Leito Durley; Ministers of Defense: H. Rap Brown, Msweusi Chui; and Special Ambassador Maxwell Stanford.

On Friday, March 28, 1969, 225 persons from various parts of the country registered for an RNA convention held at 13305 Dexter in Detroit. The meeting went on until 7:00 pm the next day when it was announced that everyone was to meet at the New Bethel Baptist Church. Almost every one of the 225 persons went over to the church.

Now I must explain that our undercover unit, always present at the RNA meetings, had taken photographs showing many armed members at each of the meetings. That was certainly true of those who gathered at the church. These pictures show the rifles carried by members around the room as the RNA membership conducted business. I have these pictures and am looking at them as I write this.

So on Saturday, March 29, 1969, nearly 225 members of the Republic of New Africa (RNA) met at New Bethel Church to finish off the conference and celebrate the first anniversary of the organization. The meeting started at 8:30 pm and the following people spoke. Queen Mother Moore, Obaboa Awolo, Hakim Jamal (Allen Donaldson of Compton, California), Virginia Collins and Milton Henry.

Milton Henry was the last speaker and concluded the meeting at approximately 11:30 pm; and as ministers of the RNA left, they were escorted by two armed members of the Black Legion (the military arm of the RNA). There were approximately 15 uniformed and armed members of the Black Legion present at the convention. Milton Henry left the church at approximately 11:40 pm.

At 11:42 pm, scout car 10-5 manned by Officers Michael Czapski (22) and Richard Worobec (28) reported to headquarters that there were men with rifles at Linwood and Euclid. The patrol officers were unaware that an undercover officer was attending the meeting.

The two officers left their car to investigate the armed men, who had their backs toward the officers walking away. The men suddenly turned and opened fire on the officers. Czapski, slightly ahead of Worobec, was shot seven times and fell mortally wounded to the pavement. Officer Worobec, who was struck twice in the back and once in the leg, crawled back to the scout car seriously wounded and still under fire. He was able to press the car accelerator, and the car careened into a pole a short distance away.

The actual transcript (which is always recorded) between Officer Worobec as he was wounded and the Police Dispatcher was this:

March 29, 1969

11:42 p.m.	Scout car 10-5: *"We got guys with rifles out here at Linwood and Euclid."*
11:42.50 p.m.	Dispatcher: *"Cars in #10 Linwood and Euclid. Men with rifles."*
11:43 p.m.	Scout car 10-5: *"Help! Help! Ow! Oh!"*
11:43 p.m.	Dispatcher: *"10-5 needs help. All units—officer in trouble."*
11:43.20 p.m.	Scout car 10-5: *"Help, help, help, help!"*
11:44 p.m.	Dispatcher: *"Two officers shot Linwood and Euclid."*

Officers arrived on the scene within five minutes and transported Patrolmen Czapski and Worobec to Ford Hospital, but it was too late for Czapski.

Minutes later, about 50 Detroit police officers attempted to enter New Bethel church. The black commanding officer, Vincent Evans, claimed the police were fired upon as they tried to enter. Once they broke down the door, police reported that they came under rifle fire from the altar and sniper fire from the loft, although the black arrestees disputed these claims. The police arrested 142 inside the church, found 9 rifles, 3 pistols and ammunition.

Among those arrested were three from California including Obaboa Awolo (RNA Treasurer), 13 from Chicago including the leader of that RNA caucus, one from Kentucky; 6 from Massachusetts; one from New Jersey; four from Louisiana including Virginia Collins who had spoken at the church, 29 from New York including Baba Oseijemen Adefunmi—RNA minister of Culture, Herman Ferguson—RNA minister of Education (indicted along with Maxwell Stanford in a 1967 plot to kill conservative black leaders Roy Wilkins of the NAACP and Whitney Young of the National Urban League); 28 from Ohio including Mwesi Chui—RNA Minister of Defense who had on his person instructions for making explosives, sketches of uniforms, and a list of suggested military targets; 7 from Pennsylvania including David Owens who was under indictment for attempted murder of a Pittsburgh police officer and 5 from Washington, D.C.

The rest were from the Detroit area including officers in the RNA Imari Obadele, Leito Durley, Janet Johnson, Warren Galloway, Selina Howard, Dorothy Sanders, and Leroy Wilds (the last four of whom were arrested on their ride to New York in October). Also from Detroit was Lorenzo Freeman who was appointed to the New Detroit Committee in 1967.

In the cell block where he was lodged on the 9th floor of police headquarters, Richard Henry (Imari Obadele) had the arrestees stand and then he stated: "Black power for black people. We accomplished more than during the 1967 riot. One pig down, and the other one will never be any good." He was referring, of course, to the death of Czapski and the wounding of Worobec.

Rev. C. L. Franklin contacted State Senator James Del Rio. I allowed Del Rio to go to the garage where the 142 were initially held to see that everything was on the up and up. He had no complaints and said that.

Then Recorder's Court Judge George Crockett came to my office about 3:30 or 4:00 a.m. to talk to me. I discussed the incident with Crockett and told him the law had not been decided about how long it takes to process people by a police department and we had 142 people. Crockett was taken aback that I knew that much law.

I told him we had to do nitrate tests and there were already more than a dozen people who had positive nitrate tests on their hands showing they fired weapons. I told him that even though this was in a church, it was a political meeting with some people in uniforms and they were intent on overthrowing the United States.

Yes, he agreed that with 142 prisoners, it takes a little more time and if he released them, he would be violating the law himself if he ordered their release.

He agreed that he wouldn't let anyone out until we completed nitrate tests. I left the office at that point.

Prisoners Were Released by Judge Crockett!

But then he apparently changed his mind when prosecutor William Cahalan came in. Judge Crockett told the press he was not sure that the Detroit police would treat these prisoners well so by 6:00 a.m., he established a temporary court room.

Crockett began releasing those who were arrested, either on small bonds or personal recognizance. By noon, saying that those inside the church had nothing to do with the shootings of the two police officers outside the church, Judge Crockett had released all but two of those arrested. This included some who had tested positive for nitrate burns, found when someone fires a weapon. Judge Crockett, who was later elected to Congress on the basis of his intervention in this event, criticized police procedures and invalidated our right to hold those arrested at New Bethel.

A storm of public controversy arose over our police "attacking" a black church filled with men, women and children (one baby and two other juveniles). Charges flew between the judge and the county prosecutor over the "premature" release of suspects. Our police were caught in the middle and the city was divided worse than ever. We (a select few within the Detroit Police Department) knew what had really happened, but we were not at liberty to reveal it because it would have exposed our undercover man.

Black youth picketed police headquarters while off-duty members of the Detroit Police Officers' Association picketed the court building at opposite ends of the same block. On-duty police kept the two groups apart. Legal opinion supported the legitimacy of Crockett's decisions, while cases were prepared against shooting suspects. The community simmered and a grim funeral was held for the dead officer.

When the New Bethel incident occurred and Judge Crockett released our prisoners before we had a chance to process them, whites denounced him but blacks supported him. When a black activist arrived at the meeting of New Detroit and threatened to burn the city down, Max Fisher, chairman, convinced that the city was on the edge of a riot, announced support for Judge Crockett. (Jacoby).

David Brown, aged 19, of Compton, California, was held for assault with intent to commit murder. Kirkwood Hall was held for possession of a gas ejecting device. Subsequently warrants were issued against three RNA members, Clarence Fuller and Alfred Hibbitt of Detroit, and Rafael Viera of New York.

Kenneth Cockrel, an attorney who belonged to the BPP and RNA, defended Alfred Hibbitt against these charges. He was cited for contempt when he called the court and judge names such as "racist pirate judge". Each day after the contempt hearings, he held a rally in Kennedy Square in Detroit telling people how racist the white courts were. Some of those who attended these rallies were: Milton Henry, other lawyers, Black Panthers, members of the RNA, and Frank Ditto (mentioned in connection with taking money from New Detroit, Inc.)

There were no convictions. Rev. Franklin never apologized for the New Bethel incident. He said the RNA would be welcome to meet at his church again, but he would prohibit guns.

Officer Michael J. Czapski, a young man of only 22 years old, was my fourth officer to die. After he died, the Detroit Police Officers Association ran a full page story (in Appendix III) about how Czapski died at New Bethel and about the fact that the following ad appeared in the "personals" section referring to the help rendered to the RNA by Judge George Crockett:

God bless you George
We thank you for your aid and encouragement last Sunday morning. We all love you. Brothers Richard and Milton

This message so incensed our officers, who lost one of their own and had another injured badly, that they had to tell the public what really happened in the shootout.

Days later, on April 3, 1969, there was a demonstration of 400 people at Kennedy Square supporting Judge Crockett's release of those arrested at New Bethel. The demonstrators included members of various groups like the RNA, Black Panther Party (BPP) and the Black United Front (BUF).

Politicians Have Not Served Detroit Well

On that same day, I addressed New Detroit who had set up an Advisory Committee to do more extensive studies of police brutality and overreaction. I knew that endless studies would tell us what we already knew by that time. So I decided to shorten studies and ask for $150,000 to bring in police and academic experts to look at executive and administrative operations for a week, to lease and equip a building for recruiting and community services, and to lease and equip another building for police-youth athletic programs and a bus for these activities.

I added that I thought as police commissioner I might have been asked for my views on what areas should be studied by their Advisory Committee. But I wanted them to recognize that some of the problems were already being corrected. I knew they were upset by the bad press about the New Bethel Church shootout and that the police were made to look like they were in error when the suspects they arrested were immediately released.

I had trouble with Common Council and the press. They laughed a lot and made jokes about the scooter cops. And New Detroit? I couldn't get to first base with them. They tended to listen to the loudest complainers and to black ones in particular. With leaders like Max Fisher and Joe Hudson, they were swayed into heeding the words of the few complainers rather than the many. The squeaky wheel gets the grease!

A week after the New Bethel incident, a meeting of the legislative assembly of the Republic of New Africa met in Detroit on April 5, 1969. I learned later from our undercover man and his materials about that meeting. The content of the meeting was reported in the *Black Panther Newspaper*, in a May 11, 1969, issue. The Black Panther Party (BPP), established by Bobby Seale and Eldridge Cleaver, was an arm of the Maoist Internationalist Movement (MIM).

Their newspaper also reported that RNA and BPP member Ron Karenga was asked to explain the death of two Panther Brothers on the U.C.L.A. campus, and having failed to respond, was removed from the position of Minister of Education of the RNA. The newspaper also carried an interesting letter about the differences between the BPP and the RNA. It was a letter to co-founder Seale from Charles P. Howard, Sr., an attorney who was the RNA minister of state and foreign affairs, who had traveled to communist countries and served as a U.N. correspondent.

Howard wrote that "Karenga represented a great deal less than the best interests of the Black Liberation struggle against domestic colonialism, white racism and world-wide imperialism." It concluded, however, that "If there are serious political differences between the Panthers and the Republic of New Africa, I do not believe they are more serious than the differences between the blacks and whites in America" (Black Panther Party Newspaper Collection, *Des Moines Register*).

On April 24, I announced the beginning of our new "Light the Night" program sponsored by the Metropolitan Detroit Council of Real Estate Boards. We urged citizens to light up their homes during hours of darkness as a deterrent to crime.

On April 26, 1969, RNA first vice president Milton Henry spoke at the National Black Economic Development Conference held at Wayne State University in Detroit. His talk was entitled, "Land Reform: The Ownership and Control of Land Is Basic to Economic Growth and Freedom."

He started his speech with a synopsis of his life and how he tried to be a "good nigger", his dishonorable discharge from the Army, his role in politics and election to City Council in Pontiac, Michigan, and the RNA. At the conclusion of his speech, he asked everyone to stand and raise his right hand. They did so not knowing what he intended. He asked everyone to repeat after him, and then recited the RNA pledge of allegiance, and advised all present that they were officially RNA members.

Among many speakers at the three day conference was Julian Bond, Georgia state legislator. He gave a speech about the role of land ownership and its relationship to freedom. He stated that the racist FHA refused to provide money for land procurements by requiring ridiculous credit standards. He also stated that racism would almost impede any progress of blacks in obtaining land and economic independence.

Another speaker was Danial Aldridge, a substitute teacher in the Detroit School District and chairman of the Black United Front. His speech advocated the overthrow of the present system of government in the United States, saying the only way we are going to achieve success is by taking such action, including the use of violence if necessary.

He urged blacks to be engaged in groups like the League of Revolutionary Black Workers (LRBW). He said their goals are to learn the management and operation of the automobile industries to eventually take them over, run them for a while and then close them down. The plants have to be closed, he said, to destroy capitalism. Interestingly, he worked for the City of Detroit on the Mayor's Commission for Human Development.

Meanwhile, on April 30, 1969, I made a presentation to the Common Council. I described the Community Oriented Patrol officers who were establishing more rapport with citizens. I told of the scooter officers who maintained peace at the World Series celebrations, the anti-war demonstration at Kennedy Square, and patrols around schools and markets, Hudson's Thanksgiving Parade, and Christmas carnivals and shopping centers.

I was happy to describe statistics showing impressive drops in violent crime, auto thefts, robberies and purse snatchings in the precincts where the scooter cops worked. At that time, we had 76 community oriented patrol officers (COPs) and 114 scooters, in six of our thirteen precincts.

I proposed to add more supervisory positions because aggressive recruiting led to some 800 new police officers with less than a year on the force. Soon, we'd have 1,000 (20% of the force). I argued that they must have the supervision, leadership and guidance of well-trained supervisory officers. My request was denied, and somehow a rumor emerged that I had demanded 1700 additional men or I would resign.

That was not so. I made a press statement at the end of May describing my unhappiness with the budget limitations imposed by the Common Council but dispelled the rumor that I was about to resign.

The second week in May was designated as Police Week in accord with a national proclamation. We celebrated by having Open House at all precinct stations, and invited citizens to attend and visit with their police officers.

On May 16th, I made an address to the widows and orphans of Detroit area police officers killed in the line of duty. Nothing could have been sadder than to lose my fifth officer the following week on May 23, 1969.

After 15 years (13 with the Detroit Police Department), Officer Carter Lee Wells was killed on Friday, May 23, 1969, with his own service weapon after making a traffic stop. Normally he rode a scooter but on that day, he was driving a patrol car. During the traffic stop, the suspect grabbed his service weapon and shot him. A passing cab driver who witnessed the murder rammed the suspect's car and held the man until other officers arrived. Officer Wells was survived by his wife and two daughters. Unfortunately, I learned that the suspect was paroled after serving only 13 years.

Soon after the New Bethel shootout, Rev. Franklin was arrested for possession of marijuana as he returned from a visit to Mexico, but the charges were dropped. Then on June 10, 1979, Rev. Franklin surprised robbers in his expensive historic old home by some men who apparently intended to steal antique windows. He shot at them with his own gun but was himself wounded in two places.

Of the six men arrested for the crime, one was granted immunity to testify against the others, one was given a 25-50 year sentence, and the others received probation. (Rev. Franklin went into a coma and died five years later on July 27, 1984. His children spent great sums to keep him comfortable during that time.)

On June 18th, 1969, I was happy to announce that we had a total of 1,350 members of the Detroit Police Reserves. These civilians underwent training that allowed them to operate as the eyes and the ears of sworn officers and to summon officers to their communities when there was trouble.

In our effort to add good officers to the police force, on June 22nd we began a program to contact servicemen with less than six months left to serve in the U.S. Armed Forces. We received help from the Greater Detroit Chamber of Commerce and Congressman Lucien Nedzi.

I was asked to address the National Industrial Conference Board's Conference on Crime and the Corporation at the Waldorf-Astoria Hotel in New York City on June 26, 1969. I was delighted to speak with the heads of corporations.

I described the tremendous help I had received when the Chamber of Commerce purchased motor scooters that the City Council and New Detroit would not approve. I described the help from the Jaycees in the Buck Up Your Police Campaign to buy more scooters. And, of course, I told them why the close rapport between police on foot or on scooters was so needed in a city like Detroit where police were feared and hated.

Additionally I told them how we had finally been able to hire a helicopter (the DPD had none) to help in the arrest of some criminals and purchase sophisticated equipment like a videotape camera with the Buck Up Your Police fund.

On July 14th, in a joint announcement with Paul Stoddard of the FBI, I explained that we were sending Lt. Joseph Joabar of the DPD to attend the FBI National Academy at Quantico at the invitation of Director J. Edgar Hoover.

When I had been in office a year, I was able to announce that we had 214 scooters in operation, as well as informative brochures on display racks in every precinct, and I had instituted Seven Minute Seminars produced by the Police Academy for training via videotape at daily roll call. All these things were made possible by the Buck Up Your Police project where citizens donated a buck.

We also opened the PAYS (Police and Youth in Sports) program in a building donated by the International Telephone and Telegraph Corporation. Other companies donated sports equipment and the rapport which developed between young men and police officers was rewarding to all as time passed.

Other Negative Influences at Work in Detroit

Also in July 1969, the news of the sentence of white hippie John Sinclair finally came down. To catch up with what he had done during my term as commish, in fall of 1968 he tried to create an arm of the Youth International Party formed by Abbie Hoffman earlier in the year. To create his political party, he used ideas from the recent formation of Black Panther Party by leaders Huey Newton and Eldridge Cleaver.

He and "Pun" Plamondon organized and named the group White Panther Party (WPP) in the fall of 1968. Plamondon, half Ottawa and half Ojibwa Indian, was a drug user and was frequently arrested like Sinclair. The two men created WPP pins, carried Mao's "Little Red Book", read speeches of Fidel Castro and Malcolm X and generally worried authorities.

Sinclair continued to write poetry, music and created a local band known as the MC-5. He also produced the Detroit Rock and Roll Revival in May 1969. After all, this is the home of Motown Records and singers such as Aretha Franklin and Marvin Gaye.

I might add that in addition to some 25% of young black men being out of work, another possible contributing factor to tensions was the increase of drug use in Detroit. The Bureau of Narcotics and Dangerous Drugs recorded an increase of 89% in Detroit's active drug addict population. Singers like Marvin Gaye made "Flying High" and other songs about drug addiction popular during this time.

Sinclair's trial date was set for July 1969. He continued to develop the WPP and was the Party's Minister of Information, edited the White Panther journal, and was later named Chairman of the WPP. This is the exact wording of the document that was distributed to describe the WPP. It was attached to other messages such as "Free John Sinclair".

White Panther 10 Point Program
July 4, 1969

We take as our heroes those that we have been told to hate and fear; Eldridge Cleaver, Huey P. Newton, Fidel. The Red Guard are our brothers; the Black Panthers are our brothers. We join with them in the liberation of the planet.

Pun Plamondon

Minister of Defense

During this same month, July 1969, Sinclair was sentenced to prison for 9 ½ to 10 years for possession of two marijuana cigarettes, which he smoked during a rock concert at the Scarab Club in the presence of two undercover police officers. This surprisingly long sentence created much unrest among the whites and blacks in Detroit, and became the subject of news stories and songs.

On August 14, 1969, I gave an annual report to the New Detroit Committee of 24, stating that my number one priority had been to increase positive communication between police and citizens. I described the success of the Community Oriented Patrol on motor scooters enhancing fact-to-face contact, and summarized the personal involvement generated between people and police in the Buck Up Your Police project, which yielded $50,000 from citizens sending in a buck.

I explained how the Love-in, the Public Information Center, the Counter Crime Clinic and the counseling of would-be victims on how to avoid potential robbery situations were paying off. I told them about the opening of the new recruiting center and the addition of training through seven-minute videotapes at roll call.

Despite progress, they continued to criticize the Department and my leadership, and much of that criticism came from the venerable Max Fisher and Coleman Young.

In September our officers arrested 50 persons who were demonstrating with a sit-in at a social service center. They were members of the group of Welfare Mothers who thought they were receiving inadequate services. But when they blocked the building entrance, the director asked us to intervene so they could continue to serve the public. No incidents occurred there but that night, a disturbance at the Michigan State Fair had to be quelled by the DPD and Michigan State Police who arrested 20 people, nine of whom were juveniles.

Time Magazine ran an article about the Detroit mayoral election after the primary on September 19, 1969, called "A Victory for Reason" as blacks used their power at the ballot box instead of through violence.

This was 1969, the year young people all over America were demonstrating against the Vietnam War. I stayed on duty at headquarters and in the field on October 15, due to the planned marches and demonstrations conducted by the Detroit Coalition Against the Vietnam War, Breakthrough and other groups.

Lots of demonstrators were en route to Kennedy Square in Detroit for a rally. On the way, they broke and shattered windows of a music store. John Nichols, my superintendent in Detroit, wanted to call out the riot troops using guns, shields, batons, face masks, etc.

I countermanded his orders. Having had success with public acceptance of the scooter patrols, I said this was not the way to handle these young protesters. I then ordered our scooters to meet the advancing rebellious crowd and it worked like a charm. Not only did the young protesters respect and engage in conversations with the scooter officers, the scooter officers became an escort for them in their march to Kennedy Square. No further incidents. The day was saved. I'm sure it would have been different with riot troops. This was the kind of interaction that I hoped would help Detroit.

On October 18, 1969, we opened a new Police-Youth Program. I participated by throwing pitches to Detroit Tiger outfielder Willie Horton and threw wavering forward passes to former Lion defensive back Dick ("Night Train") Lane. The athletics were staged to kick off a physical fitness pentathlon that was part of the DPD's Police and Youth in Sports (PAYS) program. I hoped it would bridge the communications gap between the youth of the city and the Establishment. We used the event to distribute circulars about a curfew for children. I felt that 11 to 16-year olds out late without parents had to be safe and protected from potentially harmful influences.

In October of 1969, Mayor Cavanagh was quoted by James Q. Wilson and Harold R. Wilde in an article called "The Urban Mood". This is the excerpt:

> Detroit's Mayor Cavanagh indicates that "an administration is viewed not just through its mayor—but also through its police commissioner"...Perhaps the most significant phenomenon involving the police is the increasing political visibility of the police chief...Once a relatively anonymous public servant, the police chief has come to possess an "image" as important as that of the mayor, and the most successful chiefs are those practiced in the art of public relations.

Of course, Cavanagh was referring to me and to my role as police commissioner. Cavanagh chose not to run again, partly because his personal life was suffering.

On October 25, I lost my sixth officer, Patrolman Paul Begin. He was shot to death and Patrolman William Skibo was wounded while they were transporting a prisoner to the Fifth Precinct. The suspect was handcuffed and placed in the backseat of the patrol car. Begin allowed a female acquaintance of the suspect to ride to the police station next to the prisoner in the backseat. She was not handcuffed because she was not under arrest. As they were being driven to the station, she produced a handgun and shot Officer Begin in the back of the head. Both suspects fled the scene but were apprehended several days later.

They were both found guilty of murdering Officer Begin and sentenced to life in prison. I am sorry to say that he left a wife and children, but I recently heard that they were doing fairly well after all these years.

On November 6, 1969, we were thrilled to announce that Detroit was the first police department in the nation able to check a suspect's fingerprints with the FBI. This was accomplished through the use of a fax machine which was very new technology in those days.

In November, the Detroit Police Association rallied voters to go along with white Wayne County sheriff Roman Gribbs, (an attorney, former prosecutor and later judge) who won out in a runoff as mayor over black county auditor Richard Austin.

Gribbs was the last white mayor of Detroit.

City Council Members Helped Kill Detroit

In November I returned to the Detroit City Council to ask for more manpower. What happened is an example of a terrible trend that had taken place in a lack of discipline among council members that has continued to plague Detroit for these last 35 years. That encounter foretold the future for me and is encapsulated in Clark Hallas' story in the *Detroit News* on November 11, 1969. It was entitled "Spreen bid for help falls on irate ears."

When the Detroit City Council closed the budget last spring, denying some of Police Commissioner Johannes F. Spreen's requests for more manpower, they told him: "The Council's door is always open."

Yesterday, in a bitter exchange between councilmen and the commissioner, the Council appeared to slam that door.

Spreen was before the Council to request an additional two district inspectors and eight more inspectors.

But he had barely taken his seat when Councilman Philip J. Van Antwerp, a longtime Spreen critic proposed:

"Let's hold this in abeyance until after the new mayor takes office to see whether we need more Indians or chiefs…"

At one point, Spreen and Van Antwerp, seated next to each other at one end of the table, became embroiled in a shouting match which required the gavel of Chairman Robert Tindal to silence…

Councilman Louis C. Miriani chastised Spreen for asking the Greater Detroit Chamber of Commerce to purchase radios for the scooters instead of submitting a request for funds through normal city channels.

"I did; on Jan. 10," Spreen said, "and the request was denied…"

Miriani then indirectly blamed Spreen for Detroit's rising crime rates.

"You've been here 15 months and crime has been going up." Miriani said. "When can we expect it to stop? I'm not laying the blame on anybody," Miriani said.

But before Spreen could answer, Miriani persisted, "Will crime keep going up?" he asked.

Spreen finally answered, "Yes, it will until we can get more manpower and equipment…"

Spreen said the department's recruiting was 7% ahead of last year at this time and that in October 28% of the recruits were black.

However, Spreen, whose request for 1,700 {This is an error because I only asked for 1,000 to be spread out over two years, but the error went into the article} additional patrolmen was denied by Council last spring, conceded that the department had gained a net total of only 133 new men since a year ago…

Van Antwerp, a retired Detroit police inspector, said he had heard from "several sergeants and lieutenants" that police cars are tied up for lack of manpower.

When Spreen started to respond, Van Antwerp barked: "Don't give me any excuses..."

After the hearing, Spreen rapped Van Antwerp, commenting, "He's been out of police work for a number of years. I think he could use some boning up on police administration."

Another editorial about the DPD came out by the *Detroit Free Press* on December 11, 1969. They reported that the International Association of Chiefs of Police, whom I invited to review the department, pointed out:

Weaknesses in the department's structure, promotion system, morale and physical facilities....

The strength of the police union, the resistance of the bureaucracy, the force of political habit, all these factors get in the way of an effective reorganization.

5

Why I Left as Police Commissioner

○ ○

"I do the very best I know how, the very best I can; and mean to keep doing so until the end. If the end brings me out all right, what is said against me won't amount to anything. If the end brings me out wrong, ten angels swearing I was right would make no difference."

—*Abraham Lincoln*

Why I Left as Police Commissioner

Earlier in my tenure as Police Commissioner, I suggested a "love-in" on St. Valentine's Day. In that uptight city, I thought a smile would help everybody. I think it bought us some time. Now, I hoped that a new police administration plus two cool summers would help the people of Detroit and their police to move forward as a team. This team could make Detroit the kind of city we could all live in and be proud of, without fear.

"You Can't Fight City Hall!"

As police commissioner, it was very frustrating to deal with city council members in Detroit. David Cooper, a reporter for the *Detroit Free Press,* captured some of my frustration in a 1969 article entitled "When the Council Turns on the Heat."

> Appearing before Detroit's Common Council is one thing. Making a presentation to the council without being interrupted by some councilman is another…
>
> Last Friday, for example, Police Commissioner Johannes Spreen…took the witness stand…to make a major pitch for increases and improvements to the city's Police Department.
>
> Spreen had a prepared text. He said at the outset he hoped to get through it and then would be glad to answer any questions. He had barely begun, however, before he was interrupted by Councilman Billy Rogell. Soon, other councilmen were jumping into the middle of Spreen's careful presentation.
>
> At one point during a later discussion, Rogell told the commissioner, "Don't give me that stuff!"
>
> Rogell's comment sounded more like something the former Tiger player might have shouted at an umpire whose call he did not like than what a councilman would say to a commissioner.
>
> At one point, Spreen sat silently for 10 minutes, a slightly puzzled look on his face, as councilmen began a discussion of their own not directly related to Spreen's presentation.
>
> Councilwoman Mary Beck was chairing the meeting, and kept relatively quiet until a TV cameraman placed a microphone by her side. After that, she was off and running.
>
> Earlier last week, police department officials went before councilmen on a minor request. They wanted authority to spend $900 for a consultant who would aid in the computer program portion of a study of police procedures being made by Wayne State University.
>
> The proposal was comparatively simple, but most councilmen did not seem to understand it. One of their problems may have been that various councilmen kept interrupting police officials during the explanations. Coun-

cilmen held up the proposal for several days, approving it last Friday, unanimously...

Of the city's nine present councilmen, only three, Mel Ravitz, Nicholas Hood and Louis Miriani, seem to try most of the time to listen courteously to city officials and to try to understand what they are saying. Two others, Tony Wierzbicki and President Ed Carey, listen sometimes, but occasionally join their other colleagues in badgering and harassing officials before they can complete an explanation.

At times, one of the city's new councilmen, Robert Tindal, speaks so often and interrupts so frequently that he seems to be trying to become the council's male Mary Beck...

When the Common Council learns to listen it may begin to fulfill its constitutional duty as a legislative body.

I want to summarize an article from another reporter, Mark Beltaire, who wrote an article called, "Our Secret Council" for the *Detroit Free Press*. He was quite critical of the decision-making method used by those planning the welfare of the City of Detroit. In instances like this, the press is serving the public well to reveal operational flaws in those they have elected.

If Detroit's Common Council feels itself misunderstood, it can thank its own methods of operation for leading to that condition.

All the hastily assembled press conferences in the world cannot make up for the fact that the council operates in secret. The real budget decisions were not made as David Cooper of our city-county bureau has noted, in those 22 votes of 9-to-0 to override the mayor's veto.

They were made by the council in informal sessions, away from the glare of public attention. Surely, in those sessions, there were shadings of opinion that the people ought to know about. Some individual differences were brushed aside in the drive for a show of unity.

What do the council members think the people of Detroit hired them for? Are some of them being made pawns by the candidates for mayor among them?

Maybe Mayor Cavanagh's budget was, as some of the councilmen have suggested, merely an empty public relations show. But such a show, at least, is preferable to a council that refused to acknowledge that it should have some sort of relations with the public.

Still a third article on this subject was by John Griffith, for the *Detroit Free Press*. He quoted me when I said the following, "We must solve the crime and community tensions now—today. And there is only one way, the right way. The choice is there: The tax collector or the mugger, the burglar, the robber or worse. If the police are shortchanged, so is every Detroiter."

There were more tensions as Detroit had become a hot spot for various black nationalist groups. Meetings and conferences were constantly being held, many of which fired up people against the Vietnam War, the white control of the inner city of Detroit, and it often felt to law enforcement officers that we were fighting a losing battle to control crime and violence.

Even the Good Guys Were Going Bad

FBI Special Agent in Charge Paul Stoddard probably felt as overwhelmed as I did when he fired off the following memo to Director Hoover on August 28, 1969. I have included explanatory comments in brackets in this memo obtained under the Freedom of Information Act.

> COINTELPRO—NEW LEFT
> Following the National Anti-War Conference in Cleveland, Ohio, 7/4-5/ 69, a coalition of anti-war groups in the Detroit area began meeting and an ad hoc committee called the Detroit Coalition Committee was formed. The Detroit Coalition Committee meets on Monday nights at 5705 Woodward Avenue, Detroit, Michigan, and (blacked out words).
> One of the leaders of the Detroit Coalition is (blacked out) who resides in Ann Arbor, Michigan, and who is believed to be a member of the (blacked out word) of the New Mobilization Committee to End the War in Vietnam (NMC).
> Detroit feels that the present conditions as they exist on the Detroit Coalition Committee do not make it advisable for (blacked out words) to permit the anti-war demonstration in Washington, D.C. on 11/15/69. (Blacked out sentence)
> One situation that seems to lend itself to the suggestions in referenced Bureau airtel would be some counterintelligence action directed against (blacked out name) who resides at (blacked out address), Ann Arbor, and who is a manufacturers representative in this area. Since (blacked out named) appears to be on the (blacked out words) of the NMC and one of the (blacked out word) of the Detroit Coalition Committee, Detroit feels that a counterintelligence program directed against him would have a beneficial effect.
> The specific suggestion is that a letter could be written from the BUF {Black United Front} at Washington, D.C. to the White Panther Party (WPP), 1510 Hill Street, Ann Arbor, and also to the "Michigan Daily", University of Michigan student newspaper at Ann Arbor, pleading the BUF cause. The letter which could possibly be initiated by an informant in the BUF in Washington, D.C. or which could be a fraudulent letter could ask the WPP, a white militant group that strongly supports the Black Panther Party (BPP), to

help the BUF collect the just and modest sum of $25,000.00 from the NMC by making a direct overture to (blacked out name), an NMC leader in Ann Arbor.

The letter could state that the BUF realizes that a substantial part of this sum could be easily raised by the NMC in Michigan because of the many professionals and academicians supporting the anti-war demonstration scheduled for Washington, D.C.

The letter could also state that a copy is being directed to the University of Michigan student newspaper to further publicize the very just nature of the BUF request.

Detroit feels that the *Michigan Daily* would be delighted to publish this type of a letter. It is felt that such a letter would be of a disruptive nature if presented to the Detroit Coalition Committee by (blacked out name or words) and could develop into a situation where (blacked out words).

Such a letter would also be a disruptive factor to the amicable relations between the WPP and Black Nationalist supporters and groups in Ann Arbor, inasmuch as WPP would be forced to make a choice between BUF cause and the position of the white liberals in Ann Arbor who have been critical of the war and have to this point supported the WPP. The issue in the letter would be that the BUF knows that the white liberals, who are identified with the NMC, have unlimited sums of money available through their contacts and the sole issue is whether or not they want to give the $25,000.00 to the BUF.

Comments of WFO {Washington Field Office} are requested. If the Bureau approves of this suggestion, a draft of such a letter will be prepared by Detroit.

Following this memo, Detroit FBI agents did create a letter sent to mainly white organizers of the proposed Washington, D.C., anti-war rally. The letter, under the Black United Front with a forged signature of the leader, demanded that rally organizers pay the black community a $20,000 security bond.

You will recall that John Sinclair and "Pun" Plamondon who had developed the White Panther Party referred to in the memo lived in Ann Arbor by this time.

The Black United Front (BUF) was formed by a Detroit native, Edwin Taliaferro, who entered law school at Wayne State University in 1969. He changed his name to Chokwe Lumumba when he became a Muslim. The FBI made sure that their media contacts gave the phony letter and the story considerable publicity and their efforts were successful in disrupting and discrediting the involved organizations.

Additionally, the New Mobilization Committee to End the War in Vietnam formed in July 1969 was said to be controlled by the Communist Party of the U.S.A. Col. Robert D. Heinl, Jr. wrote about it in *The Collapse of the Armed*

Forces, claiming that it was aimed at the disruption of the Armed Forces. But local citizens did not see it that way.

Detroit attorney James Lafferty, coordinator of the Civil Division of the Wayne County Neighborhood Legal Services from 1967 to 1969, was a supporter along with city council members, and formed the Detroit Coalition to End the War Now! He carried much weight as a spokesman against the U.S. war in Vietnam according to the James Lafferty Collection of papers at the Walter P. Reuther Library of Labor and Urban Affairs.

The city and police prepared for anything on the Vietnam War Moratorium Day on October 15, 1969. Some cities had problems but we were spared. The demonstrations, mainly about 1,000 people wearing black anti-war armbands in a Detroit suburb at Chene Park, passed in relative peace and harmony.

As if Detroit didn't have enough problems, I was trying to reform problems within the police department. I had outside advisors studying the department and they had concluded that we were short of at least 1,000 men. I was so upset about the off-handed refusal to add manpower that I nearly quit, but instead decided to stay on. Another newspaper story by the editor of the *Free Press* was called "Spreen's Decision to Stay Offers Council Reprieve."

Here are a few of the comments in this article, referring to ex-Mayor Miriani's comments about me:

> Louis Miriani was also conciliatory, though on Saturday he produced the inane quote of the week when he said, "I thought we had a pretty good Police Department for many, many years. I don't know what he has done with the Police Department since he's been here."
>
> The answer is obvious if Miriani or the other council members would look. During his first months on the job Spreen conducted the most effective recruiting program in the department's history. He introduced the scooter patrol, despite a great deal of ridicule, and the scooters have proved popular and effective. He's gotten more men on the streets, is currently having an efficiency study made of the entire department, from his office on down.
>
> And he's been on the chicken and peas circuit, drumming up popular support for a dispirited department, meanwhile fending off the long knives wielded by Common Council and trying to make do with one of the most undermanned forces in the country on a per capita basis.

I also had problems with micromanagement by City Councilmen. An example was in still another *Detroit Free Press* article entitled "Council Interferes with Spreen." This article referred to Philip, the son of former Detroit Mayor Eugene Van Antwerp.

In a week marked by more than its quota of silliness, one of the silliest statements was Councilman Philip Van Antwerp's hint that if Police Commissioner Spreen doesn't promote more detectives Common Council may charge him with "malfeasance or misfeasance" in office.

What utter nonsense. It is precisely because of this sort of interference and restriction that the job of police commissioner in Detroit is so difficult. How does the council know that 70 percent of the detectives deserve promotion to sergeant?

The police commissioner ought to have some latitude over promotions, and he ought not to be given a quota by the Common Council or by the detectives association. To impose this kind of restriction on him is to undermine his ability to do his job...

If there is misfeasance in office, it may instead be in the council, which bartered away the commissioner's power to decide how many detectives deserve promotions.

Will Muller wrote an article for the *Detroit News* called "Jeers Switch to Cheers for the Scooter." This reporter picked up on the problems that faced me as Jerome Cavanagh decided not to run for mayor and what that might do to my position in an administration that did not select me. However, such an article may have hurt me by being so flattering that mayoral candidates saw me as a rival or someone having my own following.

Of late, there have been indications that the former New Yorker's (Spreen's) dogged persistence in the face of recurring crises and city hall back-stabbing is getting through, at least to the people, with his message: To win the fight against crime we must have the support of the community...

There is, of course, the recent *Detroit News* poll which showed 55 percent of all Detroiters crediting Spreen's department with fair enforcement....

Last week, six women, led by an officer of the National Association for the Advancement of Colored People, went to the department and offered their best help.

From the tenor of comment around the town's ordinary people, the same question is rising generally among those concerned with living and working and feeling secure in Detroit. In the absence of leadership elsewhere, many people are looking to Spreen.

Every count was against Johannes Spreen when he took the job. He was an outsider police officer, a former operations director in the New York department, certain to be resented within the Detroit department.

He came at the call of a mayor in deep political trouble who had been hunting for months for a police commissioner to take over a city deep in racial trouble. Detroit, like every other major city, has a long reputation for pillorying its police commissioners in every real or fancied crisis.

Spreen has been here less than one year. It's something for Detroiters to say in a public opinion poll, in street discussions and by their actions that they have more empathy for him than for their own councilmen.

This city is about to undergo the trial of an election. Who is police commissioner next year hangs on who is elected mayor, and none can predict the outcome. One thing is obvious. Only a foolish candidate will make Spreen the target of his campaign.

I often had trouble with the press who rushed to publish "news" without checking the facts. On November 12, 1969, I wrote a letter to the editor of the *Detroit News* as follows:

To the Editor:

On November 1, 1969, the *Detroit News* published a letter to the Editor signed "Detroit Parents" which accused the Detroit Police Department of gross neglect of duty in a very serious incident. May I, on behalf of the officers of our Department, attempt to set the record straight.

The parents' letter indicated that while their 18-year-old son was on a date with his girlfriend, the girl had been forced at gunpoint to accompany an unidentified male and was subsequently raped by him. It was further alleged that the boy ran to a nearby street, stopped a police car, and told the officers what had happened. The officers reportedly told the youth to go home and go to bed. It was stated that, as a result of police inaction, the girl was brutalized and required hospitalization.

The investigation conducted by ranking officers of the Department reveals that these allegations are far from the truth. Ten days before the parents' letter was published in the *News*, all parties concerned had been questioned by our Women's Division in the presence of the father of the alleged victim. During that investigation, the girl insisted that she was not sexually molested on the night in question—either forcibly or otherwise. It was also learned that a considerable amount of beer had been consumed by all persons in the girl's company at the time the alleged incident occurred.

We have been unable to determine why the youth made the allegations. To our knowledge, no crime has been established; and the complaining youth now states that if he did talk to police officers, he is unable to remember the conversation.

As Police Commissioner, it saddens me that a letter such as the one from "Detroit Parents" was given enough credence by your editorial staff to be published. It saddens me, too, that many thousands of your readers probably found it credible since it appeared in a paper which has such an outstanding record for objectivity and fairness. It saddens me that every member of our fine Department bears the punishment each time the Department is pronounced guilty without a chance to have our side heard.

I appreciate the opportunity you have given me for "equal time." I still have faith in both the people and the police of our community—that we are all on the side of equal justice under fair law in an orderly society and that this applies to the Police Department's treatment of the community and the community's treatment of the Police Department.

Sincerely yours,
Commissioner

I felt that the media was rushing to judgment and taking with it the public. *The Detroit News* was not the only newspaper guilty of sensationalism. In fact, I told Lee Hills, publisher of the *Detroit Free Press* (at the Italian Ambassador's Ball in 1969), "Mr. Hills, if your paper keeps printing this way about events and policing, you won't have a rag left to publish." I was quite incensed at the *Free Press* coverage which was usually more one-sided that the other papers.

The New Mayor Was Stalling

This was happening at the same time that the public was getting ready to vote out Jerome Cavanagh and vote in Roman Gribbs.

Then I had a decision to make: whether to resign or to stay in the running for police commissioner under a new mayor. Unfortunately, I may have made that decision too rashly, after a thirty-minute meeting with Mayor-elect Roman Gribbs. That meeting left me with a very bad, even bitter, taste in my mouth.

I essentially told him that I wanted to complete some important programs and stay on at least six months. But I quickly realized he was just picking my brain to see what he could learn, so he could carry on without me. He was not a sincere man, or at least not with me.

Right after our talk, a reporter asked Gribbs if he would keep me. He put the reporter off for about three weeks, leaving me in a kind of limbo. This feeling lingered as I was left up in the air, hanging suspended. I had postponed vacations with my family since I had come to Detroit, and felt I didn't know which way to move.

When I came home from talking with Gribbs, my wife Elinor asked what the Mayor-elect said. When I told her, she asked if I was going to be able to go on a

Florida vacation that we had planned or go to New York for Christmas. That is when the frustrations piled up inside me and the commitment to my community took second place to my commitment to my wife and daughter. Elinor, in her obligation to her husband, had packed up, left the home in Lynbrook, New York, and came to Detroit to follow me despite many reservations and urgings by her friends not to do so.

I decided to tell the press that they and pressure groups had been a problem. My exact words were:

> I have felt that a few news people now and then were more concerned about titillating an audience or generating a sensational headline that they were about calming community tensions.
>
> I have felt that some of the spokesmen for the New Detroit Committee, that prestigious group to which we all look with hope, have tended to undo with injudicious comments some of the good their funds were being spent to accomplish....
>
> The Mayor-Elect has not asked me to remain...so I can only presume he has someone else in mind. Also, I understand that in some quarters, I am no longer considered acceptable because of my color.
>
> Having considered all this, I feel that I have met my original commitment to Mayor Cavanagh and the people of Detroit, and I am consequently asking Mayor-Elect Gribbs to remove my name from consideration as the next Police Commissioner.

Heather Thompson wrote in *Whose Detroit?* that Gribbs was a "leader in law enforcement who played continuously on white fears of black 'criminality' and 'dependency'". Indeed, Gribbs promised an "all out fight against crime in the streets."

She continued, "When Gribbs suggested the creation of 'small units of police' with crime-fighting responsibility assigned to certain neighborhoods, city liberals, both black and white, feared that this would only increase hostility between police and inner-city residents" (Thompson, 79-80).

As sheriff, Gribbs automatically symbolized "law and order". He ran on a law and order program to use all necessary policing to forcefully crack down on crime. He won a very narrow victory over Richard Austin, 257,312 to 250,020. It was the closest political contest in Detroit history. He didn't have a clear mandate from the people so his victory did not ease the tensions; in fact, it exacerbated them.

Thompson wrote that Gribbs' victory did not end social welfare and civil rights or sympathetic liberalism in Detroit but neither did it quiet the radical critics in the African American community. She charged that the combination of Gribbs' pro-law enforcement platforms and Austin's defeat not only led poor and working class blacks to become even more politically active, but made them far more radical than Austin had ever been.

As a follow-up on Austin who died in 2001, he eventually became Michigan's Secretary of State and went on to be elected five times to that position. He reshaped the office and changed it from a political patronage office to a more service-oriented operation. I always felt we missed a great opportunity when he lost the mayoral election. What a pity that the city was not ready for this man who could have united races and created a better Detroit.

After Gribbs took office, whites should have felt more secure but as Thompson pointed out, black and white revolutionary sentiment became more popular and powerful. This caused many whites to begin embracing politics far to the right as the only way to combat the perceived threat, she said.

I Withdrew My Name From Consideration

When the news surfaced that I was withdrawing my name from consideration as the next Police Commissioner for the new Mayor, I received a copy of the following letter. It was to Mayor Elect Gribbs on December 5, 1969 from the 12th Precinct Community Relations Committee on West Seven Mile Road.

Dear Mayor-Elect Gribbs,

We realize that you must presently be very busy formulating plans before you assume your office in January. In spite of this fact, we write now because we also know that once in office, your schedule will be an even busier one.

As concerned and involved citizens of Detroit (and we do consider ourselves as such) we desire that you know and understand our feelings regarding Police Commissioner Johannes Spreen. We would like to see him retained in his position.

During the past two years, we have cooperated with the Police Department of the 12th Precinct through an organization we jointly formed, whose name this letterhead bears. This relationship was begun with the belief that this would help Detroit remain a good place to live, work and raise our families. Our close association with our police of the 12th Precinct and the other members of the Police Department in our city convinces us that we are on the right road.

On numerous occasions, we have collectively and individually received encouragement to continue, from Commissioner Spreen. He has, as a result of personal interest, encouraged and instructed the police to help us. It has, we feel, been a fruitful effort for both sides.

Our group is composed of members of all neighborhood organizations in the 12th Precinct, as well as interested citizens and businessmen. This area, as you may know, is comprised of approximately 120,000 people. We urge you to retain, with confidence in our support, Johannes Spreen as Police Commissioner.

Should you desire further elaboration on our position, we would be most willing to discuss this with you at your convenience.

Sincerely yours,
N. R. Litt, chairman
12th Precinct, Community Relations Committee

I gave a press conference on December 9, 1969, in Detroit, only16 months after accepting the position of Police Commissioner of Detroit. I explained to the press that three studies or surveys had been conducted, none in depth.

Highlights of the International Association of Chiefs of Police were that the Department suffered from a shortage of supervisory personnel and uniformed sergeants for field supervision, in particular. They suggested that the department needed reorganization with fewer sergeants in the detective bureau. I thought this was interesting since it was the opposite of what Van Antwerp on the Common Council had voiced.

Two reports commended our personnel and recruiting operations, but agreed that the police staff needed the help of trained labor relations experts to negotiate with employee organizations. They agreed that recruit training is good but more in-service training was needed after graduation from the police academy. I certainly agreed and had instituted the Seven Minute Training videos as well as some other training, but more was definitely needed. It was like expecting a doctor to practice medicine after graduating from medical school without any additional training or reading.

The reports expressed particular interest in the community-oriented scooter patrol innovation and suggested that it be given a full opportunity to prove itself. They agreed in suggesting further study of scout car operations, and a more effective system of control for maximum utilization of available equipment and personnel. One report stated that the basic neighborhood patrol officer should be a well-rounded "generalist", which is exactly what we were trying to do with our scooter cops.

The crux of the reports was that the department needed at least an additional 1,000 police, as well as additional radios, car, cameras and tape recorders. Our women's division was highly complimented by Arthur Little researchers for their preventive work with youth, and good rapport with the community.

I told the press that it was unprecedented that a major public institution should be so forthright about self-improvement and so confident in community understanding that it would lay them out on the table. We had nothing to hide. We considered these surveys to be management tools to improve police performance.

Lawrence Carino, General Manager of the WJBR-TV2 station, delivered an editorial on his television station following that December 9th interview. He understood correctly many of my frustrations and feelings judging by his words which were as follows:

> Johannes Spreen's withdrawal from consideration as Police Commissioner in the new city administration was not entirely unexpected. Nevertheless, the reasons behind his decision should seriously concern all Detroiters.
>
> There has been, as he said, a disturbing tendency in some quarters to assume that police officers are guilty of some abuse of authority until they are proven innocent.
>
> There has been the negative attitude Spreen has so often encountered in his dealings with Common Council, with his constructive proposals for the Police Department too often lost in the endless bickering between Council and the Mayor's Office.
>
> There has been the frustration of having to spend too much time reacting to problems of the past, and too little in developing programs for the future.
>
> There has been the necessity of delaying needed improvements in the department until some outside agency completed yet another police study.
>
> More personally, Spreen has had to endure the pain of being told by his children that he is commonly referred to by their classmates as the "head pig".
>
> And now, presumably, Spreen will have the final disappointment of leaving the job just as many of the promising programs he put in motion are beginning to show results. And Detroit, in turn, will be losing a police administrator of uncommon vision and ability.
>
> When the burden of the Commissioner's office passes to someone else—as now appears definite—TV2 hopes it is a man who can serve the community as effectively as Johannes Spreen.

Earlier I asked, "Who's responsible for killing Detroit?" I feel responsible to this day! Coming out of New York, I came to love the City of Detroit and its people. I have written before that the 17 months I served as Police Commissioner were much more satisfying to me than the twelve years I served as Oakland County Sheriff.

But I also feel that many decision-makers on the Common Council, New Detroit, Detroit Police Department, FBI, and other government groups played a part in the decline of Detroit. Yes, they were usually good-hearted and tried to do the best they could. But they could have done better. That is why I have taken such pains to describe the inner workings and the decision-making during this critical time in Detroit's history. The police have been blamed too long and too often without others taking their share of the heat.

Certainly the hate groups played a large part and often operated through violence. But so did the criminals, both organized and unorganized and La Cosa Nostra in particular. The drug users, hippies who promoted a selfish lifestyle, and loudmouths who appeared before groups requesting money played a part.

The people who fled Detroit are as responsible as the businesses that moved away and left huge employment gaps. The real estate industry that made a shambles of housing for blacks, segregating them totally from whites, played a major role.

Yes, I believed when I took the job as Police Commissioner that I could help and I also sincerely feel I did. I wish I had stayed because that job was important, challenging and serious. But I removed myself from that important position when I became frustrated. So I must shoulder some of the blame.

I'm sorry and saddened by what has happened to that once great city. Why did I leave? Because of politics—damned politics! A man, if he is caring and concerned, has obligations. Obligations to the community he lives in, to his family and to himself. In the month of December, 1969, they all came into play. But I made my decision after the meeting with Gribbs due to his cavalier attitude. I thought we had been friends. He was Sheriff of Wayne County with an office across the street from police headquarters. We had met quite a few times. But again, like New York, a change of mayors meant a change of police commissioners.

You see, I have or had a dream, too! I appreciated the many citizens of Detroit who supported me and the police. I especially appreciated the Detroit Chamber of Commerce for their gifts to the police department, such as the 50 motor scooters which we used fully during the short time I had them.

But I am saddened at the condition of the city where I came to do a job. Detroit's citizens and the police were responding, but I was disappointed when Mayor Cavanagh, who had told me he would run again, did not.

In addition, he did me a disservice. He put me in two polls which included his name along with Richard Austin and Roman Gribbs for mayor. (Ed Robinson, a former top aide to Cavanagh, told me this later.) I led both polls for mayor but I did not aspire to become a mayor. I feel it soured the former friendly relationship I had with the Sheriff of Wayne County, Roman Gribbs. He became mayor by only ½% of the total vote. Gribbs may have also become embittered because Richard Austin, his opponent, named me as Police Commissioner. There probably was no way that he would have appointed me even if I had not withdrawn my name.

In retrospect I often wish that when reporters asked if I would remain as Police Commissioner with Richard Austin, I had given a different reply. I would like to have continued with many of the programs we created, particularly the Community-Oriented Police Scooter Program. After the shabby treatment in his office by Mayor-Elect Gribbs, I chose with sadness not to be evaluated by him for Police Commissioner. But as John Greenleaf Whittier said, "For of all sad tales of tongue and pen, the saddest are these: It might have been."

Just before I started to write this book, I looked over a box in my office that shocked and surprised me. When the newspapers carried the news of my resignation, people wrote me letters asking me to stay. I was given the box of letters after I made my decision. I found them poignant, touching, heartfelt. If I had been able to read them all in early December 1969, I would have reconsidered my decision to remove my name as police commissioner.

I have excerpted a few of them in Appendix IV to suggest what citizens found the most valuable in their police.

I received a nice compliment from Rev. Dr. Hubert Locke, assistant to Commissioner Girardin when the riots took place. When he gave me a copy of his book *The Detroit Riot of 1967*, he wrote the following inscription.

> To John Spreen: It's almost incredible the task you faced coming to Detroit as Police Commissioner exactly one year after the disaster which this little book describes. The fact that a year later you had achieved such major breakthroughs in building a bridge between the police and Detroit citizens, and healing many of the wounds within the Department, makes your tenure as Detroit's Police Commissioner one of the most significant in the city's history. We remember you with gratitude. Hubert 9 November 1970.

Gribbs brought in Patrick V. Murphy as police commissioner but he stayed only eight months. Murphy had 25 years experience as a New York police officer, just as I did, and served under me when he was a sergeant. He went from captain to deputy inspector before he left to become a police chief in Syracuse, New York, even while he was still employed by the New York City Police Department. Murphy was tapped for New York City police commissioner in October 1970, a post he held until 1973. He went on to become Executive Director of Drug Policy Foundation and has an excellent reputation.

In Detroit, Murphy was followed by John Nichols, my former police department superintendent. Nichols served as police commissioner until he ran for mayor and was defeated in 1973.

The STRESS Program Created Stress

Gribbs' most publicized accomplishment was the creation of STRESS (Stop The Robberies, Enjoy Safe Streets), which was composed of about 100 mostly white police officers working in high crime areas (which were mostly black neighborhoods). STRESS engaged in surveillance and decoy operations.

As an aside, when John Nichols who replaced me asked me what I thought about STRESS, I told him I could not be for it. I said, "You put Officer Worobec who had been shot by blacks at New Bethel in the STRESS program. How do you think he's going to feel toward blacks? You need more men and then you won't have to fire on blacks running from a scene who get shot in the back. If you have enough men, they're surrounded and if they need to be shot, they are shot in the front coming at you. There's no question of the police action then." In my newspaper column after I left as commissioner, I simply couldn't support STRESS.

Twenty-two Detroit citizens (mostly black) were killed by the STRESS officers, mostly shot in the back. It came to be known as a "killer squad". There is no danger to an officer when the suspect is running away from him! To do STRESS properly, officers should be stationed at either end of the street where the decoy officer was. That officer who has the assailant running at him, after demanding him to stop, could legally and properly shoot if he did not stop, but in the front—not the back.

I could see tension between the city blacks and the Detroit police increasing rapidly. Black militants and black radicals made their voices ring in rebellion. STRESS became a rallying point for black militants. Many pages are devoted to it in the book by Dan Georgakas and Marvin Surkin. That book refers to me (page 56) when the Black United Front states that "public opinion was being misled by Governor Milliken, Police Commissioner Johannes Spreen, Mayor Cavanagh, Prosecutor Cahalan, the DPOA and *The Detroit News*, all of whom were guilty of racism."

That book made no mention of the many positive programs put into place following the riot of 1967, and strikes me as a bigoted book with many pages devoted to tearing down the police and the government of the city. Still, I have to agree with their assessment against STRESS. It was a bad concept badly executed.

The STRESS program was ended by the next mayor, Coleman Young. However, there was lots of pushing by Sheila Murphy Cockrel. I was very aware of her because she formed an Ad Hoc Action Group to monitor police activities after the 1967 riot.

She became a lawyer and eventually married Detroit attorney, activist and leader Kenneth Cockrel in 1978 and served two terms on the Detroit City Council. She is a life member of the NAACP and in 1968 was nominated by anthropologist Margaret Mead to receive the Mademoiselle Award honoring 26 young women who carved niches for themselves beyond traditional areas.

After I left my service as Police Commissioner, I resumed teaching at John Jay College. Having made my home in Michigan, I flew into New York weekly to handle a full teaching load of 12 semester hours in addition to being Director of the Law Enforcement and Protection Program at Mercy College of Detroit.

I brought in some Detroiters to be guest lecturers in my police administration courses, including a course called "The Impact of Media on the Administration of Criminal Justice", a course which I developed with the author of the well-known book *Sybil*, Flora Rheta Schreiber. She was a colleague and English teacher at John Jay.

6

Who Killed Detroit?

○ ○
"Politics are almost as exciting as war, and quite as dangerous. In war you can only be killed once, but in politics many times."

—Sir Winston Churchill

Who Killed Detroit?

The white citizens living in the suburbs by the late 1960s were unaware of the simmering problems eating at blacks in the inner city. Their recollections of Detroit matched those of my wife, Sallie, who described growing up near Detroit. As a New Yorker, I enjoyed hearing her describe the town I came to know. This is her account:

The Detroit I Knew:

Growing up in the small town of Algonac, Detroit was always the shining city, the place to go to see "stars". What a beautiful city it was. I'm talking about my teenage years and twenties and even my thirties.

The Greyhound bus would take us into Detroit and the last bus home was 11:00 p.m. We would spend all day downtown and sometimes end the day at a movie. There were so many movie theaters then.

We were young girls 13 or 14 years old, and we felt very safe. We would meet under the Kern's clock, if we went different ways to shop. There was a great Woolworth's that took up a whole block, and Hudson's was a wonderful place to shop. Lunch at Greenfield Cafeteria was a must. Always before heading home, we stopped for a Hot Fudge Cream Puff at Sanders, because we never had hot fudge as good as at Sanders.

I remember standing in line to see Frank Sinatra—the line went around the block. I was a bobby-soxer. I remember seeing Ella Fitzgerald. In those days, they would show a movie and then have live entertainment. Ella was watching the movie before she had to go on. Not many were at the theater because it was early afternoon, so my friend and I sat next to her and asked for her autograph. We had no pen or pencil so she used my brand new lipstick that I had just purchased. I still have that autograph.

I have so many wonderful memories of Detroit: the Grand Circus Park, the Book Cadillac Hotel, the streetcars, the train station; so many beautiful buildings. Later, when we were old enough to drive, we would drive to Seven Mile, park our car and ride the streetcar downtown. Today, if you parked your car at Seven Mile, and left for a couple of hours, good-bye car! We had no such fears back in those days.

I remember going to Eastwood Park on Eight Mile Road. It had a wonderful amusement park. Again, it was very safe. It had a great dance hall where all the big name bands came to play—Harry James, Benny Goodman, etc. It was special to be a teenager in the late 40s and in my teens and twenties in the 50s. Detroit was a classy city, bright, shining, and safe. What happened?

When my grandmother was a girl, they had the D&R, a train that ran from Port Huron to Detroit with all the stops in the small towns along the way. She would travel to Detroit twice a year; once for her new summer outfit and once for her winter outfit. The Tashmoo boat would dock in Algonac and sail to Detroit with all the young lovers dancing the night away.

My sons never had a chance to know the Detroit I knew. It was never a place for them to go. Malls were where they shopped, all far away from downtown Detroit. People said "Detroit? Oh, no! Don't go there!"

What's a pity is that a gorgeous city is gone. Can it be brought back? Oh, I hope so. But I won't hold my breath.

There is also a 19-year-old friend of ours who wrote us about how Detroit is now. Danielle wrote the following:

My brother attends Wayne State University. He took me for a car ride around the campus because I love historic buildings. The buildings at Wayne State are truly one of a kind, but if your eyes move slightly to the university surrounds, you would think, it's time to get out of here! It's like you're in a bad movie, in a horrible part of town. Seven years ago, my cousin was murdered here. She was 18, one year younger than I am now, and she was in the wrong place at the wrong time. I always worry for my brother. I can't imagine losing him to the crime-infested city of Detroit, all because he is educating himself...

I'll never forget the experience of one Saturday night. We were headed to his living quarters on the campus. We had to take side streets but this was anything but usual. We had to pass this club/bar that overflowed with people. You could tell the gangsters were hanging out there. They were all scattered on the road as if they owned it, with their pants halfway to their knees, and guns at their waistline.

As I saw the sight before me, I have never seen anything like it except in the movies. I said a prayer that God would protect us as we barely passed through. My brother quickly stated that to be in control is to keep the car rolling. Once you stop, they have control of you.

They wouldn't move out of the way. They stood in front of our car as if they had a plan. His hands gripped the wheel so hard that I knew this was serious. That's when fear was overwhelming me. I felt like my blood circulation stopped. I was numb all over, but the key was not to look like you're sacred, otherwise you're in trouble.

There were about a million things running through my mind. What should my facial expression be as the guys looked at me through the front windshield? Should I cross my arms to make it look like I wasn't afraid? The scariest part was the fact that we were surrounded with gangster guys, two on each side, five in front. Were we going down?

Somehow our car managed to keep rolling at 1 mile per hour. Eventually we got out of the ordeal.

As we entered the gated parking lot, gated for the sole reason of car theft and break-ins (surprise, surprise) the gate opened with his code. As we just passed the opening, he made a complete stop. I was so confused I asked what was going on. Well, he had spotted a car slowing down as he entered, and to block this car from entering, he made a complete stop.

It's amazing to me to see how your mind has to strategize every move. It's been his experience to witness some "outsider" pass through the gate before it closed on the student. Therefore, naturally, a theft occurred that same night.

Interestingly enough, when we settled in his condo, he told me that just the week before; someone from school went through what we just went through. The same setup, guys around the car, except this student wasn't lucky. The gangsters pulled out their guns and tried to rob the guy. As he started to drive off, they started shooting…

In my future years, I hope to establish myself in a place that I have always dreamed of. A place far away from the great city of Detroit.

My wife's recollections and Danielle's are like so many others who are white. But the whites aren't the only ones who are shocked by present day Detroit. Laura Berman wrote a story called "The Detroit That Was" for the *Detroit News* on July 20, 2004. She wrote about Thyris Hughley, a black Detroit ex-convict. He had called her in a state of despair for the city's future. She was surprised that a man who once appeared lawless had such a strong reaction to the lawlessness in Detroit. She wrote:

> Hughley describes himself as "an early model of the thug and gangster", a 59-year-old man who launched his criminal career as a Black Panthers' follower in the 1960s….
>
> Hughley sat out the 1967 riots: he was already in the state prison in Jackson.
>
> What I really didn't expect was the rest of what he said—nostalgia for the vanished city where he'd been raised. "I remember when Detroit was a nice place to live. Now it's terrible."
>
> And: "It's scary here, even for me. There are shotguns everywhere. Somebody was shooting off a machine gun the other night. I know that sound. And nobody did anything. I listened for sirens. There weren't any."
>
> …"It was my generation that started this behavior…but when Detroit picked up the gun, it never put it down."
>
> A "hip-hop mayor", he argues, reinforces a negative stereotype. "Everybody wants to be a thug, and I should know."
>
> Hughley says his sister insisted he move back to Detroit, where his two children and other family members live. But after only a month here, he finds himself disturbed by the changes in the city where he grew up. And even more concerned by the apathy of the city's residents who tolerate what people in other places do not.

Thyris Hughley's lament is a familiar one. Too much crime. Too few legitimate businesses. A racial divide that seems unbridgeable. A feeling he can't quite put his finger on, of people being suppressed, shut down.

One day, he waited on Seven Mile three hours for a bus that never came. "In any other city," he argues, "people wouldn't stand for that. They would protest and demand change."

After a lifetime behind bars, Thyris Hughley sounds optimistic about his own life. It's the city he worries about.

To me, Thyris Hughley is complaining that police no longer pay attention to crime in certain communities because they have come to expect it. This emphasizes the fact that police no longer prevent crime but act only, and often not quickly enough, to enforce laws. That is dead wrong.

What Saves a City?

The officer should be influenced by a concept well known in policing for at least 40 years, called the "broken windows" policy. This means that crime is reduced by citing, arresting, and reminding others of minor violations to maintain community peace and pride. "Broken windows" means that criminals regard an area with broken windows and damage as a target because nobody seems to care about their property. It signals that nobody is minding the store, so to speak.

Sometimes politicians can make a big difference in crime. I want to describe one such instance, "the New York Miracle". This was the remarkable drop (over 60%) in that city's crime during the 1990s during the term of Mayor Rudolf Giuliani.

Giuliani championed the "broken windows" theory of crime after he learned about it from William Bratton.

Bratton, the first Police Commissioner appointed by Giuliani, used "broken windows" as the key to changes in the police department. He explained that individuals who are prepared to commit serious crimes will also disregard laws regulating everyday interactions. For example, those prepared to commit serious crimes won't bother to pay their subway fare. Arrests for every little thing, including subway fare dodging, is sometimes called the "zero-tolerance" theory, clamping down on all crimes.

Here is a brief review of the different types of policing that Giuliani and Bratton considered. "Broken Windows" is policing of the "little things" and often includes intelligence-led policing. "Intelligence-led policing" is using technology and intelligence information to target hotspots and potential offenders. "Zero-tolerance" is a total clampdown on all crime without individual police decisions or targeted arrests. "Community policing" is community and police partnerships to identify and solve problems. "Problem-oriented policing" includes intelligence-led and community policing to tackle specific problems.

Other things played a part in the New York Miracle. Prior to the implementation of "broken windows", New York's police force was increased by 10,000 officers (a 25% increase). Ah, if I had been given another 1,000 officers, perhaps Detroit could have been turned around.

Another factor was a change in the drug market. Still another was a decline in the number of young males in New York City, the most crime-prone group. Bratton had already learned, as head of the New York City Transit Police, that fare dodgers often had outstanding warrants, and their arrests cut subway crime significantly.

Giuliani's initiatives included arresting jaywalkers and speeding cab drivers, and rezoning sex shops. Additionally, statistics were used to note the highest level of disorder and crime called "hotspots." More crimes were committed in small areas, which could be reduced by police making random stops of around 15 minutes in these locations. The structure of the NYPD was decentralized to give precinct commanders flexibility to deploy officers to hotspots and relentlessly follow criminals as they shifted about.

I have to mention that I had scooter police officers do this in Detroit and also as sheriff. We had SCAT (Sheriff's Criminal Annoyance Team) where we zeroed in on those whom we knew were criminals and would commit future crimes.

The concentration on "hotspots" reduces crime and so does the concentration on certain individuals. It has been shown that a large proportion of crimes are committed by a small number of offenders. So police can aim to reduce the crime rate by getting repeat offenders off the streets.

A study in the United Kingdom aimed at known, suspected, and potential burglars found that by targeting these individuals for arrest, burglary rates fell by 62% in the target neighborhood. Later when I became Sheriff of Oakland County, we had such a program called SCAT (Sheriff's Criminal Annoyance Team) to get criminal repeaters.

In New York, they netted repeat offenders by policing softer crimes. But New York is different from many cities. There was a highly criminal population with many outstanding warrants on the streets and these people were caught when the police toughened up on minor offenses. Other cities do not have this same problem and the same strategy may not be as effective elsewhere.

What communities learned from the New York Miracle was that if criminals believe there is more likelihood of getting caught because of police presence, they are not as likely to engage in criminal activity. Furthermore, if police patrol high crime hotspots, stopping randomly for around 15 minutes, their possible presence deters crime. If a district has fewer troops and cannot arrest everyone for every crime, targeted arrests of repeat offenders will get many criminals out of circulation. And finally, if a district has a small police force, statistics can help target the areas of greatest criminal activity and these can be patrolled more frequently.

Overall, some 60,000 violent crimes were prevented in New York City from 1989 to 1998 because of the "broken windows" policing.

That was not Detroit's policy. Perhaps a man named Frank Owens had it right when he wrote "Detroit, Death City" in *Playboy* magazine's August, 2004, issue. He wrote a story about his father-in-law and his brother-in-law who were involved in the riots of 1967. He opened the article with this dramatic statement:

> It's a throwaway city for a throwaway society, a place where the American dream came to die. No other U.S. metropolis has suffered a decline as steep as Detroit's. From the "arsenal of democracy" during World War II to a blue-collar Shangri-La in the 1950s and 1960s, where a man could go straight from high school to the factory floor and earn enough money to buy a house and a car and support his family for the rest of his life—to a global symbol of what happens when cities go bad, a byword for violent crime, urban decay and racialized poverty, today Detroit is America's forgotten city...
>
> It's the story of the Detroit I came to know through marriage. It's a journey from hope to heartache, a drama that combines race, politics, violence and its victims. And it begins as many Detroit stories do, with the 1967 riots, an event old-timers still talk about as if it happened yesterday...
>
> The riots deeply scarred Detroit. The devastation was so extensive that, 37 years later, some neighborhoods have yet to recover. Whites fled the city in panic. Within five years Detroit would become a black-majority city.

Detroit is not the same as when I arrived June 1968. I embarked on a wild ride in the once great Motor City when I became the police commissioner.

After I left my post in 1970, I became Sheriff of the adjoining county (Oakland) and I have followed Detroit's story through magazines, newspapers, radio, television, talk shows, etc. I have been saddened by all that has happened in our area.

I love Michigan. I loved the city of Detroit. I felt most people were great, and that they also cared about their city.

I stayed in Michigan and was talked into running for sheriff by both Democrats and Republicans. I served three terms as sheriff (12 years) running as a

Democrat in a Republican County, but somehow overcame that to win three times.

I enjoyed my 17 months as police commissioner in those tough times, even more than the 12 years as sheriff of wealthy Oakland County. Today Oakland County is richer and Detroit is much poorer than it was at that time.

In 1968, taking office as police commissioner, I saw burned out houses, vacant and boarded up store fronts, as well as abandoned stores and factories. But I also saw much promise. I stayed at the beautiful Book Cadillac Hotel and later received 30 police scooters in front of the Statler Hilton Hotel. Both structures have since been vandalized and probably will vanish.

I was told before I came that Detroit was not a sophisticated city, it was a working man's town; that it was, but not now. Detroit was a city of churches, synagogues, great restaurants; a city of working families. Now all are mostly gone.

The riot of 1967 and its aftermath turned Detroit from a city that could have been a beacon of hope into a city to avoid.

The Five P's Killed Detroit:
Police, Politicians, Press, People and Pressure Groups
Other Cities Beware!

Detroit has never recovered from those fateful days and nights in 1967. Los Angeles has struggled with race riots and race problems as has Toronto, Newark, Minneapolis, Hartford, Dallas and other cities that have also seen massive decreases in population, a loss of businesses, a decline of economic vitality and slums developing in the downtown area. Other cities should beware because if we don't pay attention to history, it may repeat itself.

Who or what was responsible? I call it the 5 P's: police, politicians, press, people and pressure groups. We all had a hand in it. I say "we" even though I was not there at the time of the riot.

I feel that while I was police commissioner, the police and the people of Detroit became more favorably disposed to each other. But in my opinion, the politicians, the media and specific pressure groups, good and bad (e.g. Black Panthers and New Detroit, Inc.) left much to be desired and lent disturbing support to rebellious and militant blacks.

Police Helped Kill Detroit

The police certainly play their role in killing a city. Detroit's homicide rates make it America's deadliest big city. Reporters have said that it's too easy to die in Detroit—and too easy to get away with murder.

Cops often face the street code of violence, then silence. Murder can often result from drug use or the drug trade. The code of silence occurs when people are reluctant to speak out, fearful for their own safety, and don't want to get involved. The other side of the code of silence is when police officers don't report on each other when they see wrong being done.

The police profession must strengthen its relationship with the people of the community they serve. Police cannot solve crimes or protect the neighborhoods if people aren't talking to them. Yes, police must do more, do better, to win the hearts and minds of a community. And they must do more to root out their own bad apples lest the whole bushel become rotten.

Terrorism is now a way of life. It requires good training for police and requires citizen help, trained volunteers, as the eyes and ears of a community, not a code of silence. The federal government agencies must share information with local police. Now that we may be attacked from without or within by terrorists, we need our police and good communication with the public more than ever.

Police must become proactive. They must establish good relationships with residents. People know what's right and wrong in their communities. Police must get them to share that information. Today most policing is based on simply responding to emergency calls. But that depends on residents reporting crime and other incidents to police.

The police must bear the blame in many cases for ruining relations with citizens. They use unnecessary force, they intimidate and insult citizens in totally unprofessional ways, and they don't take the time to offer help and protection. Part of this is because they work with some paranoia fearing that they are seen as the enemy, and this is part of the reason they may act as aggressors before they are acted upon. Part of it is that they work daily with the worst people in our society, and they see the results of terrible crimes that make them lose faith in the goodness of man. And part of it is because some individual officers have become corrupt and seek personal gain or vengeance.

The key to changing the relationship between citizens and police lies more in the hands of officers than it does in the hands of citizens. But the message to change it in a positive direction must come from the top. The top means not only the top cops, who should be role models, but the leadership of the police union, who are supposed to speak for the police and their best interests.

Pressure Groups Helped Kill Detroit

Police unions are only one of many pressure groups. I certainly had my problems with the Detroit Police Officers union. Out of those problems, I created some guidelines in the final chapter to guide police executives as they deal with their own police union for best results.

Other pressure groups represent a section of the public on some particular issue. A group may become popular when people feel that the government doesn't listen to them. Other groups pressure local government to undertake projects that would benefit them financially. A good example in Detroit was Super Bowl XL. Backers maintained that the big game would generate $302 million.

"The Super Bowl is to be the catalyst for creating some 50 businesses, 100 lofts and $20 million of street improvements in blighted downtown, civic boosters contend," wrote Louis Aguilar in *The Detroit News*, Oct. 23, 2004.

He predicted that 125,000 out-of-towners were expected to come to Michigan in the dead of winter to spend an average of $2,500. However, economists who had reviewed every Super Bowl from 1970 to 2001 conclude that an estimate of only $90 million will benefit the local economy.

The real beneficiaries are the National Football League, the stadium owners and big businesses. The losers are the taxpayers and local businesses. Imagine if the $302 million was invested directly in schools, the police and local businesses?

Politics, many say, is a "blood sport". Allegations of voter intimidation and fraud abound around politicians. There are often charges of dirty tricks and Watergate style break-ins at campaign headquarters of both parties. Politics often means political warfare, accusations and irregularities. Politicians are too easily swayed by pressure groups.

Prominent public pressure groups include trade unions such as the AFL-CIO. In 1984, the AFL-CIO had about 18 million members, about 20% of the workforce. But it has been weakened by allegations of racketeering, corruption and infiltration by organized crime. The weakness is also due to the fact that individual trade unions within the AFL-CIO have their own autonomy. These were at work in Detroit but have weakened with the passage of time.

Headlines in the press vividly display conflicts between the leaders of police unions and city mayors and councils. Who really controls law enforcement today? Is it law enforcement management? I believe readers want to know what police executives think so I'll tell you. We in management don't have dues paying members but unions do. Members and money mean clout! We're kidding ourselves if we think a police chief totally runs his police department.

Some cooperation between unions and management is most essential. We should be working together for each other in the people's interests. But management must believe in and retain our right to manage while recognizing our fundamental accountability to the public we serve. Let us be the managers of our enterprise and be the main man in that seat with our hands firmly on the throttle. We can certainly ride together with unions on the same track that leads to professional status of law enforcement, but we must control the train. That is what we were hired to do!

People Helped Kill Detroit

The people, Detroiters, must team up to fight crime and violence. Luther Keith of *The Detroit News* made some important points in an article on October 21, 2004:

> If Detroiters want to make some real headway in the fight against crime and violence, they will have to get past "me-ism" and into "we-ism".
>
> This means stop waiting on the Detroit police, the Wayne County Prosecutor, Mayor Kwame Kilpatrick and the Detroit City Council.
>
> Stop waiting on the NAACP, the Urban League...New Detroit, the Detroit Public Schools, Save Our Sons and Daughters (SOSAD), the Detroit Regional Chamber of Commerce and—yes—the media.

Keith stressed the importance of all groups working together, pooling resources, and getting the business community to pay for positive messages to reinforce the efforts all over the city.

Rev. Olen Bruner, pastor of Trinity Community Presbyterian Church, made an emotional appearance at an anti-violence rally on October 16, 2004, in downtown Detroit. The rally was sponsored by the Men in Action (MIA), a grassroots anti-violence group that sprang up in response to the September 16, 2004, tragic murder of Robert Reynolds, 72, a deacon at Trinity. Reynolds was shot, allegedly by two teenagers during a carjacking near the church.

Rev. Bruner told the audience that the problem is too many various factions and organizations that aren't working together. He ended on a positive note when he said that the MIA was God's way of making something good come out of tragedy.

In black communities, 85% of babies are born out of wedlock. Now, let's deal with the truth about human nature. When a man wants to feel he's a man, he proves it by the number of women and the number of children he has. Where are the black leaders who will deal with this more directly? These young black men, the children of other young black men who put notches on their belts, are unable to get decent jobs, education and housing. They have contributed to part of the deterioration of the inner city of Detroit.

Of course, the housing authorities and auto industries must take their share of the blame for their ostracism of blacks in favor of whites. The unorganized and organized criminals, the Marxist agitators and many other groups played their part in the collapse of the city.

The 5 P's must shoulder the responsibility not only for the destruction of Detroit but for failure to aid in its recovery, thus causing the exodus of white people. The whites fled in fear of blacks, there was the cross district bussing nonsense, and a succession of top police executives who came and went like a revolving door because of mayoral turnover. Really no city can survive all this and Detroit has not.

If Detroit can recover and resume its former place among America's premier cities, it will depend on all the above developing more soul searching. They must all realize that proper policing is a must and engender more awareness of ethics and integrity. Adherence to a code of morals and values will be the first step toward the unity necessary for this divided city.

Yes, morality, moral courage, ethics and values must be used for the good of the people of America. And I believe that unity will come from cooperation and communication rather than political partisanship and law enforcement jurisprudence jealousies.

The Press Helped Kill Detroit

Even the diverse pressure groups and the for-profit press could show more concern for the welfare and good of the people of the community than for their own interests and profits. The news media tend to cater and pay more curious attention to the abnormal than the normal. Just as curiosity killed the cat, such media philosophy helps to kill a city.

Our TV media news programs now have 17 minutes of news in a 30-minute segment. There is a general lack of community news and important information, in favor of "smart shoppers" plugging products and "investigative journalism" with reporters trying to create sensationalism through exposing bad business practices.

Controversies abound. Dan Rather's *60 Minutes* story on President Bush's National Guard service during the Vietnam War ended his career, as the media rushed forward with the supposed results of "investigative journalism".

Network news is slipping. People have deserted to cable news, websites, videogames and whatever. Thus the major news programs and anchors try to bring them back with dramatic news stories. A citizen named Al Kwasniuk of Walled Lake, Michigan, wrote in to *The Detroit News* not long ago complaining, "Nothing really strikes me as 100 percent true anymore. I miss the old days when you knew what was what."

Extremists get a disproportionate amount of attention in our media, and therefore create a false sense of alienation between those in the mainstream of life. The media often give people a chance to vent their spleen. Good news gets the back page because controversy is what sells. If it bleeds, it leads, as they say in the media.

Today, there is dissension among the media as they fight for their share of the audience. CNN's Ted Turner criticized and lashes out against Fox News. Both cable news shows are making inroads against network news. When Fox News overwhelmed CNN during the Iraq War, Ted Turner warned his competitors that just because ratings were higher, they weren't necessarily better. I think he's feeling the effects of the ratings and audience shares war.

Advertisements cater to basic appetites, as do news stories. Sexual material sells well and stories about sex sell well also. Big disturbances and loud noises catch the headlines, the camera and the microphones. People who are quiet, reflective, and weigh all the issues acting with moderation are toast in the papers.

The press should be fair, even-handed, giving equal space to all sides of issues. Consumers of media, you and I, have a special impact on a city's image and therefore a special responsibility. They and we should balance negatives with positives to keep a city's image in balance. I've often wondered why the newspapers can't have one page, at least, called the "Good News Page." It may not sell papers but it can sell the city's favorable image. Improper or erroneous reporting can wreck a police department and it can wreck a city.

Let's look at Detroit today. It still is a city devoid of hope. Top department stores, Hudson's, Crowleys, Sears, Kern's, and many other retailers have left the city of Detroit. The *Detroit News* Business Section editorial on May 14, 1992, stated:

> Once Sears closes its Highland Park store at the end of this month, it could be a decade or more before another major department store chain opens in

Detroit, according to developers and retailers attending the nation's largest shopping center convention this week.

New stores spring up like mushrooms in the suburban Detroit metro area but no large national retail chains will market in Detroit city. They shun Detroit. Kmart and Wal-Mart have no interest in doing business in the city of Detroit. Nor are any of the other major department stores interested. Yet other cities such as Indianapolis, Pittsburgh, Chicago, and Atlanta flourish.

By 1990 the one-time fifth largest city in America was becoming an also-ran. The police were not the only players in the drama of a dying city. The politicians, businesses and the people were to blame, also. And the media, the fourth estate.

What will Detroit be tomorrow? That's a great unknown. Today, Detroit faces many problems: high unemployment, rising crime—especially murder, race issues, poor and problem schools, fear of living in the city, and fear of going to the city.

Detroit as a comfortable, livable city has greatly diminished its image. Many of Detroit's neighborhoods are old and unattractive, and almost unlivable. The scars and blemishes of the 1967 riots are still highly visible.

White flight from the inner city and now black flight to new homes and jobs in Oakland County, Macomb County and Western Wayne County are symptoms of Detroit's problems.

Black resentment and distrust of whites, and white distrust and resentment of blacks compound the problems. The result is a city of about 85% black residents with much political squabbling internally. With suburban resentment and non-cooperation, distrust or inertia hampers efforts towards solutions.

How Can Detroit Be Revived?

What will happen to Detroit? In the 1960s and 1970s, President Johnson's "War on Poverty" and "Great Society Program" provided federal monies to rebuild older cities, provide job training, equal racial opportunities, affirmative action programs, etc. Monies were provided to build or improve superhighways. This stimulated employment, growth, and the automobile business, but it also served to spur white flight.

In the 1960s, Detroit and other cities were seen as deserving of federal support for renewal and revitalization. But now, we have rings of suburbs around older central cities creating animosity between suburban and central cores. The flight of whites into a ring around black Detroit is the most distinctive feature of this city.

Farley, Danziger and Holzer, authors of *Detroit Divided*, wrote that skills, space and race all matter in the labor market, and that matters in the housing market as well. They believe that educational improvements to provide labor market skills offer the best prospect for raising employment/earnings and closing both the city-suburban and black-white gaps in socioeconomic status.

They think that central city residents should be moved to homes in the sub-urbs, firms should be moved back to the central city, and transportation must commute workers from the suburbs to central city jobs. Those are interesting and important ideas but they haven't been tested. They have been discussed for 35 years but policies have not been instituted to try these suggestions nor have success stories emerged.

I know that public service employment programs have a long history in the United States, but they are not politically popular. President Ronald Reagan eliminated the Comprehensive Employment and Training Act (CETA) in the early 1980s. Even so, *Detroit Divided* authors claim that federal and state laws ban racial discrimination, but enforcement is lax.

Judge George Crockett (who released so many prisoners in the New Bethel church case) surprised many in 1992 when he asked his old friend Coleman Young to step down as Mayor in favor of Dennis Archer. Crockett and Young resolved their differences in a phone call according to Crockett's obituary in *Detroit Free Press* in 1997.

Another thing that can kill a city is when it is at war with itself. The police were caught in the middle between orders from the top of the FBI to the Detroit branch to proceed with covert repression of radical organizations within our midst. Incidentally, I've got to tell a funny saying among cops. There are three things no cop needs because they cost too much in the long run: a yacht, a mistress and the FBI. All kidding aside, I've always loved working with the FBI but they do have a different agenda. The average citizen has very little contact with FBI special agents but they have daily contact with police officers.

The FBI Wasn't Perfect Either

The following information and memos show something of the crime, criminals and unworthy as well as worthy FBI methods used to deal with them in Detroit in earlier years.

Within three months of my departure, FBI Special Agent in Charge Paul Stoddard received the following letter from FBI Director J. Edgar Hoover written April 17, 1970.

Counterintelligence and Special Operations
Research Section

Captioned title is used to coordinate and develop sophisticated intelligence and long-range counterintelligence operations. Through this control file suggestions for the development of new intelligence approaches and techniques are afforded serious consideration.

Over the years it has been a tendency of some relatively minute extremist groups to publicly project themselves as large membership organizations. Long-time communist Homer Bates Chase operates in an almost solo fashion out of the Boston area as the New England Party of Labor (NEPL). He is the Editorial Board of "Hammer and Steel Newsletter", far-out Marxist-Leninist publication. NEPL membership consists of Chase, the sometimes participation of his wife, and the periodic association of several relatives.

Nevertheless, Chase has established contact with a large number of Chicoms (Chinese communists) and pro-Chicoms throughout the world. He has engaged in an international conference of pro-Chicoms in Albania, and he has made several trips to Communist China, conferring on at least one occasion with members of the Central Committee of the Communist Party of China. Chase apparently finances his international Marxist-Leninist activities on his salary as a truck driver for a lumber yard.

Similarly, Michael Lasky has for a number of years acted as the chairman and almost sole driving force behind the Communist Party, USA (Marxist-Leninist) (CPUSA, M-L)

This organization, which describes itself as "the only true Marxist-Leninist party", has rarely had more than a half dozen members and, in effect, all activities have been those of Lasky himself. Last year Lasky merged his group with the Proletarian Revolutionary Party in New York City, this latter organization consisting of three effective members. In spite of questions regarding (blacked out name) his aggressive egotism enabled him to operate an "International Bookstore" selling literature furnished by the Chicoms.

He periodically published a newspaper, and he traveled to Europe where in England he was afforded red carpet treatment by a number of pro-Chicom organizations who looked upon him as a Messiah seeking to form a new Communist International sympathetic to the Chicoms. Lasky suffered a serious gunshot wound inflicted by a comrade in December, and this action apparently destroyed his West Coast branch of the CPUSA, M-L, and the three member East Coast branch earlier this month reconstituted itself into the Marxist-Leninist Party.

The Committee of Correspondence of Seattle, "Antithesis" of San Francisco, the Committee for Political Studies of New York, the Maryland Socialist League, the California Communist League, the Cousins Coordinating Committee of Upstate New York are but representative of a number of organizations which in actuality are the instruments of one egotistically minded militant seeking to develop fraternal relationships with other extremists.

Even the extremist Student National Coordinating Committee, which endeavors to project itself as a militant national organization, operates out of New York City with eight individuals, only three of whom are considered active. (Some paragraphs are blacked out.)

It is requested offices receiving copies of this communication call this matter to the attention of all agents interested in investigations of an intelligence nature, and that thereafter comments and recommendations be forwarded to the Bureau relating to (rest of sentence is blacked out.)

The following month, during which Stoddard left his position, he and the new Detroit Special Agent in Charge sent this memo to Director Hoover on May 18, 1970, proposing to create a phony organization to mess up black nationalist and other groups.

Counterintelligence and Special Operations
Research Section

ReBulet, 4/17/70 (Re: Bureau letter quoted above.)

In accordance with Bureau instructions, SAs (Special Agents) of the Detroit Office interested in investigations of an intelligence nature have reviewed and discussed reBulet.

Detroit concurs that it is desirable to organize and operate a cover organization intelligence operation in the Detroit Division, and suggests that such an organization (committee) in Detroit be set up to be portrayed as an anti-war, anti-capitalistic organization, sympathetic to the oppressed and exploited people, not only in the U.S., but in other non-Socialist countries. This image would appeal not only to the "New Left" and the militants, but also to "peace" groups. (Paragraphed blacked out.)
<u>Request of Bureau</u>
Bureau authority is requested for Detroit to contact (name blacked out) in line with the above.

On June 2, 1970, Director Hoover responded to new FBI Special Agent in Charge of Detroit, Neil J. Welch. Welch had become famous before he got to Detroit over the following incident in 1968.

During a routine transfer of a prisoner (Winston Moseley, a black man) to a hospital in Buffalo, Moseley overpowered a guard and stole his gun. He then took five people hostage and raped a woman in front of her husband. Welch, special agent of the Buffalo FBI office, entered the apartment where Moseley held the hostages. In a nail-biting half hour, Moseley and Welch pointed guns at each other in a point-blank position while they continued negotiations. Moseley eventually surrendered (Gado).

Later Welch became even more famous for redirecting office resources into the organized crime investigative program, according to Steve Pomerantz, former FBI agent and current partner of Mitretek Organization. Pomerantz told co-author Holloway, "The Detroit field office under his (Welch) direction led the way in the Bureau's ultimately very successful fight against La Cosa Nostra."

From 1960 to 1990, the Detroit Family of La Cosa Nostra (LCN) was very active with about 30 "made members" and between 200 and 300 associates. They were involved in illegal gambling, loan sharking, money laundering, drug trafficking, and the infiltration of legitimate businesses, according to the FBI. (FBI, Investigative Programs, Organized Crime, www.fbi.gov)

La Cosa Nostra collected "street taxes" from illegal gamblers, loan sharks, and extortionists and committed acts of violence to support these activities. They also controlled the Aladdin and Edgewater Casinos in Nevada during the 1970s.

The FBI investigations led to indictment of the Detroit LCN and admission by the head (Vito Giacalone) that he was a member and that the Detroit LCN existed. Giacalone was one of two people Jimmy Hoffa was supposedly waiting to meet when he disappeared in 1975, but Giacalone died before being brought to trial.

Hoffa became a stockboy in Detroit warehouses until he became active in union organizing during the 1930s. By 1942, he became president of the Michigan Conference of Teamsters. He was elected international vice president of the Teamsters Union in 1952 and become international president in 1957.

In 1964 he was found guilty of misusing the union's pension funds. He was sentenced to eight years in jail on bribery charges and served four years in prison. It was rumored that La Cosa Nostra was responsible for his rise in the union. But Hoffa refused to leave his union successor in office when he was released from jail.

His refusal to stay out of union affairs may have led to his disappearance on July 30, 1975, when he was to meet with Teamster boss Anthony Provenza, a reputed LCN figure, along with Giacalone.

There have been some indications from the FBI that other Detroit mobsters operated during the 1970s. They have included such men as Michael Polizzi, Anthony Zerilli, and Matthew (Mike) Trupiano, all identified by the FBI as involved with the Detroit LCN syndicate.

Welch and David Marston wrote *Inside Hoover's F.B.I.* in 1984. Welch was one of several men interviewed by President Jimmy Carter to be the next director of the FBI after Clarence Kelley, but Carter chose Judge William Webster instead.

Ernest Volkman wrote about Welch in *Gangbusters: The Destruction of America's Last Mafia Dynasty*. Volkman wrote that after Hoover died, Congress passed the Racketeer Influenced Corruption Organization (RICO) statute and Detroit Special Agent in Charge Neil J. Welch became convinced the government could use it along with surveillance to ruin the major mob families, and they did.

But let me return to Hoover's obsession with Black Nationalist Hate Groups. He sent a memo to Welch in Detroit on June 2, 1970, giving permission for Detroit to create a phony organization:

> Counterintelligence and Special Operations
> Research Section
> Counterintelligence Program, Black Nationalist-Hate Groups.
> Bureau concurs the cover organization, proposed by Delet 5/18/70, may very likely be used for counterintelligence as well as intelligence-gathering purposes.
> When the cover organization has been established, the Bureau will consider the advisability of using (name blacked out) to attack the organization if this action would serve to authenticate the cover. Also consideration should be given to using (sentence blacked out). Specific recommendations regarding counterintelligence use of the cover should be submitted at an appropriate time after the cover is established.
> It is requested all correspondence relating to the development and operation of this cover be submitted under above caption (COINTELPRO-Black Nationalist-Hate Groups).

On June 25, 1970, Detroit SAC Neil Welch sent this memo to Director Hoover:

> Counterintelligence and Special Operations
> Research Section
> On 6/23/70, (name blacked out) was interviewed in accordance with re Bulet. This informant immediately and enthusiastically endorsed this endeavor and stated that he would cooperate to the fullest extent.
> (Next two paragraphs blacked out.)
> Based on further discussion with the informant, he suggested that the name of the organization be (name blacked out). Detroit feels that this name would lend itself to development of an organization along the lines suggested in relets and recommends that the organization be so entitled.
> (Next two paragraphs blacked out.)
> <u>Requests of Bureau</u>

(First paragraph blacked out.)
Bureau authority to obtain two post office boxes in line with the above.

Authority to file with the County Clerk, Wayne County, application to conduct business under an assumed name, in line with the above.

Authorization to instruct informant to begin preparation of initial communication to be directed to selected target organizations.

Provide Detroit with list of suggested target organizations.

While the FBI continued the COINTELPRO dirty tricks in the background, there were also dirty tricks being planned by local Black Panther Party and White Panther Party members. An informant reported to the FBI on June 20, 1970, that three BPP members intended to ambush policemen at midnight on the night of June 27, 1970. The FBI notified the Detroit Police Department and they were ready.

When the three snipers fired on the officers, they were arrested and three others were arrested in connection with the shooting. A cache of weapons and ammunition were recovered from the home of one of those arrested.

On July 25, 1970, the same informant notified the FBI that a member of the Detroit National Committee to Combat Fascism and a member of the White Panther Party stole some dynamite two weeks earlier. He advised the FBI as to the location of dynamite on the farm of the mother of one of the two. On September 16, 1970, the mother gave the FBI agents permission to search her property and they confiscated 50 sticks of dynamite (Final Report of the Select Committee to Study Governmental Operations, April 23, 1976).

Neil Welch was known as an independent thinker, according to James A. Abbott, former Special Agent in Charge of the Dallas FBI office. Welch refused to follow Hoover's request for phony letters in 1970 and switched his agents over to routing out organized crime and La Cosa Nostra members. By 1971, an FBI dragnet snared 16 Detroit police officers along with other citizens and LCN members. Directed by Welch, his 400 agents struck simultaneously in 37 Michigan cities, in the largest gambling raid in FBI history. Welch announced that the gambling industry had grossed nearly $1 million daily (*Detroit Free Press*, May 7, 1971).

It broke my heart to hear of so many Detroit police officers being involved with the syndicate. I had known there were probably some, but the code of silence was unbelievably strong in those days. Neil Welch described it in his book.

> I've seen police corruption in New York and Detroit where an entire precinct systematically shakes down the prostitutes, gamblers, after-hours places. Cop cases are never just one cop—it's the captain, the lieutenant, the inspector, the sergeants, the whole pad, as they say in New York (216).

I have to hammer one more nail in the coffin for Detroit according to some. I'm not sure I agree with the following position because every police force needs to have intelligence officers. They are part of the prevention component of the law enforcement profession. But they can be overused and certainly were overused when the FBI began creating fake documents and organizations. Such actions stain the law enforcement profession and that affects police officers as well as FBI agents.

A paper by Frank Donner, who later wrote *Protectors of the Privileged* in 1990, was published in April 22, 1971, in the *New York Review of Books*. His paper was entitled "A Special Supplement: The Theory and Practice of American Political Intelligence". He wrote that since the early 1960s, political surveillance and association practices have spread throughout the nation. Surveillance has expanded largely because of the scale and militancy of the protest movements that erupted in the 1960s. He added that many of the red squads run by city police were growing so fast that they are hard put to find enough agents. He claimed that the official membership of Detroit's intelligence unit, which was formed in 1961, grew by 1968 to 70 members.

I don't recall the numbers and perhaps he is right. But a police department can no more operate without advance notice of criminal schemes from undercover operatives than America can operate without undercover operatives detecting anti-American and terrorist activities. Our duty is to protect citizens before bad things happen rather than just responding after the fact when it's too late.

After I left as Commish, blacks were filling the streets of downtown Detroit and gathering political strength. Coleman Young won support to become the first black mayor of Detroit in 1973 by a narrow margin over Police Commissioner John Nichols, who would later follow me as Oakland County sheriff.

It was a funny election, with both Young and Nichols as gun-toting candidates. Additionally, lame duck Mayor Roman Gribbs fired Nichols as police commissioner during the election campaign, saying he needed a full-time police boss. The nearly all-white Detroit Police Officers Association again supported a white candidate, Nichols, for mayor but Nichols lost.

Forces had been in motion for many years before Coleman Young became Mayor. Those forces had gathered considerable strength and produced a mayor that wrecked the city. Mayor Young became the conductor of a train named

Detroit that headed downhill without any brakes. I'll summarize the forces that gathered so much steam that nobody could stop the mayor and the decline of the city.

Why Do Blacks Resent White Government?

Put yourselves in their shoes. Three hundred or more years of slavery, torn from their roots, shackled in chains to be shipped to America, used and exploited on plantations and cotton fields in the South, later further used and exploited for their labor in the North, treated as subhuman, lack of jobs, substandard living, substandard schools and so on and so on. Frustration upon frustration. Separate facilities, separate schools, separate travel accommodations, separate restaurants and stores, separate drinking fountains, etc., etc.

Anyone old enough has seen many of these things and most caring and thinking people have been revolted by them. It was there, though, and not enough was done by white government leaders.

Blacks have to look at life so differently than whites. The great James Weldon Johnson (1871-1938), mentioned earlier, described some of the problems faced by parents who know that the future for a black child is more limited and difficult than for a white child.

> Awaiting each colored boy and girl are cramping limitations and buttressed obstacles, in addition to those that must be met by youth in general; and this dilemma approaches suffering in proportion to the parents' knowledge of and the child's innocence of those conditions.
>
> Some parents up to the last moment strive to spare the child the bitter knowledge. The child of less sensitive parents is likely to have this knowledge driven in upon him from infancy (56).

The lack of freedoms encountered by blacks throughout their lives can be handled constructively by people like James Weldon Johnson or vengefully. Eldridge Cleaver wrote in *Soul On Ice* that every time he had sex with a white woman, it was like a moment of freedom and a revenge against white males who constrained him.

The South has now changed greatly, but not enough. I and my family saw on a couple of driving trips to Florida on Route 303 the shacks, the poverty, and the unfairness.

I remember well what happened in a Georgia restaurant with my wife and daughter. Betty was about ten years old. A white "gentleman" suddenly said to her, pointing out a young Negro lad bussing tables, "See him—that's a nigger, honey." We had thankfully almost finished our meal and we made haste to leave. That was life in the South.

As Detroit Police Commissioner I met many fine people, and some not so fine. I have complained about several blacks in this book but I met many fine blacks as well. A man I admired was Damon Keith, a black citizen of Detroit who rose to be Circuit Judge of the U.S. Court of Appeals for the 6th Circuit. An article in the *Detroit Free Press* August 1985 quoted him as he spoke about blacks and racism. Much as I admire him, his words are sometimes hard to take.

> There are people in America who say that blacks should be pulling themselves up by their own bootstraps and that race is not a factor in the upward mobility of blacks in America today.
>
> Let's face it. We live in a racist society. We have been enslaved, segregated, rejected, excluded, mistreated, locked out, exploited, despised, disenfranchised, and discouraged for one reason only, and that is the fact that we are black. If the society that we live in has damaged us because we are black, and it has, then the society must now remedy the situation.

America is the land of the free and the brave, but really there has been a limitation of freedom for black Americans, and up to 1920 women did not have the freedom to vote, certainly indicating a lack of fairness for many in our land.

This remarkable man is the grandson of slaves. Keith Damon's father moved the family to Detroit to take advantage of the better wages and working conditions in the auto industry for blacks.

During the year of the riot, 1967, Keith, who practiced law in Detroit with John Conyers and others, was appointed to the Circuit Court of East Michigan. A friend of his, Willie Horton, grew up in a neighborhood near 12th Street where the riot began. He came over as soon as he finished playing baseball for the Detroit Tigers the night of the riot to talk people out of their mob reactions and violence, along with John Conyers and Damon Keith.

Damon Keith was one of the original members of New Detroit, Inc., and he always gave the group wise counsel. But he spoke little and groups were the poorer for it.

Keith's famous five words, "Democracies die behind closed doors", were rendered in a famous case against John Ashcroft, and led to the open trials of 9/11 immigrants, among others. He also issued famous verdicts in cases of school and workplace discrimination, including a 1977 decision that the Detroit Police Department had the right to remedy racial discrimination in their ranks by hiring and promoting equally qualified blacks over whites.

I think the good citizens of Detroit and Michigan, like Damon Keith, worried and watched but could not stop the rapid downhill motion of the city. They could not control the mayor, city council and actions that worsened Detroit's condition. And those same forces are in action in many other cities at this time. As Hubert Locke said in his book on the riot, "As the cities of America go, so goes the entire nation."

Now the blacks in Detroit no longer feel excluded from city affairs and city government. Now it is their city—with a black leadership. One city employee told me recently that Detroit is turning into a "third world city—leaderless and rudderless".

One other American city has been classified similarly. David Rieff wrote a book entitled *Los Angeles: Capital of the Third World.* He dealt with the polyglot of races immigrating to Los Angeles and their effect as the economy strains and nearly bursts at the seams to absorb them. The 12 million occupants of Los Angeles have had to endure riots, disorder, crime, decay, white flight and problems similar to Detroit but amazingly their crime rate has recently begun to subside.

In the 1960s the young black males among the rioters complained about police brutality, unemployment, quality of their housing and their schools. Sidney Fine wrote,

> They did not, however, think that there was anything inevitable about this state of affairs. Since they did not believe that the existing political system was responsive to their needs {which I question concerning all that Cavanagh and his administration tried to do} they turned to rioting...as their means of protest, as a way of signaling to those in power that they must pay attention to the black ghetto and its problems. In this sense, the rioting of 1967 was born of hope, not of despair, the hope that improvement would follow the disorder in the streets (462).

I'm not sure that the rioters had any sense of hope or had anything planned out about bringing attention to their problems, because that's not in the nature of rioters. But I do agree with Fine's conclusions:

> One has to recognize the difference in outlook of Detroit blacks in 1987 {his book was published in 1989} as compared to 1967. Their mood, it would seem, was now one of despair rather than hope. Their material condition, having deteriorated during the preceding twenty years and with the Civil Rights Movement a fading memory for them, they may very well have sensed that although rioting might possibly serve as an outlet for frustration, it was unlikely to lead to an improvement in their circumstances (462-3).

Fine closed his book sadly by quoting reporter Barbara Stanton, a life-long Detroit resident who had covered the 1967 riot for the *Detroit Free Press.* "The inescapable reality," she remarked, "was that there was far more destruction and violence in Detroit in 1987 than in 1967...It is as if the riot had never ended, but goes on in slow motion. Instead of a single, stupendous explosion, there is a steady relentless corrosion."

To the question, "Could it happen again?" Fine's answer was "It is happening right now, a riot without end, a tragedy still without resolution" (463).

And that was 18 years ago.

Another writer, Julia Vitullo-Martin, said simply:

> Detroit's decline is a textbook case of how to kill a city. The table of contents reads like this: a history of poor race relations, a shrinking industrial base, the U.S. auto industry's collapse in the seventies, and Coleman Young's mayor-alty" (2).

That doesn't even include people like white hippie songwriter and White Panther Party co-founder John Sinclair. I'll just finish up the story of what happened to him. While in Jackson and Marquette prisons in Michigan serving his sentence for 9 ½ to 10 years, Sinclair was indicted for the September 29, 1968, bombing of the Ann Arbor CIA office.

I ought to comment that I heard a group wanted to kidnap me when I was police commissioner in January 1969. It was thought that the group was the White Panthers. I joshed with the officers who told me this and said, "Hey, wait a minute. If they know how much I eat, they'll think twice!"

On April 30, 1971, the White Panther Party dissolved and was reformed as the Rainbow People's Party. Despite being in prison, Sinclair worked with party members to guide its actions. It re-formed with a Marxism-Leninism focus on promoting the struggle for a "communal, classless, anti-imperialist, anti-racist, and anti-sexist...culture of liberation" (Morris & Nolan).

Two and a half years into his 9 ½ to 10 year sentence, after numerous legal battles, a rally was held on December 10, 1971, to "Free John Now". It was head-lined by John Lennon and Yoko Ono and attended by Jerry Rubin, Bobby Seale (co-founder of the Black Panther Party), Allen Ginsberg and others. John Len-non wrote and played a song criticizing Sinclair's sentence, including the line, "They gave him ten for two" meaning ten years for two marijuana cigarettes.

About $45,000 was raised for Sinclair's defense. Finally on December 13, 1971, the Michigan Supreme Court ordered him released and overturned his conviction, ruling that Michigan's marijuana statutes were unconstitutional. The CIA bombing charges were dropped.

It was my friend, respected Judge Damon Keith, who caused the charges to be dropped. He issued the opinion to reject warrantless electronic surveillance on domestic groups that posed a threat to national security in what later became known as the "Keith case". The Supreme Court upheld his opinion that the government should not use surveillance on those who only express dissenting opinions in a democratic society. It was another thing to commit to a plan of destruction, said the court (Damren).

Upon his release, Sinclair continued to spout acceptance of free love, marijuana and urged a cultural revolution. He later worked for the city of Detroit as editor of Detroit's City Arts Quarterly magazine. However, he was terminated after opposing Mayor Coleman Young in a disagreement over what should be done with Tiger Stadium. He then settled in New Orleans for 12 years but passed through Detroit in 2003 on his way to Amsterdam for a marijuana festival (Provenzano).

As a follow-up on Rev. Albert Cleage, in 1972 he wrote a second book called *Black Christian Nationalism*, renamed his denomination Pan African Orthodox Christian Church and renamed himself Jaramogi Abebe Agyeman ("liberator and savior of the nation" in Swahili).

Later, the Shrine launched a political group that claimed to help Mayors Coleman Young and Kwame Kilpatrick, as well as U.S. Representatives Carolyn Cheeks Kilpatrick and U.S. Rep. John Conyers, according to a *Belleville News Democrat* article in 2003.

Politicians Helped Kill Detroit

Many thought Commissioner Girardin had been unduly influenced by black leaders when he urged a policy of police restraint during the riot on July 23, 1967. Many black leaders, the black middle class and even many Twelfth Street residents and merchants criticized the police toleration of looting and arson.

State Senator Coleman Young, however, defended the police behavior on July 23rd. Later, with regard to the Algiers Motel verdict, where there were limited police convictions for what had taken place on July 26, Young declared that law and order is a one-way street. He warned that with mostly white cops, there was no law and order where black people were involved. Coleman Young was never a friend of the police in my estimation and tended to use the race card far too much.

In August 1969, State Senator Young proposed the creation of a civilian review board to judge police actions. The effort by proponents of the measure failed to have their proposal submitted to a referendum of the voters in the 1969 election although it did have the support of the Detroit NAACP, the Human Relations Council of the Detroit Archdiocese, the Metropolitan Detroit Board of the American Civil Liberties Union, the National Lawyers Guild, and the Association of Black Students of Wayne State University.

I supposed that most of those groups would represent black demands but the Detroit Archdiocese was somewhat of a surprise. However, I understood more when I visited the Catholic Church on Woodward Avenue and saw the banner in the church with the words POLICE BRUTALITY.

I really was incensed. Later when the Archdiocese purchased video cameras and gave them to white activist Sheila Murphy (later Cockrel), in order to film "bad police", I was even more incensed. Why was there no offer of cameras to film the vicious actions of some militants against the police? Sheila Murphy was a Catholic worker employer and leader of the Ad Hoc Action Group—a "cop watching" organization.

Coleman won favor when, upon being elected mayor, he abolished STRESS (Stop the Robberies, Enjoy Safe Streets), the undercover police unit that Nichols had begun in October 1971. The program was said to have caused police to kill as many as 20 young black men prior to Young's election.

Then later as part of the new city charter that was approved by the voters, the five person civilian Board of Police Commissioners was approved by the mayor and Common Council. This abolished the position of police commissioner, and administration of the police department was vested in a chief of police.

Then Mayor Coleman Young had free political control of the police department, the 5-member board of commissioners and the chief. The Board of Police Commissioners are approved by the mayor to be the policy-making body for the police department, but in effect serve as Review Board, with the ability to investigate citizen complaints against the police.

Coleman became known for instituting affirmative action in hiring, especially for the uniformed services of fire and police, and for managerial positions. This, in almost 13 years, resulted in a 50% black police force and it is much higher today. Sidney Fine wrote, "Police-community relations, which had inflamed race relations before, during and after the riot, took a decided turn for the better as the result of Young's election and the substantial changes in the police department that ensued" (458).

The voters re-elected Young over and over with these election results:

1973	Young 233,674		Nichols 216,933
1977	Young 164,626		Browne 63,626
1981	Young 176,710		Koslowski 91,245
1985	Young 141,551		Barrow 90,907
1989	Young 138,312		Barrow 107,073

The annual share of city contracts awarded to black firms grew from $25,000 in 1973 to $125 million by the 1990s. But I ask if the City of Detroit is better off because of Coleman Young's administration of some 20 years?

Although black incomes grew, the poverty rate tripled as auto plants closed and job opportunities dwindled. While buildings and companies moved or closed, he used resources for a few projects like sports stadiums, gambling casinos, the expansion of Cobo Hall, Millender Center and the People Mover. During the 1980s, he cut the budget and city jobs, used police to break strikes, and presided over many scandals.

Among these are business scandals; conviction of his police chief, William Hart, for embezzlement; conviction of a relative for using Detroit police to protect drug dealers; and fraudulent contracts awarded by city departments. He cried "racism" for every conviction, claimed to defend black Detroit against white suburbs, and made race the issue for virtually every challenge the city of Detroit faced.

In addition, Coleman Young often simply made bad decisions. In 1979, Saddam Hussein donated hundreds of thousands of dollars to a Chaldean church in Detroit after Rev. Jacob Yasso of the Chaldean Sacred Heart had congratulated Hussein on his presidency. Yasso traveled to Iraq in 1980 and was received by Hussein, whom he presented with the key to the city, courtesy of Mayor Young. There are tens of thousands of Chaldeans among the roughly 300,000 Americans of Middle Eastern descent in the Detroit area (*CBS News,* Mar. 26, 2003).

Reports were rife that Mayor Young was the target of investigations and even that he was to be indicted on federal charges, but that never happened. Chief Hart did serve several years in federal prison for embezzling 2.6 million dollars from the city (Jacoby, 347).

Mayor Young's administration was beset by financial crises, charges of corruption, and a lack of jobs in the city. His third Deputy Police Commissioner, Ken Weiner, was convicted of stealing $1.3 million from a secret police account and sentenced to ten years in prison for masterminding a phony investment scheme.

Weiner arranged the purchase of gold Krugerands (coins of South Africa), yet the mayor was denouncing apartheid in South Africa at the time.

Detroit is now a city with many problems. Its economy is in bad shape, far worse than in 1967. Many more are jobless now than then, particularly among young people. Manufacturers, auto companies, retail and wholesale businesses are gone. There has been a massive white exodus from Detroit. In addition, there has been a growing trend of educated blacks to also leave the city, creating an ever wider city-suburban economic gap.

"Blacks look on this as our city now," declared the black vice president of Detroit Renaissance in 1978, as Mayor Young started his second term. At that time, the mayor, five of nine council members, the superintendent of schools, eight of the thirteen members of the Detroit Board of Education and the police chief were black. Yes, there was now black political control of Detroit, but, at what price? As whites fled and white businesses and industries fled, so did the economic power.

Last year, I was talking to a friend who is a top black political leader. He said, "Detroit will be like a third world country—without hope."

I am not the only one to suggest that Coleman Young really cared more about making the police force blacker than better. Reforms were undoubtedly needed but his policy of firing those police officers who lived outside the city was clearly an attempt to get rid of whites. He achieved that goal by promising to promote one black for every white officer who was promoted. He lowered recruitment standards and allowed blacks to take exams until they passed, so it is no wonder that Detroit's crime rate went up dramatically and came to be the highest in the country. As crime rates rose, whites fled. Black pride has always been a noble goal for American blacks, but only when there is something to be proud of (Wilson, 1998).

Since Coleman Young, we have had two more black mayors, Dennis Archer and now Kwame Kilpatrick.

As for Coleman Young, I had problems with him. In my opinion, he was a racist mayor, with his black talk, using words like "mother fucker", causing many whites as well as blacks to look askance in shock. I think such words are unprofessional, unwarranted, and foul. I have the same opinion of whites who use cuss words, such as the former New York City Police Commissioner Bernard Kerik in his book *Lost Son*. I feel that lowers a person in my estimation and others may feel the same. Bill Cosby has similar objections to the language being used by black adults and now children.

In my opinion, the great city of Detroit went downhill during Young's admin-istration. White flight was hastened with Mayor Young's statement in his first term, warning all dope pushers, ripoff artists and muggers to get out of Detroit. It had the unexpected effect of making whites fear that bad guys would soon be moving out of central Detroit into the suburbs.

While I was sheriff in Oakland County, some more of Coleman's remarks really irked me—and I then called him a "damned liar". That statement hit the front page of the newspapers. I did not have the chance to spell out exactly where and what he had lied about to reporters. In essence, Mayor Young had said all previous white police commissioners had lied, were racist, misused promotion lists, promoted their chauffeurs and aides improperly, etc. I bristled at that. Com-ing from New York after being in command of Operations Bureau, President of American Academy of Police Sciences and having been involved in the study and practice of policing for 33 years then, I resented it.

There may have been some truth in what he stated about previous police administrators. I was surprised at the promotions of some previous chauffeurs and aides. I adhered strictly to professionalism and approved of promotions based only on tests and the results of performance scores. I even turned Mayor Cavanagh down three times on his requests to promote officers and sergeants quite a ways down on the list because Bobby Holms of the Teamsters Union had requested it.

As I was leaving my post as commissioner, I did not promote my own aide and chauffeur, Sgt. Joe Loesche, to lieutenant. But I did him a favor. Irving Bluestone of the UAW asked me to suggest an officer for Walter Reuther's security guard. I suggested Joe Loesche—and he was almost killed in the line of duty.

Walter Reuther was killed in a plane crash at Blacklake, Michigan, the site of the UAW campgrounds. I've heard that Joe was saved only because the other security officer alternated weekends with him and it was not time for Joe to go. Joe continued many years with the UAW security post, to each succeeding presi-dent.

Dennis Archer: A Turnaround Mayor?

Dennis Archer was the second black mayor of Detroit. My belief is that the Young administration's racial relations between the city of Detroit and its sur-rounding suburbs were considerably turned around because of the election of Mayor Dennis Archer. Dialogues were opened up between whites and blacks and there was, in my opinion, some movement forward by those who sought to rebuild the city after the debacle of July, 1967.

After Mayor Archer was sworn in, I sent him a letter of congratulation and later sent him a letter praising his appointment of Isaiah (Ike) McKinnon as police chief in 1993. For the most part, Archer and McKinnon improved Detroit. However, in May 1997, several police officers were found to have cheated on police promotional tests by using advance copies of the test, including McKinnon's driver. Nearly 2,000 Detroit police officers had to retake exams at a cost of more than $250,000.

In addition in November 1998, four officers were found guilty of corruption when they kept money, guns and drugs seized from crack houses, planted phony evidence and falsified police reports between 1995 and 1997.

In July 1998 Archer appointed Benny Napoleon, my former student at Mercy College (now University of Detroit—Mercy), as chief. I again sent the mayor a letter of congratulation on that selection. Napoleon worked his way up in the Detroit Police Department where he served DPD for 26 years.

After another incident of corruption among three policemen, Napoleon introduced an Integrity Testing Program in 2000. However, after the city paid $8.6 million to settle six lawsuits of officers shooting citizens during the five preceding years, Archer asked the U.S. Justice Department to investigate the shootings. Napoleon resigned after three years in the job. Archer appointed Charles Wilson as the chief in July 2001.

7

What's Happening Now?

○ ○
"Those who cannot remember the past are condemned to repeat it."

—George Santayana

What's Happening Now?

In 1998, James R. Miller, a patrol officer of the Detroit Police Department, wrote a stunning research paper on "The Failure of the Detroit Police Department to Provide Adequate Police Services to the Citizens of Detroit." In his summary he wrote,

> I have concluded through interviews, personal experience and listening to the way things used to be done, that the police precincts in the City of Detroit are in desperate need of an overhaul on how things are done. With additional personnel, the officers would be able to clear up the calls for services and would have time for routine patrol. Routine patrol would include something as simple as just talking to citizens or stopping by a high school football game. This would create a friendlier environment between the public and the police and after a short time, would begin to reduce crime because the community would be working alongside of the police.

Some more highlights of Miller's document confirm that little has changed since my tenure as police commissioner there. (The city no longer has a single police commissioner but a board of five police commissioners, all appointed by the mayor.) Miller wrote:

> Basically upper management of the Detroit Police Department looked down on the uniformed patrol officers....
>
> While the mere presence of police may not be sufficient to deter crime, the manner in which they approach their task may make a difference....
>
> Not only more officers on patrol but better equipped and trained officers would make for a much better police department to serve the community. Not only would you significantly reduce response times for calls for service, but you would also see a greater cooperation between the public and the police department. The officers would have much more time for community policing and would be able to "clean up" their scout car area. I feel that proactive problem-oriented policing would work extremely well in the City of Detroit. If officers had to stay in their assigned scout car areas for eight hours not only would the calls for service be handled but the officers would also handle all the non-emergency complaints within that scout car area as well.
>
> Like I stated before, officers just simply talking with neighborhood people on a nice sunny day sure would go a long way toward bridging the gap between the public and the police...
>
> In addition I feel that the department should also give officers business cards so that they could pass them out to citizens. If the officer wished, he could even give a citizen his pager number or his cell phone number.

This entire recruiting problem is essential to improving the patrol function. It involves creating new ranks in the patrol force along with a varied range of responsibilities keyed to the education, experience and potential performance of the individual officers involved.

Just after I was Police Commissioner of Detroit at the end of 1970, the department's actual strength was about 10% under authorized strength, so the force had room for about 500 additional police. About 12% of officers were black but the black population of Detroit then was more than 40% of the total population. To reach a comparable level in the police department would have required the addition of about 1,400 more black officers.

About 13 to 16% of white applicants were successful, but only 3 to 4% of black applicants were successful.

Analysis showed that the written examination, year in and year out, was the biggest single factor in the disproportionate elimination of black applicants.

Within a percentage point or two, some 60% of both black and white applicants were screened out for failure to meet a variety of preliminary standards. These included age, education, medical background, previous police record, and traffic record, in which there was no significant difference in the number of blacks and whites rejected. Many more whites than blacks were screened out for failure to meet height, vision and weight standards.

However, three times as many blacks as whites, proportionately, were eliminated for failing the written examination. About 60% of the blacks taking the examination were screened out by it, compared with about 20% of the whites. In all other screening areas, differences were negligible.

A number of possibilities stemmed from these statistics:

- Blacks in general were intellectually inferior to whites. This, of course, is untrue, genetically or hereditarily, and even if it were true, it would be unacceptable.

- The caliber of black applicants attracted to police work was intellectually of lower quality than the caliber of white applicants. The success of blacks in many fields, while it was not distributed as widely as whites, made this conclusion unacceptably abrasive.

- A cultural gap exists between young blacks and whites, which was highlighted by conventional written examinations. School surveys lent some credence to such a conclusion, since they revealed that teenage blacks came from public schools with lower educational attainment levels than teenage whites, who attended public schools on the periphery of the "inner city."

If certain young people, from whom future police prospects were to be drawn, were receiving an inferior education, it was inevitable that due to no fault of their own, they should do poorly on tests reflecting the results of schooling.

The police department could not wait for changes in the educational system to turn out a larger number of better-educated young people. Different types of tests were sought that would eliminate such cultural bias, if such were the fundamental reason for the problem.

New testing methods were tried in 1969, 1970 and 1971. Uncertainty as to their validity remained. An undercurrent of dissatisfaction was discerned about officers who felt that special examinations, although applied to all applicants, represented a lower standard than previous examinations. The touchy point was, "I want my fellow police officers to be just as good as I am, to back me up in an emergency. Will these tests bring in individuals I can trust in a pinch, individuals who are just as capable as I am?"

This dissatisfaction was multiplied in the 1980s when racial quotas were used by police departments to fill openings. Thus the highest scoring black or Hispanic might be named to fill a position even though his or her score was lower than the highest scoring white.

Currently, the city of Detroit has lost population and is now under one million, which reduced the size of the police force. In 2002, the Detroit Police Department had 4,235 sworn police officers, of which 120 were community policing officers, a slight increase from my time.

In 1997, a consultant was hired to review the Detroit Police Department. Merrick Bobb's report stated that the department's recruiting minimums (18 year olds with a high school diploma or GED) were too low. He suggested age 22 with two years of college. Police Chief Benny Napoleon said state law prevented him from raising the hiring age and increasing educational standards would severely shrink the hiring pool.

The Detroit News issued a special report on June 29, 2003, entitled "Police Brutality Comes Full Circle: Force has a 30-year history of abuse," by Norman Sinclair and Francis X. Donnelly. Here are some of the highlights:

> Two dozen former police executives, current department leaders, scholars and activists say the department's downward spiral was accelerated during 20 years of political interference by former Mayor Coleman A. Young. His successor,

Dennis Archer, relied on the two chiefs he appointed to make changes to improve the department, but they failed to do so.

Following a public outcry three years ago over questionable shootings by police, the department is now being reformed under the supervision of the U.S. Justice Department.

Retired police executives, who spoke publicly for the first time, and others who have studied the department told *The Detroit News* that its troubles were hastened by:

- The failure of mayors Young and Archer to recognize that their choices for chief were insiders lacking vision or broad police experience to reform and modernize the department. Except for Stanley Knox, who was a precinct commander before his promotion, the other chiefs spent nearly all of their careers doing undercover street work with little exposure to community policing, patrol or other critical branches of the department.

- The effort by Young to integrate the predominantly white department soured with two botched recruitment drives in 1977 and 1986 that added nearly 1,700 officers. The department under Chief William Hart hired many unqualified and poorly trained candidates because it lowered standards and cut training to comply with Young's timetable to get them on the force.

- Young's appointments of cronies to key civilian department jobs, and his promotions of others over more competent individuals, decimated morale, the department executives said. Kenneth Weiner, a Young operative and a civilian deputy chief, was convicted in 1991 of stealing $1.3 million from the department, which was less than Hart was convicted of stealing.

- Young's demand in 1983 that all executives from inspector up submit undated letters of resignation shook the top command and hastened the exit of some of the force's brightest officers...

- Archer's determination not to repeat Young's mistakes made him adopt a hands-off approach to the department until it was too late. The mayor put his faith in Chiefs Isaiah McKinnon and Benny Napoleon, neither of whom acted upon signs of trouble.

Sinclair and Donnelly's excellent long article mentioned other things which I'll just summarize. In addition to 47 people shot by police under the administrations of McKinnon and Napoleon, at least 18 prisoners, some arrested on minor charges, died suddenly in police department lockups between 1992 and 1999. From 1987 to 2000, the city paid $123 million to settle lawsuits stemming from complaints of police misconduct.

The reporters wrote: "In the years after the 1967 riot, the department, under two chiefs brought in from outside, Patrick Murphy and Johannes Spreen, enjoyed a national reputation for superior training and a crack homicide section that solved more than 80 percent of its cases."

He added that when Young was elected mayor in 1973, he finally picked the little-known Bill Hart to lead the department. He became the longest-serving chief in Detroit history, holding the post until 1991. But despite winning recognition in his tenure for community policing efforts and expanding the neighborhood mini-station network, Hart's career ended in disgrace. He was indicted and convicted of stealing $2.3 million from a police undercover fund and spent seven years in prison.

Hart was succeeded by Stanley Knox, who in his two years as chief, put more officers on the streets and did a better job of supervising them, but he did not address the deep-seated personnel problems on the force.

Two of the crucial issues in the U.S. Department of Justice's investigation that led to its oversight of Detroit police involved the use of fatal force by officers and the homicide section's illegal practice of rounding up people and holding them until someone cooperated or confessed to murders.

In both those abuses, the department was forewarned of the practices years before the Justice Department stepped in, according to the retired commanders.

Another major part of the Justice Department's case against Detroit police—the indiscriminate roundups of potential witnesses until someone confessed or cooperated—came to light in a 1997 lawsuit.

When Archer became mayor, he appointed McKinnon and Napoleon, and stated that he didn't intend to interfere with the police department. He admitted he wasn't a police officer, didn't know how departments were run, but trusted the judgment of those in command. Archer remembered turning over to McKinnon a report in 1993 that identified major problems such as lack of direction, poor use of resources, politicization of the department, corruption, lack of training and poor labor-management relations.

This article also had pictures of the next six police chiefs from 1976 to 2003, with the following captions:

- William Hart: Cut police academy training from 12 weeks to eight. Appointed by Young.

- Stanley Knox: Brought in after Hart was convicted of embezzling city money. Appointed by Young.

- Isaiah McKinnon: Failed to confront serious personnel problems. Appointed by Archer.

- Benny Napoleon: Focused on narcotics, missed signs of trouble. Appointed by Archer.

- Charles Wilson: Held post for six months. Appointed by Archer.

- Jerry A. Oliver, Sr.: Implementing police reform. Appointed by Mayor Kwame Kilpatrick.

This article was disturbing to me as well as almost everyone, I'm sure.

As a matter of interest, Ken Weiner and Bill Hart wanted me to join them in writing a book about police work. I had given them lectures at the University of Michigan. Can you imagine me writing a book with these two men who were convicted? I didn't do it.

The article also had graphs stating "The city spends about 3.5 times more on its police department than it did in 1970." It showed Detroit police staffing at 5,607 in 1970 and 4,686 in 2002, with the comment "Police have helped bring down Detroit's violent crime rate. But that rate is still substantially higher than the national average."

I have added this list of Detroit Police Commissioners to aid readers.

Detroit Police Commissioners

Herbert W. Hart	9/2/58-1/2/62
George Edwards	1/2/62-12/19/63
Ray Girardin	12/19/63-7/21/68
Johannes F. Spreen	7/22/68-1/5/70
Patrick V. Murphy	1/6/70-10/1/70
John F. Nichols	10/16/70-1973
Phillip Tannian	1974
William Hart	1976
Stanley R. Knox	1991
Isiah McKinnon	1994
Benny Napoleon	7/96-7/2001
Charles Wilson	7/2001-2002

| Jerry Oliver | 2002-10/2003 |
| Ella Bully-Cummings | 11/2003-present |

After Tannian, Coleman Young changed the format so that William Hart and the rest were police chiefs, not commissioners. Now the chief and the board of five commissioners are political appointments made by the mayor. Talk about a political police department—that's it!

Kwame Kilpatrick: Nepotism Sinks a City

Kwame Kilpatrick (whose mother is U.S. Congresswoman Carolyn Cheeks Kilpatrick) became the next mayor after Archer by defeating Gil Hill, (former DPD homicide commander) who had played Inspector Todd in the *Beverly Hills Cop* movie with Eddie Murphy. Gil lost, I believe, because of a poor campaign and because of being some 40 years older than his rival.

I tried to help Hill in various ways, including correcting some spelling errors I found in campaign posters and materials. I also suggested keeping the accent on a *protective, preventive patrol presence* using both male and female officers working together on motor scooters. His campaign advisors, mainly lawyers, saw no merit in my suggestions or those of other worthy people. I remember leaving one of the campaign meetings saying, "You are going to lose!" and they did.

After Kilpatrick's election, his inaugural speech stated, "Mediocrity will not be tolerated." I sent him a thoughtful letter of congratulations, offered suggestions, but never received an answer.

Kwame Kilpatrick developed the nickname of the "Hip-hop Mayor" early in his administration because of his attendance at rap concerts and his knowledge of the rap musicians in the Mo-town music industry.

Unfortunately, the mayor is in trouble up to his eyeballs. He did not swear off nepotism and political patronage. He appointed his uncle Raymond Cheeks to run $3.3 million neighborhood city hall department. He appointed a distant cousin, Ayanna Benson, as general manager of the Detroit Building Authority (M. L. Elrick, *Detroit Free Press,* July 3, 2002).

Another questionable appointment is the mayoral chief of staff Christine Beatty, a high school friend of the mayor. She apparently was stopped for speeding by police officers, and asked officers, "Do you know who the f.... I am?" She then placed a call to the police chief, Ella Bully-Cummings. She did not receive a speeding ticket. Beatty has been in the news for other reasons such as using government stationery to apply for a personal home loan, and urging Kwame Kilpatrick to remove Deputy Chief Gary Brown for investigating negative rumors about the mayor. The news story of these events was interestingly entitled "Kilpatrick's team needs a dose of ethics" (*The Detroit News*, October 17, 2004).

Kilpatrick is in the media almost daily with shenanigans and turmoil within his Executive Protection Unit, events at the Manoogian Mansion and his political fund-raising. He set up Next Vision Foundation intended to be a charity. It is not exactly that, according to a *Metro Times* (Nov. 3-9, 2004), article which said,

> A charity set up by his politically ubiquitous family with much fanfare soon after he assumed power isn't being all that it can be...The foundation's public mission is teaching leadership to high schools and awarding them scholarships. Leaning on city contractors and other charities for cash support, the foundation has awarded around $50,000 in scholarship dough.... And for carefully administering that largesse, it paid close to $400,000 to Kwame's wife's sister and the wife of one of the mayor's posse members.

Some call the Next Vision Foundation a Kilpatrick Clan Production that seems to be doing a better job of giving financial assistance to the mayor and family and friends than to the Detroit youngsters it was intended to help. Daniel Borochoff, president of a Chicago-based watchdog group that evaluates charities (American Institute for Philanthropy), told reporters that there were too many Kilpatricks on the board of Next Vision. The mayor's mother, father and sister are three of the nine directors. Borochoff commented that there's a risk that family could operate in their best interests, rather than what's good for the charity (Elrick and Schaefer, *Detroit Free Press*, October 29, 2004).

Two police officers have sued Mayor Kilpatrick and the city of Detroit for alleged violation of the state's "Whistleblower Protection Act." The civil suits are being brought by officers Harold Nelthrope, a former mayoral bodyguard, and Gary Brown, a former deputy chief who previously headed the DPD Internal Affairs Unit.

Nelthrope went to Internal Affairs with allegations that some members of the mayor's security team were getting paid for overtime hours they did not work, also about a wild party at the Mayor's mansion involving strippers. Brown says he was fired for letting members of his Internal Affairs unit investigate Nelthrope's allegations.

The Michigan Attorney General's office investigated these allegations. Attorney General Mike Cox announced the results of their investigation at a press conference on June 24, 2003:

Five weeks ago, I promised the people of Detroit and the citizens of Michigan my office would conduct a thorough investigation into the allegations surrounding Mayor Kwame Kilpatrick and members of his Executive Protection Unit....The Attorney General's Office began this investigation on Monday, May 19, to investigate a number of charges that grew out of press reports concerning the firing of Detroit Police Deputy Chief Gary Brown, an alleged incident at the Manoogian Mansion, and allegations concerning police officers Loronzo Jones and Michael Martin involving overtime fraud, drunk driving and the failure to report automobile accidents involving property damage. Additionally, the reports raise the specter of possible obstructions of justice...

The focus of this team was on determining whether any criminal charges should issue...The task was simple: do we have evidence of crimes being committed? The answer is "no".

First: The allegation of a party at the Manoogian Mansion involving strippers, the Mayor and members of the Detroit Police Department....These allegations appear to be founded solely on wild rumor and speculation...

A second set of allegations concerned alleged automobile accidents involving unmarked police vehicles driven by officers Martin and Jones while they were on-duty and intoxicated....The investigation was unable to uncover any evidence of an accident, a date of the alleged accident or cause of the purported accident.

The more serious charges involving officers Jones and Martin involved allegations of fraudulent payment of overtime.... We conducted an extensive investigation of these practices which confirmed overtime abuses and shoddy recordkeeping within the Executive Protection Unit.... Against this backdrop of poor management and the lack of written policies, it is literally impossible to prove a criminal intent to defraud the Police Department by any of the EPU officers.

Finally, the most serious allegation as it relates to possible public corruption concerns the firing of Deputy Chief Gary Brown and whether this firing was an attempt to obstruct justice...We do not find any evidence of an obstruction of justice.... Undoubtedly, Ms. Beatty's actions and recommendation (that Brown be fired) were arguably premature and heavy-handed, yet there is nothing to suggest that she obstructed a criminal investigation....

In short, while a number of decisions were arguably shortsighted and the indications of bad judgment or inexperience, there is not any evidence of an obstruction of justice or other criminal wrongdoing.... Whether any of the decisions made equal bad politics, bad policy or a wrongful termination, we leave to the civil court system and the voters of Detroit. (www.michigan.gov)

Still another issue is a political action committee called 21st Leaders PAC which has received press attention.

A political action committee funded by U.S. Rep. Carolyn Cheeks Kilpatrick and Ambassador Bridge owner Manuel (Matty) Moroun has spent more on the Congresswoman's family and friends, including a $350 wedding gift, than it has on political candidates (M. L. Elrick and Patricia Montemurri, *Free Press*, Dec. 16, 2004).

The Michigan Secretary of State says that political action committees are formed to support or oppose candidates or ballot issues. However, the congress-woman's 21st Leaders PAC has instead spent money on people and causes close to her. Among its payouts are donations for college expenses, wedding gifts, flowers, and photos for friends and family.

Founded in March 2003, 21st Leaders PAC has gotten all its money from two sources: $40,000 from Cheeks Kilpatrick's congressional campaign coffer and $15,000 from the Moroun family. The Free Press reported that Mayor Kilpatrick had chosen the Moroun-owned Michigan Central Depot for a new police head-quarters. The 91-year old building has been an abandoned eyesore since closing in 1988.

I'll just add that "Matty" Moroun's wife, Nora, ran into my old Lincoln on a cold December day when I was leaving a shopping area. After that, I learned a lot about the Moroun family, including the fact that they owned the Ambassador Bridge between the U.S. and Canada, a toll bridge that has the most traffic of any U.S.-Canadian crossing.

Speaking of Lincolns, Mayor Kilpatrick purchased a red Lincoln Navigator valued at $57,000 with city funds to transport his wife and children around. When questioned by the press in January, 2005, he denied it was for personal use. He asked his new police chief, Ella Bully-Cummings, to deny it and she went along, saying she approved the lease of the car. He asked his director of commu-nications and his police spokesman to deny it and they did. But he admitted it was for his own use in January, 2005. This came at a time when the mayor was asking the city to sell its cars and lay off hundreds of employees to help with a projected $230 million shortfall.

Kobe Bryant spent $4 million on a purple diamond for his wife and $50,000 to renew vows (Jay Leno quipped that maybe he should listen to the vows this time) after he was accused of sexually assaulting another woman. My wife said, "Unlike Kwame, at least Kobe spent his own money on his wife—not the taxpay-ers' money" (Young, "Kobe, money can't buy love", *Arizona Republic*, April 26, 2005).

Mayor Kilpatrick is guiding a city that is neck-deep in red ink according to the *MetroTimes*, Feb. 23, 2005. They reported that the city has a $93 million deficit from the 2003-04 fiscal year that has not been completely addressed. Then there is also a projected deficit of $65 million from this year, and a probable $230 million shortfall for next year. The news story presented a humorous piece about those deficits called, "What if Detroit held a garage sale?" They joshed about the money that might be realized from the sale of Belle Isle, the Detroit Zoo, the Cobo Conference/Exhibition Center, the old Tiger Stadium and even an estate sale of the Manoogian Mansion, the official residence of Detroit mayors since 1965. Could this really happen? How sad!

The mayor is alienating many of the white residents still remaining in Detroit and almost all of those whites who fled the city. And I think more will flee.

As one black man told me, "They burned down the city. Now they own it. Let's see how they do."

After Kilpatrick's win, he appointed Jerry Oliver as the new chief in January 2002. Oliver made eliminating corruption a top priority and approved of federal help to do internal investigations. Four months after taking office, Chief Oliver told reporters that he was going to run off a lot of people because the DPD had some criminals working there. Nine months later, nine people including one Michigan State Police lieutenant and one DPD police officer were indicted for stealing cocaine from the police property room and selling it.

In June 2003, 17 Detroit cops were charged with extortion, robbery, stealing money from drug dealers and prostitutes, searching houses without warrants, reselling drugs, and falsifying reports. The FBI and experts from Washington, D.C., will be monitoring a federally ordered reform of the Detroit Police Department until 2008 in areas such as the use of force and the detention of witnesses (Shepardson and Grant, *The Detroit News*, June 19, 2003).

A recent issue of *Time* magazine (April 25, 2005) featured five of the best mayors and three of the worst in the country. Kilpatrick topped the list of three worst in a short story by Jyoti Thottam, and reporters Amanda Bower, Joseph R. Szczesny and David Thigpen. The brief account begins with the mayor's admission in January, 2005, of leasing a car for his wife that cost taxpayers $24,995. This was, said the article, despite Detroit's $230 million budget deficit that has prompted the mayor to eliminate city jobs, end 24-hour bus service, yet maintain 21 security guards for himself. And now we have the unfolding saga of Kwame's credit card capers in May, 2005.

One good thing that has occurred in Kilpatrick's administration, however, was the creation of a joint task force in 2003 to catch fugitives by combining police officers and sheriff's deputies. When I was sheriff for 12 years, I spoke often on the need to combine forces with other agencies for greater efficiency and cost-effectiveness and to avoid duplication of efforts.

I cannot help but believe that the police chiefs in recent years have let Detroit down and have contributed to its demise. I've outlined the problems of many chiefs. I reluctantly have to include Jerry Oliver. Most recently, Oliver knew exactly what he was doing when he did not declare a .25 caliber pistol in his luggage before taking off on a flight from Detroit to Philadelphia October 18, 2003. Oliver was the first outsider police chief since I became police commissioner in 1968. He had not yet become a licensed sworn police officer in Michigan when he boarded the airplane with his gun. The controversy led to his resignation.

Oliver set a bad example when he pleaded ignorance of the law, saying he didn't think he had to register his personal weapon in Michigan. Yet he had been hard on other Detroit officers during his 18 months as chief when they committed criminal acts (Detroit News, October 31, 2003).

Who Can Control City Council Members?

There are more problems in the Common Council or City Council of Detroit than the mayor and police, of course. The Council's action or inaction in the face of economic recession is an example of misused power. The problem is that once elected, no council member is responsible to anyone—except the whole city—which practically means they are not really held accountable at all.

I believe council members should be elected to represent neighborhoods or districts. This means a change in the city charter. I spoke against the charter after I was police commissioner.

There are frequent allegations against Common Council members in Detroit. On Dec. 1-7, 2004, Ric Bohy, editor of *Metro Times Detroit,* wrote,

> Barbara Rose Collins is one of the most glaring examples of what's wrong with Detroit's entrenched, inbred politics. She's made a career in politics, often a very lucrative one, since first elected to a Detroit regional school board in 1971. She then filled a seat in the legislature, then City Council, then—only in America—in the U.S. House of Representatives, where she earned her place in history as one of the worst ever members of Congress before being voted out. Finally—only in Detroit—she was re-elected to the City Council in 2002.

Collins' troubles began when after serving on the City Council she went to spend four rocky years in the U.S. House of Representatives (1993-1997). There she violated campaign finance rules, was absent more almost any other member, slept and snored loudly through many sessions she attended, held a fund-raiser in a strip bar, and missed an important vote when she refused to fly coach and waited for a flight with a first class seat (Lessenberry, "Hopes and horrors", *Metro Times Detroit*, Oct. 31, 2001).

When she tried to be re-elected, she invited Nation of Islam leader Louis Farrakhan to speak with her at the New Bethel Baptist Church in July, 1996. He urged thousands at the church to forgive her and support her with money and votes. He promised to mail her a check for $1,000 the next day. She was at that time still being investigated for misusing office, campaign and scholarship funds. Before Farrakhan's speech, she described herself as a little person, a sister from the east side of Detroit, and compared her re-election to a "holy jihad". She said her home had been broken into and her mail with checks stolen so she could not pay her bills. She added that she had been under some of the most vicious and racist attacks since black Harriet Tubman (Jennifer Loven, AP, *The Detroit News*, July 20, 1996).

However, she lost in a landslide vote to Carolyn Cheeks Kilpatrick, Mayor Kwame Kilpatrick's mother. Carolyn campaigned that Collins' alleged ethical violations made her undeserving of serving the district. She attempted to sue the *Detroit Free Press* who quoted her on July 17, 1996, as saying she hated the white race. They apologized and issued a retraction showing that she merely said, "All white people, I don't believe, are intolerant. That's why I say I love the individuals, but I don't like the race" (Gorchow, *The State News*, Aug. 7, 1996).

Barbara Rose Collins returned to Detroit, ran for the City Council again, and was elected. She receives an $81,000 salary while serving as a councilwoman. She sponsored an ordinance which passed in June, 2004, requiring that Detroit contractors must tell the City whether they have benefited from slavery. Contractors must search their backgrounds, and then sign an affidavit disclosing investments and income from the slave industry. Companies with slave ties would not be banned from city contracts, but any with a false slave history would have contracts voided. Many believe this brings blacks a step closer to receiving reparations (Moore *The Detroit News*, June 25, 2004).

In January 2005, Mayor Kwame Kilpatrick said the city must cut salaries and workers to save more than $231 million. The council sought a 4 percent increase in its budget, and Collins led a discussion to update video equipment to expand the budget of the council (Bello, Detroit Free Press, Jan. 27, 2005).

Another councilwoman, Kay Everett, died in November, 2004. As Jack Lessenberry of the *Metro Times* wrote on Dec. 1-7, 2004,

Nobody wanted to see Kay Everett dead. Yet everyone knows that having her off council is an enormous blessing, since we will be spared the distraction and cost of her bribery, fraud, conspiracy and corruption trial....

Listen, people, Detroit is dying. The schools are failing...The neighborhoods are crumbling eyesores, the downtown is a shell and anyone who can afford to is leaving. What's needed are civic leaders who are willing to tackle this, and do something about it; as Malcolm X might have said, by any means necessary...

Detroit is the way it is in large part because of white flight from the city, white racism to a degree, and, most of all, economic selfishness. But it's also being held back by pigheadedness, irresponsible behavior and corruption on the part of the black politicians who run the place. Everyone needs to face both things, and do it soon.

On October 25, 2004, the U.S. Department of Justice issued this press release:

United States Attorney Craig S. Morford announced today that Detroit City Council member Kay Everett, age 63, was indicted by a federal grand jury in Detroit on charges of wire fraud, extortion, bribery, conspiracy to commit those offenses, making false statements to investigators and filing false tax returns.

The 27 count indictment charges that between 1997 and 2002, Everett demanded and accepted over $150,000 in payments from a local contractor who held contracts with the City of Detroit during that time period. The indictment further alleges that Everett failed to disclose her financial relationship with the contractor, despite repeatedly voting in favor of contract awards, extensions and change orders for the contractor's companies.

According to the indictment, Everett was also charged with filing false tax returns for the 1997-2001 tax years, because she did not report the additional income she received from the contractor on her tax returns. In addition, the grand jury charged Everett with making false statements to the FBI in relation to its investigation of those offenses.

More details of Everett's offenses were described in a news article. Everett demanded regular payments in exchange for helping Detroit businessman Frank Vallecorsa, owner of American International Inc. She also received free meals, 17 pounds of sausage, roundtrip vacation tickets for herself and aides/family members, and even a $5,950 payment for Everett to stay at the Greenhouse Spa in Arlington, Texas (Shepardson and Moore, *The Detroit News*, Oct. 22, 2004).

After she died, another article described the former schoolteacher as having dialysis three times a week for diabetes, and family problems. After a divorce, she lost her son in a house fire he set to obtain money. Her daughter was sentenced on charges of attempting to extort money from DaimlerChrysler executive Frank Fountain, Jr. She was also criticized for hiring her other son, Walter, for $20 an hour as her legislative analyst (Lin, *The Detroit News*, Nov. 28, 2004).

Alonzo Bates, another council member, is under federal investigation for using his office payroll to finance an aide, a 23-year old New York University graduate student, who spends most of her time in New York. Her reported $30 an hour pay rate apparently has resulted in an income of $38,000 since January. Bates defends paying the aide saying she works in Detroit during the summers and on holiday breaks. He additionally caused a stir when he went on a radio talk show and said that was standard procedure in the City Council (Bello, *Detroit Free Press*, Jan. 27, 2005).

Bates has a record of abuses including a taxpayer-funded trip to Acapulco. When asked why he always sticks taxpayers for first-class seats, he said that he was a big man (Lessenberry, "Hopes and Horrors", *Metro Times Detroit*, Oct. 31, 2001).

Council President Maryann Mahaffey said, "Each council member has their own budget…There's no oversight of that budget; it's an honor system."

I say, "Wow!" That is another problem that must be addressed by the Detroit City Council where members can decide how many aides they want. There is a current range of 7 to 14 aides per council member. And by the way, according to Bello's article, Kay Everett's 14 aides will be permitted to draw salaries until June, 2005, while helping other council members, even though Everett died in November, 2004.

Another tough city council member was Attorney Sharon McPhail, the first female attorney to be elected to Detroit's City Council. After she served on the Common Council, she became the President of the National Bar Association, Chairperson and member of the Detroit Branch of the N.A.A.C.P. Later she was appointed by President Bill Clinton to participate on a Council for Justice and Civil Rights. In fact, in 1993 she was the first woman to win a primary election for Mayor of the City of Detroit but did not win the general election. I have always felt she couldn't appreciate the police perspective because she was totally focused on the black perspective.

Detroit's Hotels Died

Another example of what has happened to Detroit is the story of its famous hotels. The fact that the city is in ruins is obvious to anyone who sees its two dilapidated major luxury hotels. The Book Cadillac Hotel with its fabulous fixtures and luxurious accoutrements now lies in shambles.

The Statler Hilton is to be razed despite the State of Michigan spending $4.4 million to clean up and remove asbestos from the abandoned hotel because the City of Detroit thought it had a hotel developer to renovate the downtown eyesore. This was the luxurious Statler Hilton that set a new standard of excellence when it opened in 1914. It had 800 guest rooms. I remember it well and I even met Baron Hilton. It was the site of a banquet in September 1969 where Mayor Cavanagh spoke when I, as Police Commissioner, was presented with 30 scooters—forming a most thrilling and rewarding day.

I had stayed at the Book Cadillac in the Presidential Suite when I was brought to Detroit to discuss the position of Police Commissioner. I dined there with Cliff Owens and Jim Trainor before the press conference that next day, June 21, 1968, when they announced that I had accepted the position as Commissioner.

Yes, two once grand hotels in a once great city—that is until July 23, 1967—and its aftermath.

Crime Is Now Tolerated in Detroit

True! Today the City of Detroit has changed dramatically. It is now over 85% black and growing more so. It's a city in trouble.

Detroit led the nation's murder rate in 1999, 2000, 2001, and dropped to second place behind St. Louis in 2002 according to Morgan Quitno Press and U. S. Census data. The *Free Press* published a series called "Special report of Violence and Homicide in Detroit" beginning on December 4, 2004, because of the shocking increase in murders. They stated that in the first 11 months of 2004, 1,279 people had been shot in Detroit, (247 more than in all of 2003) and 341 more have been killed.

City leaders have tried to stop the violence in Detroit by flooding areas with cops, targeting the drug trade, buying back guns, teaching children tools for conflict resolution and even holding a day of prayer. Yes, Mayor Kilpatrick got together with his new woman Police Chief, Ella Bully-Cummings, and a group of ministers to pray for guidance in response to the city's violence. However, the situation is getting worse.

The spike of violence is generally attributable to a mix of unemployment, poverty, illiteracy, drug use and hopelessness.

Thousands of Detroiters, children and adults, are touched by this extreme violence. Such violence and murder have a chilling effect on Detroit's national image and keeps people, business and culture away from Detroit.

The violence and hopelessness affects everyone. Almost all the victims are black and are males in this now nearly totally black city. Most the violent acts and murders are drug-related.

Two police officers were killed in February, 2004, a family of five was murdered on April 1, 2004, after hours of torture, and nine people were shot at the Freedom Festival fireworks in July, 2004.

The cost to Detroit is enormous in dollars and perception. It makes me think of July 23, 1967.

According to the *Detroit Free Press* Special Report, "It's not uncommon to see a scene with multiple gunshots. The violence in Detroit has morphed into something new, something truly evil. The code of the street has changed. Ten or 20 years ago, there was a morality to street violence. There were unspoken rules: Never kill children. Never kill family members. Take one person at a time…But now, the killers shoot at anyone. They empty a clip into the crowd. They shoot in any direction."

How does this effect Detroit's citizens—the children? What's the legacy of this violence?

What do the black militants say today? What do some of the white activists against police say today? What do the mayors and the city councilmen and women say today? Do they feel responsible for the parts they played? It's their city now, and Kwame's. It's a black city now. The police department is mostly black. It's black on black crime! It's a shame.

Bill Cosby Can't Save Detroit

In 2004, Bill Cosby attracted a lot of attention by spilling out his frustrations at an event sponsored by the NAACP. He said, "The lower economic people are not holding up their end in this deal. These people are not parenting. They are buying things for kids—$500 sneakers for what? And they won't spend $200 for 'Hooked on Phonics'."

That started debates on talk shows and articles by columnists that have not died down. Many saw his comments as criticism of black leaders. He took to the air on a Detroit radio station in July, 2004, to clarify himself. He urged blacks to offer more mentoring programs for parents and children based on tough love concepts. He urged parents to "parent hard" and give children the full benefit of their philosophy. He told audiences, "It isn't just the white man. We've got to run the drug dealers out of our neighborhoods" (Keith, *The Detroit News*, July 26, 2004).

This caused many cities to invite Cosby to speak and he set up a tour that was to include Detroit, Newark, Milwaukee, Chicago, Baltimore and Norfolk, Virginia. The event was hosted by *Detroit Free Press* columnist Rochelle Riley, since the newspaper was a cosponsor. The other sponsor was the Detroit Public Schools. Riley invited people to attend the free event in her column on December 17, 2004. She wrote that he intended to discuss what makes people kill someone over a video game. Cosby was referring to the news that a little 7-year old Detroit girl had been shot in the chest two weeks earlier in a dispute that started over a video game.

Riley wrote that Cosby was going to be on a panel with the directors of ten community programs that are positively affecting parents and students. Programs wanting to be on the panel were to contact Mayor Kilpatrick's office.

Cosby intended to discuss how violence had become routine in Detroit, according to Riley. She quoted him saying, "I'm talking about these people who cry when their son is standing there in an orange prison jumpsuit. Where were you when he was 2? Where were you when he was 12? Where were you when he was 18, and how come you didn't know he had a pistol?"

An article the next day reported that some 1,800 attended Cosby's conference January 13, 2005, at Western High School. They wrote that Cosby told the audience that blacks had become No. 1 in the nation for teenage pregnancy. Cosby said, "But I tell you, now 87 percent of the city is black. We are not a minority…It costs no money to open your mouth. It costs no money to tell people to stop." The others on the panel made two-minute speeches offering information on tutoring, how to reach teens, teaching youngsters to read and volunteer. The reporters added that if Cosby had any critics, they didn't show (Angel and Pratt, *Detroit Free Press*, Jan. 14, 2005).

Cosby has many critics but one of the most important is black reporter William Raspberry. Four days after Cosby's appearance in Detroit, Raspberry contrasted Martin Luther King, Jr., and Bill Cosby in an article called "How to reach black America".

King, he said, urged an alternation between attacking the causes and healing the effects of black problems, with an emphasis on being judged by the "content of our character". Cosby's message is that white people can't save you if you won't try to save yourselves, and his escape plan is to behave and speak in better ways. But according to Raspberry, youngsters don't see evidence that changing their behavior will pay off. They see middle-class life as unavailable to them.

Raspberry concluded, "But we need to help them understand that life can be made to open up, at least for the children. Calling them knuckleheads or accusing their parents of dereliction won't do it. Patience and teaching and example just might. What is needed is "a rhythmic alternation between attacking the causes and healing the effects" (*Washington Post*, Jan. 17, 2005).

Unfortunately, a short time later Cosby was accused of drugging and fondling a woman and this was shortly followed by a similar accusation by another woman. He abruptly canceled his speaking tour. He is yet another black icon who may have feet of clay just when he could have been an important role model. That has been true of so many role models in today's world.

An unfortunate practice among black leadership, especially in Detroit, has been an emphasis on labeling every problem a result of racism. This was exactly what Bill Cosby attacked. An example of harping constantly on racial matters is the Traffic Stops Statistics Act of U.S. Congressman John Conyers, D-Detroit. After some blacks in metropolitan Detroit complained that they were dispropor- tionately pulled over for minor traffic offenses when they drove through white communities, Conyers proposed the Act.

Do Politicians Blame Too Much on the Police?

There has been a national debate on whether blacks and other minorities are tar- gets of an alleged practice blacks refer to as "Driving While Black."

Except in a minority of police districts, traffic tickets do not include race. Conyers' bill would force police departments to keep detailed records of traffic stops, race, ethnicity, age, whether a search was conducted, how long the stop lasted, etc. The Justice Department would collect these to see if there are patterns of "Driving While Black" in select communities. Police would be required to keep records of every stop, including those that don't result in a ticket or arrest.

Law enforcement officials oppose it saying that it is burdensome and unneeded. The local American Civil Liberties Union responded to the problem by issuing a "Bustcard: Pocket Guidelines on Encounters with the Police."

These guidelines of what to do if stopped include common sense warnings such as: Be polite and respectful, never bad-mouth an officer, stay calm and in control, keep your hands where the police can see them, don't tell the police they're wrong or that you're going to file a complaint, etc. They also inform peo- ple, "In certain cases, your car can be searched without a warrant as long as the police have probable cause. It is not lawful for police to arrest you simply for refusing to consent to a search."

No reasonable person wants profiling to unjustly target ethnic minorities and subject them to harassment or undue scrutiny. Even in this post 9/11 time when airports must screen targeted travelers for weapons, the perception is that travelers are being randomly checked rather than ethnically targeted.

But what about the *perceptions* that police are harder on blacks? This perception was backed up by a telephone survey of 925 randomly selected American police officers from 121 departments about attitudes toward abuse of authority by police. The National Institute of Justice printed the results in May 2000. Mostly police said they didn't use too much force in arrests and mostly they believed abuse of authority should be reported, even though whistle blowing might lead to bad reactions by fellow officers.

However, when they separated black and white officers, reactions to whether police were tougher on blacks, results were striking. Of the sample, more than half (51.3%) of black officers agreed or strongly agreed that whites receive better treatment by police than blacks. Only 11.9% of white officers agreed or strongly agreed with that statement. Although only 5.1% of white officers believe police officers were more likely to use physical force against blacks and other minorities than against whites, 57.1% of blacks thought they were more likely to use physical force against minorities.

Leaders can encourage young people to excel in more than the sports and entertainment arenas. They can encourage youth to excel in the use of the mind. That's the answer for all of us: black, brown, white, yellow, and every mixture of these. We all need to use education of the mind, effective coordination of the body, and development of the spirit (morality).

Yes, it takes work to be a good tennis player. That racquet has to swing thousands of times. Basketballs must shoot through hoops thousands of times. In the area of education, one must to go to class, listen to the teacher, learn, work, study and remember thousands of things. But it can be done!

More respect should be given to blacks for their intellect. New leaders must inspire youth to develop a balance in their way of life, fostering excellence in every way, not just the body. New leaders must work with and support good policing. Good men and women should look upon policing as a moral calling, not just a job. That would prevent corruption and conflict such as the Detroit Police Department is in now.

Even black police officers in the telephone survey cited above believed that community-oriented policing would reduce the number and seriousness of incidents of excessive force in arrests. Additionally, some 85% of the entire sample agreed that a police chief's strong position against the abuse of authority could make a big difference in deterring officers from abusing their authority. Almost 90% believed that a good first-line supervisor was an effective role model in preventing officers from abusing their authority. Over three-fourths of the officers thought that training in ethics, interpersonal skills, and cultural sensitivity would help prevent abuse of authority.

Do Politicians Blame Enough on the Police?

Edward J. Tully, Executive Director of the Major Cities Chiefs Association, wrote in January 2002, that in this age of litigation, the "actions of one poorly trained officer can result in liability to the governing body" ("Regional Consolidation of Law Enforcement Services in the United States", *National Executive Institute Associates*).

To this day, Detroit has never really recovered its image. Straight from the shoulder, the police can often be a major problem. Police officers that do not measure up to professionalism are police that are biased, bigoted or brutal, including police who do the wrong thing or do improper things. Yes, a few bad apples will infect the whole box, the media will see to that. And that hurts all other police officers nationwide.

Police officers today must combat the feelings or attitudes of cynicism. That's somewhat difficult because their duties expose them to the many bad experiences of conflict and hostility with people. Police feel a constant frustration with human imperfection. Police work mostly at night so who do they see? Who do they have to handle? Of course, it's the bums, the pimps, the prostitutes, the criminals, and the parasitic scum that abounds. Police must have more opportunities to meet and interact with some of the decent, caring people they protect.

The soaring economy of the 1990s caused the number of law enforcement applications to dwindle. Thus administrators across the country had to pick the best from a small pool of poor applicants. Therefore, many departments hired officers they never would have hired ten or twenty years ago. In fact, some hired the kind of people we used to put in jail according to a friend of mine.

The recent firing of Dallas Police Chief Terrell Bolton on August 26, 2003, is an example of what has been happening in many departments. Bolton came into office under a cloud. The Dallas Police Department had a policy of selecting the highest test-scoring minorities to fulfill quotas. It was rumored that Bolton was selected for promotion at least once when he had scored below white officers, a move which always hurts police morale. Later he became the first black police chief in Dallas and served in the position four years, with a total of 23 years of service in the Dallas Police Department.

His four years were marked by the highest crime rate among large cities for each of his years. He was accused of hiring problematic officers and was involved in lawsuits by demoted commanders. In addition, there was a scandal in which officers reportedly planted fake drugs on innocent people. Since his firing, he has sued the City of Dallas for wrongful termination saying that he could have been demoted but was fired with insufficient cause.

His firing led some to believe that racial turmoil would result (Aynesworth, *The Washington Times*, Aug. 27, 2003). Dallas has some characteristics that make it similar to Detroit. The Dallas Independent School District is currently (2005) 62.6% Hispanic, 30.3% black and 6% white.

Did Bolton's leadership serve as a role model to his men? Only they can say whether his character inspired them to do well or badly. Character does not change easily. As time goes by, the bad character of a leader affects staff through the usual cynicism and frustration, which soon becomes misconduct and corruption.

I've always thought that chiefs and supervisors must be models of integrity for their employees. This must start with attention to hiring. Psychological and background examinations must be connected with proven predictors of good performance and bad performance to select the best applicants. Once hired, carefully selected people must do Academy and field training, and ethics training should be included along with other subjects.

I believe that promotions, discipline and terminations must be made fairly, consistently, and objectively, based on performance instead of "good old boy" favoritism. There must be an open policy requiring officers to report each other's serious misconduct and violations of policy standards. It must be clear that the organization will protect those who report misconduct.

Furthermore, I believe that the highest level of administration must visibly support these policies. We must be willing to have ourselves and our agencies open for inspection whenever there is any question about corruption.

My objective is to restore American policing to respectability, to see law enforcement as honorable and needed, but also ethical, moral, proper, and wanted by all communities; black, white, brown, young, old and in-between.

Affirmative action has been used because of long-denied opportunities for minorities in various businesses. There should be affirmative action in getting educated. Blacks could put in similar hard work in the classroom, learning the basic skills to achieve prominence and a better quality of life as they make more money and become someone admirable.

New black leaders are needed to emphasize realism, not always racism. Hard work is required to pull oneself up by the bootstraps. In order to have more, one must do more! And as we consider doing more, we mustn't forget the law enforcement profession.

To be a police officer requires good physical qualities (like the athlete) and good mental ability (which should be fostered in minority communities.) It can be developed and should be. It really is more important than athletic proficiency. Above all, a police officer must have good moral qualities and that seems to be poorly lacking, even in today's law enforcement world.

I was so disappointed to learn that the percentage of full-time black sworn personnel increased so little over the last few years. From 1990 to 2000, the average number of full-time police officers in cities larger than 250,000 increased by 17%. Minority representation among local police officers increased from 29.8% in 1990 to 38.1% in 2000. Hispanics recorded the greatest increase, from 9.2% to 14.1%. But black representation only increased from 18.4% in 1990 to 20.1% in 2000. I hoped it would increase much more.

Policing Can Improve: Here's How

Let's get back to policing, a term I prefer to law enforcement. Good, respected policing is what any community can get behind and support. That requires good officers, assigned to an area of responsibility, knowing and known to the community, as was the old time beat cop of yesteryear. We must change from almost total emphasis on response enforcements, from wild car chases to safe controlled apprehension.

We must favor slow moving protective patrols over an area known to the officer, who is concerned about its environment and its safety. Such an officer will be alert to the best means for the prevention of crime and the removal of environmental hazards. This appears to be a trend that is catching on. Statistics on cities over 250,000 showed a substantial increase in the use of bicycles with 98% of departments using them in 2000 compared to 39% in 1990. On average, departments operated 44 bicycles per 1,000 sworn personnel in 2000 compared to 3 per 1,000 in 1990.

Slow-moving vehicles and police assigned to a specific beat become familiar with residents and their problems. Often they are considered community police officers. By 2000, 71% of departments of large cities had a formal community policing plan and 29% had an informal plan. Indicators of community policing include meetings with citizen groups to discuss crime-related problems, assignments of responsibility and cases for specific beats or geographic areas, citizen training in mobilization and problem-solving, upgrading technology to support community policing, and taking the time to talk with individuals and proprietors.

Such police and deputies, bringing some of the good qualities of the past, working with modern electronic marvels, can do much to keep America safe in all our communities. In the black and Latino communities, new leaders should emerge. They should be leaders committed to excellence for their followers, setting examples, not harping constantly on racial matters, wrongly or rightly.

Police will get no respect until they harmonize with the citizens they serve. They currently play two roles; either they are a protector or an enforcer. When they protect, they work among the people in slow patrols like scooters or bikes or on foot. In that role, they listen to people, see wrongs, serve as the eyes and ears of police executives and tend to prevent crime from happening. When they are enforcers, they respond quickly in patrol cars to problems that have already occurred and their job is punitive as they arrest lawbreakers. When they play that role, they are not in harmony with the citizens.

When police and citizens work together as a team to protect their communities, they each respect the other. I used to tell citizens that crime prevention "takes a team, you and your police." In Detroit I promoted the concept of Citizen Watch Patrols. Later as Sheriff, in addition to my posse, I had volunteers on scooters and volunteers on Harley Davidson motorcycles.

Uncaring police who simply respond to incidents and are not known by residents cause riots in American cities. This could be avoided if police served as both a protector and enforcer. Police departments could embrace a dual purpose role, and include "dynamic duo police officers," in the words of my wife Sallie.

I propose a dual purpose police department which could do much to prevent crime, alleviate the drug evil, greatly reduce vandalism, and secure a safer and better looking environment.

The surest method of crime prevention is the foot beat, which puts the officer in close contact with the neighborhood he is paid to protect, or so thought Robert Peel who created the role of the policeman. Many excerpts in Appendix IV from Detroit citizens who wrote me verified the effect and importance of seeing officers in the neighborhood. But population growth, urban sprawl and municipal economics have so taxed the ability of police departments to provide sufficient foot patrolmen that police agencies have had to try other methods of increasing the range of the individual officer.

Aggressive service patrol officers look for what is right and wrong in the neighborhood. They try to be active servants of the people, guardians and protectors rather than enforcers. If they don't prevent crime, this puts them in the position of being punitive enforcers of the law once the crime is done.

The most popular means of spreading available police personnel over miles of city streets is the police car. As the use of the automobile has increased, the original preventive function of the police officer has gradually shifted to response.

The all-weather comfort, convenience and versatility of the automobile have indeed been assets to quicker response once a crime has been committed. But this has been of small comfort to the thousands of victims of crime who wish they could have been spared the experience in the first place.

Cocooned in their steel and glass vehicles, the response-oriented police officers of today lack personal visibility. They lack the opportunity to know and be known by citizens as personal protectors who can be recognized and trusted. Some of the alienation that has developed between police and some community segments has its basis in this lack of personal contact on a one-to-one basis.

Only in recent years has there been a serious attempt to re-examine patrol methods and to develop innovative practices to correct police thinking that motorization was the answer to effective crime control.

Obviously, the record indicates that motorization has not been the answer to crime control, if by motorization is meant the total disappearance of police into scout cars.

Authorities have assumed for too long that the essence of patrol is simply movement, and the greater the mobility, the better the patrol. But if observation and contact and the gathering of useful intelligence to anticipate and hopefully prevent crime are also characteristics of effective patrol, then emphasis on the mobility aspect at the expense of other essentials is misdirected.

Mobile foot patrols (scooters) can change all this. Turning this assessment around, the disadvantages of the foot patrol method are the advantages of the car. But few if any have taken equal pains to point out that the advantages of foot patrol are the disadvantages of the automobile. The undeniable advantages of foot patrol simply do not carry over into automobile patrol. Motorization of the police force trades off one type of service, which foot patrol did better, for another type of service, which the scout car does better.

On the basis of movement and economy alone, most police departments over the past 40 years have simply written off the advantages of foot patrol. No one has taken the concept of mobility and visible, protective presence and combined them to use both manpower and technological power to offer something better than total commitment to the automobile.

Research done on early community policing strategies clearly shows that they made residents feel more secure, increased trust between the police and the citizens, and enhanced citizen perception of police services. Community policing causes increased contact between the citizens and the police and results in a police force more aware of the criminal activity in a given community and more able to collect and analyze information that will contribute to prevention of crime as well as apprehension of criminals.

Yes! Research goes on! Community policing is based upon the following principles:

- Preventing crime is as important as arresting criminals.

- Preventing disorder is as important as preventing crime.

- Reducing both crime and disorder requires that police work cooperatively with people in neighborhoods to (1) identify their concerns, (2) solicit their help, and (3) solve their problems.

Co-author Holloway found many community-oriented police officers doing additional preventive tasks in Dallas when she was that city's "Drug Czar" in the late 1980s.

The police visited people's homes and made recommendations about how to make them harder to burglarize. They identified problems before they become serious, such as unsafe housing conditions. They became neighborhood ombudsmen and obtained services from the city and politicians for the needs of the community. They came to know and be known by their community. They helped the community obtain cameras to photograph drug dealers in action so that they could be arrested and removed from neighborhoods. They helped citizens march the streets to clog the usual routes of drug customers coming in to buy from drug dealers. This forced dealers to move on out to other areas not so well protected.

The police even helped youngsters gain access to the physical workout equipment in fire stations. This created valuable rapport between young men and the uniformed services. They also helped groups build and renovate community facilities by obtaining the use of parolees and probationers who were required to contribute service hours to the community.

It is important that police officers do many new tasks if they are to be protective and preventive. But it's equally important that they don't do unethical tasks involving the use of force, misuse of discretion and police corruption.

Unfortunately, there are many new kinds of criminals that operate presently. Today's police must be "trained for change" because the bad guys have developed new operations that require complex training to stop them. A good example is the computer spammers. Sometimes police get some help from corporations whose business is hurt by criminal activity.

AOL, Microsoft, Yahoo and Earthlink joined forces to sue Alan Ralsky, who operated 20 different computers in his $740,000 home in West Bloomfield, Illinois. He was called the "Detroit Spam King" because his operations began in a suburb of that city (Wendland, *Detroit Free Press,* Nov. 22, 2002). These companies overlooked competition with each other to help law enforcement arrest and convict someone who hurt them all. Their joint action set a good example for other businesses to work with police.

Here is how this new type of criminal works. In the basement of Ralsky's 8,000 square foot home, computers controlled 190 e-mail servers across the world, each capable of sending out 650,000 messages every hour. He used hundreds of internet addresses to send his spam, and many of his e-mail servers were located in Israel. His e-mails touted debt reduction loans, breast enlargement and penis growth, and various other products. Two associates helped him monitor his computers, one adding new names and deleting those who have asked to be deleted, and the other connecting with banks of e-mail servers and watching e-mails.

Every time a user opened one of his e-mails, Ralsky received a message and could monitor the effectiveness of his subject line on the e-mail, and adjust it accordingly.

He was earlier sued by Verizon and settled by paying an unpublished amount to the company for sending out unsolicited e-mails to their customers. Now Ralsky is a graying 59 year old man who poses for pictures in his office with a plaque behind him saying "Reform School Certificate, Grade D".

Ralsky tries to keep his business going by avoiding legal entanglements. He avoids the term "spam" and says he sends marketing messages. He promised his wife, Irmengard, that he would not send pornography or sexual messages. He came to spamming rather late in life, only seven years ago, after being in trouble with the law several times.

In 1992, while selling insurance, he was sentenced to 50 days in jail and ordered to pay $120,000 for failure to deliver on unregistered securities contracts. In 1994, he was convicted of falsifying documents and bank fraud in Michigan and Ohio and had to pay $74,000 in restitution. In 1996, his insurance license was revoked and he declared personal bankruptcy. In 1997, he sold his Toyota and used the money to pay back taxes on his house and buy two computers.

After he bought the computers, a friend told him about mass marketing on the internet. He bought some mailing lists from advertising brokers, and launched a computer career that quickly made him thousands every week.

Ralsky was not the only spammer in the small community of West Bloomfield. He was involved with some other spammers in his suburb. The four other spammers were charged with violating the CAN-SPAM Act by the U.S. attorney's office on April 29, 2004. They were brothers Daniel and James Lin, Christopher Chung and Mark Sadek. They were accused of illegally sending millions of spam messages offering diet patches and other devices through companies like Phoenix Avatar.

The U.S. Federal Trade Commission claimed the men earned about $100,000 monthly offering the useless diet patches for $59.95 through many websites. They illegally used the known websites (Ford Motor Company, Amoco, Unisys, U.S. Army Information Center, and Administrative Office of the U.S. Courts) to send the spam so that it would appear to be legitimate.

The West Bloomfield home/office of the four was raided on April 28, 2004, and U.S. Postal Inspection agents found that they were far beyond young computer nerds. Over a dozen computers, hard drives, modems, records, half a dozen guns (including a Glock 26), boxes of ammunition, a "how to" book on white collar crime, drug paraphernalia, $3,300 in cash and e-mail complaints were confiscated.

This brings me to how law enforcement officers must be "trained for change". Today's criminals are developing new and complex methods that require new and complex training methods if we are to catch them. To describe this training, I will go into findings of several groups.

Much attention has always been paid to the findings of the Police Foundation, a privately funded independent organization established in 1970 to support innovation and improvement in policing. The former president, Patrick Murphy, and I were instructors together at the New York City Police Academy. When I became the first New York City Police lieutenant to attend the Southern Police Institute in 1954, I asked then Sergeant Murphy to take over my promotion classes for three months. Pat has had an excellent and extensive career since then, becoming Detroit Police Commissioner in 1970 after I left. And then he went on to become Police Commissioner for the City of New York.

The current president of the Police Foundation, Hubert Williams, and I played tennis together at a police conference held in Jamaica some years ago. This fine man served as police commissioner of Newark, New Jersey.

The Police Foundation has assembled the National Advisory Committee on Higher Education for Police Officers to examine the question: How can the quality of police education be improved to make it a more effective force for changing the police?

I've read many books about police education. One was *The Quality of Police Education* by Lawrence Sherman and the National Advisory Commission on Higher Education for Police Officers but it had its problems like most books on this topic. It was published in 1978 but it addressed many things that are important today. It stated that conservatives criticize the police for failing to control crime, liberals blame them for brutality, corruption, racism and failure to provide due process, and the media find police troubles a favorite topic. Has there been much change nearly 27 years later? Nope!

This book argues that a primary objective should be "educating the police for change". But like other books I've read, it stated that police education should be left to "the elite" four-year universities instead of the two-year community colleges. I don't agree.

When I served as national president of the American Academy of Professional Law Enforcement, I addressed the February 4, 1979, annual meeting. As a matter of fact, Hubert Williams and Patrick Murphy attended the address.

I urged coordination, teamwork and articulation between the two-year colleges and four-year colleges and improvement of the transferability of credits. I lamented the "academic iron curtain" where many liberal arts institutions exclude the educationally qualified *practitioner* from teaching law enforcement in a four-year institution. Isn't it better to welcome such colleagues and have them work in cooperation with other disciplines at the college? I stressed, of course, how college is only a beginning for continued lifelong learning.

To bring this up-to-date, an education bill in Arizona was just narrowly defeated on April 6, 2005. It would have allowed four-year undergraduate degrees to have been offered by community colleges in health, teaching, fire and law enforcement professions. I was so sorry to read this because that was exactly what might have been helpful and innovative (Colleges bill dies in Senate, *The Arizona Republic*, April 6, 2005).

8

Epilogue—Conclusion: Hope?

o o o o o o o o o o o o o o o o o o o o o o o o o o o o o o o o o
"Men should be taught as if you taught them not
And things unknown proposed as things forgot."

—Ben Franklin

Epilogue-Conclusion: Hope?

The real answer to the challenge of crime in America

People commit crimes. Other people see such people commit crimes, or learn and know of it. Such people must convey those facts to their police. This must be done willingly, and with an understanding that the police are simply an extension of themselves and their responsibilities in a free and democratic society.

The vital question, then, is how can such people come to regard the police as an extension of themselves? How can we get them to come forth to cooperate? How is it possible, when it seems the police today are continually alienating themselves from the individual public? The answer is that the police must return to the people, and so get the people to return and respond to them.

This phenomenon of non-involvement, of public anomie or outright alienation from their police must change—but how? The individual member of society cannot be expected to make such a change—the police must. Yet, the police, despite all the recent emphasis on public relations programs and community relations programs, are still alienating themselves from the people.

The answer? It lies in some means of bringing policing back to a community function—with local feeling and with local identification. The local police officer—once accepted—is a better public and community relations example than all the departmental lip service and press articles, important as they may be.

Indeed, I suggest that the very surge of professional advances over the years may have served to make policing more remote and distant than ever.

One such advance, the automobile, is today perhaps the worst culprit in the present alienation of the police officer and the public he serves. Ever since early police authorities held that the patrolman on foot was obsolete and showed how motorization amplified enormously the striking power of the force through increased mobility, maneuverability and speed, police administrators everywhere have fully employed the use of the automobile. Too fully!

Police administrators now have expanded and fully utilized fast response until today, police cars are almost entirely engaged in responding to a myriad of calls, *after* the crime has been done. Very little preventive patrol is effected or even possible by overburdened police car crews. The former neighborhood "cop on the beat", visible to all, has now been replaced in an impersonal vehicle of glass and steel. Extensive localized foot patrol might be an answer to the crime problem and might return the police officer to closer contact with the people, but the prohibitive costs make this approach almost impossible.

No, something different must be found. A happy medium is needed between the costly but identifiable personal foot patrolman and the more economical but impersonal car. Call it a scooter, or a motorized two-wheeled vehicle that will enable a neighborhood foot patrolman or the second man of a two-man police car to cover enormously more territory, more often, and still be identifiable as a community officer. Sometimes a three-wheeled vehicle might be needed, or a bicycle, or a Segway. Motorcycles are not the answer because they are built for speed and are used to chase people and cars, not to prevent crime.

The very presence of a scooter, bike or golf cart with a uniformed officer (security guards, neighborhood patrols, volunteer posse members or police officers) deters criminals who fear being observed and reported, as well as making people feel more protected.

When police officers serve in that role, different and more professional motivation, supervision, esprit de corps, and pride in the community emerge. More information is likely to be given to protective police officers. The omnipresence of a mobile friendly police force conveys safety and deters crime.

In a day of escalating costs for technology and personnel, the tax-paying public would perceive an attempt by police administrators to do more with available manpower.

The renewed pride of the patrol officer in regaining proper regard and respect as a key member in police operations should bring a greater sense of individual contribution to the police effort. At the very least, a certain amount of respect for helpful police officers will develop among delinquency-prone youngsters, simply because pursuit is removed from their relationship.

Police Must Become Professional

The failure of police to become professional became apparent, wrote Sgt. Jeffrey Patterson of the Clearwater, Florida, Police Department, in the 1970s. In his document, "Community Policing: Learning the Lessons of History," Patterson described the problems that have plagued community policing efforts.

He said a good example was urban riots such as the one in Detroit, which led to my appointment as Police Commissioner. Police, politicians, press and people complained about how the police were no longer close to those they were to serve and protect. They had lost the respect of everyone. They weren't seen as professional but they were seen as tough!

Charles Gruber, Chief of Police in Barrington, Illinois, is the past President of the International Association of Chiefs of Police. He gave a speech called "The

Chief's Role in Prioritizing Civil Rights" which was printed in the *Police Chief Magazine* of March 2005. He wrote:

> No institution is more visible than the police. We are scrutinized daily for our actions and inactions, what we did, what we didn't do, our intentions. Our policies and procedures are debated daily in the newspapers and reviewed countlessly in the courts around the country…
>
> In one sentence, our job as police chiefs is to put in place a policing organization that institutionalizes the proper values that emphasize the power of authority over the power of force. And the most visual area in policing, the use of force, continues to be the pinnacle issue for civil rights infractions…
>
> For law enforcement, the advent of community policing has greatly contributed to changes for the better. Law enforcement leaders want to become more responsive to our citizens in protecting their civil liberties while serving the police mission effectively.

The Code of Silence Must End

Joseph D. McNamara wrote an article for the *Sunday Oakland Press* in Pontiac, Michigan, on October 1, 1995, called "Code of silence must come to an end." He reported that the number of bad cops is rising. He detailed cases such as the following:

Some Los Angeles County Deputy Sheriffs got caught robbing and extorting money from drug dealers. A New Orleans policewoman murdered her partner and shop owners during a robbery she committed while she was on patrol. While performing drug stings in Atlanta and Washington, D.C., police were found to be stealing and taking bribes. Two white police officers framed a black man for murdering a white woman in Boston. New York State troopers falsified evidence that sent people to prison. Counterfeit evidence and evidence tampering forced a number of cases to be reopened in San Francisco and Philadelphia. A former police chief of Detroit, William Hart, was sent to prison for stealing drug-buy money. A Drug Enforcement agent was sent to jail for stealing laundered drug money.

He argued that the "essential task is to create within police agencies an incentive to break the code of silence among the rank and file and encourage cops to police themselves." He believes that mayors and police chiefs should not use the "few bad apples" defense to cover the fact that the code of silence is allowing bad cops to operate, and tell good cops they will be rewarded instead of punished if they expose bad cops.

When police misconduct surfaces, many administrators attempt to remove the department from public scorn by blaming the incident on "rogue cops." Their position is that "certain rotten apples" acted on their own and will be dealt with to the fullest extent of the law. This position denies the existence of the code of silence. The "rotten apple" strategy allows the agency to distance itself from the incident and the public is satisfied that the guilty officer is being prosecuted. But it behooves us to investigate how things came to be this way and why officers seem willing to endure personal loyalty that forces them into an unnatural relationship which the organization neither requires nor needs.

Police commanders can clean up their departments and cut down on the code of silence by developing career development programs, providing ethics training for all officers, encouraging officers to participate in community functions, ensuring that officers know lying will not be tolerated by administration, training in the importance of truthfulness, ensuring that management rights are not negotiated away, and holding supervisors accountable for the acts of their subordinates.

The person at the top of law enforcement agencies must be a good role model for his men. His principles must show in the decisions he makes. In large departments, officers may have little contact with the chief and may learn more about what he stands for from in-house word of mouth and the press than from their contact with him. I had occasion to get press coverage many times and used the opportunities to get my principles across to my men and women. I hoped they understood that I would not tolerate bad cops. One of those incidents or defining moments came when I had to go to jail to avoid taking a bad deputy back on the payroll. That incident is covered in Appendix V.

Good police officers and administrators abound thankfully and many examples of their good works can be given but none can wipe out bad actions by others.

Crack Down on Corruption

Neal Trautman (National Ethics Institute, June 21, 2004) has defined stages in the growth of organizational corruption.

1. First officers perceive that there is administrative indifference toward integrity.

2. Next is the perception that obvious ethical problems are ignored as leaders intentionally look the other way or even cover up misconduct.

3. The third stage is the growth of fear as officers perceive that to survive as a leader, one must abide by the unwritten rules of internal politics. This stage may be accompanied by bitterness, officers rationalizing unethical acts in conversations with each other, and the hopeless conclusion that "everyone else is doing it."

4. The fourth phase is the survival of the fittest as good employees fear the corrupt dishonest ones, and the code of silence prevails as administrators hide misconduct rather than try to resolve it.

Deep within us, we assess the behavior of individuals, agencies, institutions, and societies by the measuring stick of integrity. Law enforcement must have integrity if it is to be acceptable to the people.

Events in the 1990s such as I have described rocked public trust in the integrity of law enforcement agencies. This motivated the National Institute of Justice (NIJ) and the Office of Community Oriented Policing Services (COPS) to create a symposium to examine the issue of integrity.

The National Symposium on Police Integrity was held in July 1996 in Washington, D.C. The 200 participants included police chiefs, sheriffs, police researchers, police officers, professional disciplines, community leaders and members of federal agencies. It attracted international interest and was attended by representatives from the Netherlands, Belarus, Nicaragua, Haiti, El Salvador, Honduras, Sweden and the United Kingdom.

During the 2½ days, there was a clear understanding of the tragic consequences in the profession as well as the country if integrity was seriously eroded. Brainstorming of "healthy" organizations with little or no problem around the issues of integrity took place in small and large group sessions. The attendees felt they could learn at least as much from examining what is right in police organizations as what is wrong in them.

The conclusions were set out in a report submitted to the (then) Attorney General by Joseph E. Brann, Director of COPS, and Jeremy Travis, Director of National Institute of Justice. The recommendations were categorized into short-term and long-term recommendations. Many of them are so important that I have summarized them.

Police leaders were urged to infuse integrity and ethics into curriculums and build it into those in charge of recruits, in-service, and training programs. They also suggested using model media relations programs that have focused successfully on police integrity. Then they suggested a survey of participants to learn which actions were instituted and how they worked out.

Long-term recommendations included assessing entry-level screening and hiring processes to see if they reliably predict ethical behavior, and determine the best predictors. They wanted to do research on whether officers with more education maintain a better track record of professional performance. They wanted to explore alternatives to methods of receiving and responding to citizen complaints about officer performance to avoid adversarial environments.

I was glad to see that they wanted to delve deeper into the issue by these recommendations:

- Identify the kind of training that keeps recruits from becoming cynical and critical of their work early in their careers.

- Research officers with integrity violations and explore why they were not deterred.

- Track incoming recruits and officers during their careers to determine why some commit integrity violations while others don't.

They also made recommendations about how supervisors are being oriented, guided, educated and held accountable for maintaining integrity among officers.

Their recommendations even touched on unions, politicians and the press. They suggested conducting research on trends over the past five years in arbitration rulings for and against police agencies in matters of integrity. Interestingly, they suggested training for politicians about police integrity and police culture so they may help chiefs set realistic expectations and change programs. They recommended a survey of successful marketing strategies used by police agencies with good integrity records and how they could be applied to other agencies.

Opportunities for Positive Public-Police Interaction Must Increase

The Police Chief of March 2003, journal of the International Association of Chiefs of Police, spotlighted specialized patrol vehicles, which gave "opportunities for positive interaction between the public and the police." They described electric bikes, scooters, multi-terrain vehicles, and mobile substations. I continue to believe that crime would be reduced by more contact between police and citizens.

Remember the local policeman, assigned to patrol traffic and to see that each child safely crossed to the other side of the street? We recall how he wore a smile, had pockets full of bubble gum, asked the children how they were doing and listened to those who reached out to him. Parents didn't worry about their children on those daily walks home. They rested assured that the community caretaker for the children at the school was on duty and was a family friend.

Tenure of Police Chiefs Must Increase

Law enforcement in the big cities is not working well for many reasons. One reason is that the commissioner or chief at the top doesn't last long enough, even if we assume he is selected professionally. In the City of New York since 1898, commissioners have lasted on an average of just over two years, hardly time for proper planning, implementation and continuity of programs. In Detroit, from 1968 to 1978, there have been six chief executives averaging a little more than a year each.

Today's chief must be all things to all people. A chief must be a leader, decision maker, confidante, politician, disciplinarian, therapist, mentor, administrator, taskmaster, spokesperson, community leader, educator, change agent, facilitator, partner, negotiator, role model, steward, student, parent figure, visionary, manager, minister and leadership developer. Of course chiefs can't be all these things and sometimes unions don't want him to be all these things.

Police unions have become very sophisticated. They have realized that they can influence politicians by using the no-confidence vote. It is now one of their most powerful tools and they use it to influence wage negotiations, decision-making, and removal of the police chief. However, unions and police benevolent associations have a few ideas that may help a chief to survive a dreaded no-confidence vote.

Unions may threaten or actually take votes of no-confidence against the police chief hoping that the negative publicity will embarrass local officials who appointed the chief, thus serving as leverage for higher wages. They use it to gain the attention of top management, to force the chief to listen, and to indicate their frustration. The no-confidence vote is used after other attempts have failed or when the union believes the chief to be incompetent, disinterested or uncaring. It is used to request that the chief be removed from office. When a no-confidence vote occurs, the chief should determine immediately why it was taken.

In 1991, the FBI National Executive Institute Associates issued the results of a five-year study of 35 such votes and reported that over half of the chiefs involved were removed from office. Thus such a vote is disruptive and demoralizing to a chief.

The usual reasons for such a vote is lack of leadership or lack of communication or lack of support for employees. There may be union doubts about the chief's integrity or his interest in supporting the needs of his employees. The union may want input into the decision-making process. They may perceive the chief as being aloof, dictatorial, unfair in promotions and discipline, and they may get back at the chief through the vote of no-confidence.

Chiefs Must Be Open and Show Support for Employees

What can a chief do to avoid the end of his tenure if such a vote occurs? The Southern States Police Benevolent Association published an opinion in "The Front Line" in their January-March 2003 web site about this. They said that how the chief reacts might determine whether he stays or leaves!

A chief must determine how many employees (union members) voted and how many were eligible to vote and how many expressed no confidence. Next he must determine if employees have been treated unfairly. He must examine whether he has been open to communication and whether he has shown support for his people. And he must learn the answers to these questions quickly. Then he must acknowledge and correct mistakes, promise to solve the problems cited, and take other appropriate action as needed. To deny mistakes or refuse to recognize problems will probably doom his administration.

If there is no validity for the vote of no confidence, the chief must clarify this immediately and set the record straight by actively defending his or her character. Although the tendency is for the chief to lash out at his accusers, he must react professionally and not take it personally or show emotions. Those chiefs who withdraw usually lose their jobs. Those who remain as visible as possible and walk through the department and the ranks show care for employees.

Of course, an inept union leader may take reckless steps for his/her own advancement and cannot control the militancy of a few members. The chief who speaks out on behalf of employees and cares what they want and how they feel may be able to overcome this. A chief must show good character through fairness, respect, dignity and compassion. He must consider what is right rather than who is right.

A chief must ensure that union leaders do not have to go through a complicated chain of command to communicate with him. There must be many avenues for communication with the union such as informal contacts, periodic scheduled meetings, and participation of the union in staff conferences. There can be labor-management retreats, committees, advisory groups, newsletters, suggestion programs, surveys, etc.

The chief must demonstrate trust and fairness. A chief must avoid playing favorites, give credit to others, treat employees with respect, give them the freedom they need to do their job, listen to different opinions, treat others as they want to be treated, value individual diversity, support and encourage people, and give fair performance feedback.

The chief should also develop good relations with community leaders, the mayor, the city manager, city council members, and others. These will be valuable if a no-confidence vote occurs. Chiefs should also treat employees like community-oriented police treat citizens, as customers who need respectful service.

Finally, to maintain a chief's tenure, he/she must show the employees that he cares about them. This will avoid no-confidence votes.

Find Common Ground with Unions

Can management and police organizations travel the same track in the interest of law enforcement services and protection? Frankly, I am pessimistic. Why? Because of the narrow viewpoints and positions of our many organizations representing law enforcement personnel.

However, let us remember some of the benefits of unions to their members. They protect employees job security and guard against unfair labor practices. They obtain higher wages, fringe benefits and safer equipment. They enable employees to collectively exercise political strength through the bargaining process and endorse prospective elected officials. They provide legal assistance to members. Lastly, unions have the force to change the status quo and to redefine the police role.

Some police unions are simply resistant to departmental changes in procedures and policies. Sometimes they lack consideration of the ability to pay their higher wage demands. Sometimes they challenge administration through strikes and work slow-downs, which weaken the overall mission of peace and order in a community. Sometimes their political involvement unduly polarizes a community. And sometimes unions are the refuge and protection of lazy employees and those unwilling to upgrade themselves, insisting upon senior rather than the most qualified personnel for job assignments, and offering protection or legal assistance for those that are below professional standards.

At the bargaining table today are three interests: the union, with their various economic and non-economic demands; the political subdivision such as the city or county; and the law enforcement chief executive such as the chief or sheriff. As Police Commissioner in Detroit, I watched and felt the rise in power and influence of the unions.

In 21st century America, there is more effort to include union representatives at police administrative meetings, administrative training functions, and on corporate boards than ever before. Lee Iacocca said it well in his autobiography:

As a board member, Doug (union representative) found out firsthand what was going on at Chrysler from the perspective of management…

When there's a plant closing, he advises us on how to minimize the dislocation and suffering that go with it…

Until then (1980), no representative of labor had ever sat on the board of a major American corporation. But it's pretty standard in Europe. In Japan, they do it all the time…

I want labor to understand the inner workings of the company…

America's economic future depends upon increased cooperation among government, union, and management.

Give Press Good Plus Bad News and Handouts to Ensure Accuracy

The crippling malady afflicting police management today is that management cannot effectively achieve its legitimate goals. In some departments, management has allowed employees to virtually determine their own working conditions and the level of services to be delivered to the public. Other agencies have failed to understand the nature of collective bargaining and surrendered basic management rights. And then there are those departments that have attempted to fend off some of labor's illegitimate demands only to find themselves manacled and shackled by either the courts or labor arbitrators.

The press is out to make a profit. Since the goal of the press is to sell their work, they often select news to entertain or titillate the senses rather than providing objective information to readers. Many media executives believe that conflict sells. If there is no conflict, there is no news. Often they attempt to create conflict where there is none. To do this, they may ask provocative questions to stir up emotions and make a more interesting story. On the wings of controversy, often you can get your message across.

On a daily basis, reporters need material for stories and all they have to offer in return is media exposure and sometimes flattery. Those who seek attention may be happy with exposure and flattering or even non-flattering coverage, as long as they get the coverage and attention.

The cynical handling of some issues by the media and their preference to depict conflict make society's problems harder to solve than they would otherwise be. Often, the press gets in the way of society solving its own problems. In fact, their sensationalism often incorrectly exaggerates menaces, making citizens more fearful than they need to be.

Reporters often irresponsibly convince the public by their slanted articles that public officers cannot be trusted. They do this by claiming to look into issues and calling it "investigative reporting." These "investigative reports" often yield alarming results that must be disclosed by reporters because they are being hidden from the public. The media then proceeds to bring out the worst in every person in public life, driving serious candidates away and rewarding gutter-fights. Our "news" is the result of hundreds of judgment calls made by reporters and publishers instead of objective news reporting.

It is clear, however, that campaign media consultants can make or break presidential candidates. It has been ascertained that television's interpretation of primary election results can influence voters as well as candidates.

The press claims to have the license to criticize and defame but I fear that they shun the license to be responsible in serving the public. Rather than serving only the selfish side of the human spirit, they should serve the striving, inquiring side. They should help voters and readers sift through facts, information, and propaganda, equipping them to evaluate issues intelligently. The press could ask the readers what issues they want candidates to discuss instead of putting their own questions to candidates. When they plan to interview public officers, they could ask readers to submit questions for the interview instead of reporters creating questions themselves.

It is true that speeches, wars and violence must be reported but how it is presented determines whether the reader feels happy, angry, powerless, betrayed or involved with their institutions and political system. The focus of television is image, 30 second sound bite phrases, and only incidentally upon the definition of real issues.

Investigation, explanation and fair-mindedness should be the tools of reporters. If they are not, the media gets in the way of society solving its own problems. Irresponsible reporters contribute to the public's anger and distrust of their own public officials. The media's real goal should be to make what is important also interesting enough to learn about, understand, and use to improve life.

Sometimes members of the press recognize and write about these problems. I was delighted to read an article by Kathleen Parker of *Tribune Media Services* in September, 2003. I will quote some of her salient points.

> It is indeed too soon to pass judgment on Iraq, but bad news is what compels and sells. Journalism's once heroic goal of seeking truth has been subjugated, it seems, to the more commercially expedient mandate of "sexing up" the news.
>
> With notable exceptions, the media increasingly are perceived as the world's pimp, selling cheap stories for slicker suits and flashier careers. In the absence of salable truths about lying politicians—the Woodward and Bern-

stein template that introduced careerism to newsrooms—reporters are increasingly willing to fictionalize.

Not all, of course. And honest mistakes admitted and corrected are something else. But too many of today's mistakes are of a different order. Too many reporters maliciously alter truth, from fabricating stories and sources (Jayson Blair) to selectively using partial quotes to purposely distort meaning.

Just last week, the *Washington Post* ran a correction on a story that took one of Vice President Dick Cheney's quotes so out of context that the impression presented was exactly the opposite of what Cheney obviously meant.

We so want bad news, apparently, that we'll avert our eyes from the good. But do we so want bad news that we'd rather fail in Iraq? That we're willing to compromise American lives? Not consciously, perhaps. Not the way France wants us to fail, as *New York Times* columnist Thomas Friedman described in that same paper. (Friedman's column was entitled, "French appear bent on becoming enemy.")

But our obsession with the downside, ignoring the progress that is being made in Iraq (too extensive to list here) in favor of items that suggest failure and quagmire borders on the pathological. Has our self-loathing come to this?

It is refreshing that a prominent reporter like Kathleen Parker would point out the problems of her own profession. Beneath her picture with this article was a quotation by her, "Apparently we take such glee in bad news that, lacking any, we'll make some up."

Have a Press Schedule for Responding to Incidents

Silence on certain aspects of investigations may be viewed as stonewalling when in fact the agency does not yet have the information. The Community Relations Service of the U.S. Department of Justice published a *Conciliation Handbook for the Police and the Community* on the topic of "Police Use of Excessive Force". The handbook suggests developing a protocol on information dissemination.

There could be a meeting within the first 24 hours focusing on where the other agencies are with the investigation and what processes are in play. Another meeting scheduled within two days of the incident would be more formal and would describe what is known about the incident. From then on, meetings would be held on an as-needed basis to offer the formal findings of fact from the inquest. Processes such as this can counteract the perception of the police as trying to hide information.

Community Policing Combines Responsive Police and Community Partnership

Police lost their role as protectors serving the community when they isolated themselves inside patrol cars and resorted to two-way radios for communication. Community policing makes the community a partner in the police mission because it demonstrates attention to the concerns of residents. It fosters an atmosphere of cooperation and mutual respect by one-to-one rapport, attendance and participation of community meetings, and surveying residents as to their priorities.

Police officers' confidence in their job depends upon the satisfaction and encouragement of those they serve. When this support is lacking or buttressed by animosity, a breeding ground of excessive police force is created. Building rapport, combined with awards for officers who contribute the most to communities, brings out the best in effective crime prevention, reduction and community safety.

In New York I introduced the concept of motorized, two-wheeled scooter patrol, first in parks and then to all 79 police precincts in the city. Despite much bureaucratic opposition and roadblocks, they were successful. In the city of Detroit, again against much political opposition and after some police opposition, I instituted motorized scooter patrols with great success.

In Detroit in 1968 and 1969, I referred to scooter patrols as "Community-Oriented Patrol Services" or COPS. Now years later, our federal government Department of Justice has an office called COPS and dispenses millions of dollars to police agencies for various types of community services policing (but not scooters.)

Later after Detroit, I was a professor at John Jay College of Criminal Justice in New York City and also at the same time became Director of the Law Enforcement and Protection Program at Mercy College in 1970 until almost 1980. (Note the term Protection. I felt then that Law Enforcement was not enough). My theme in courses was that we need both law enforcement and protection. Yes, we must take proper action when crimes are committed. But we must also serve as protectors and preventers of crime, which police in police cars really cannot do well.

Conciliation Builds Common Ground Between Police and Groups

So often when a minority person is wounded or killed by a white police officer, word spreads and crowds gather resulting in arrests, injuries, quick accusations and premature indictments by minority leaders, and uninformed responses by various police personnel. Conciliation can bring opposing parties together short of legal or legislative actions. If efforts to work things out fall short, the police or minority community still has other ways to pursue action, with no party having lost anything.

There are many parts of an event that can create overreactions: the nature of the incident and type of force used, pre-existing conditions, the circumstances such as the age and mental condition of those involved, police and witnesses reactions at the event, statements made by police about the incident, media portrayal of the event, what community leaders say and do, the investigation of the incident, the community tension and reaction to the incident, the announcement of the results of the investigation, the court/jury decision, and any new incidents.

The International Association of Chiefs of Police recommends steps to avoid such overreactions and to avoid use of excessive force in the first place. These steps include arranging for community and religious leaders to accompany police on patrol in their neighborhoods, meeting precinct commanders, discussing community concerns with police and with citizens on these walks/patrols/meetings, and using their influence to help communities remain calm while things are being investigated and worked out.

It is necessary to inform these leaders of the two types of investigations needed in such incidents: internal investigation of whether an officer has violated rules (which results may remain confined to the police department) and external investigation of whether an officer has committed a crime, which will be public information. Community leaders can cooperate and calm their constituents if they understand the process and can check on the steps as it goes along. Without their cooperation, police silence can be interpreted as protecting one of their own or dodging blame. Assurance that leaders and the public will receive timely information on each step of the process can demonstrate responsiveness to the community's concerns.

Identify the correct spokesperson for the police in communicating information to the media, community leaders, and concerned citizens. If community organizations want to arrange a march or a demonstration, assist them with barricades, traffic control, speaking platforms, routes of travel, and necessary permissions.

Sugrue illuminated the basis of white resistance during the years before the 1967 riot which emphasized the importance of homeowners associations. He described how those associations gained support from various white groups such as churches, labor unions and real estate agencies. For blacks, their support organizations came mainly from the NAACP, Urban League and a very few churches. It would behoove law enforcement organizations to work with these very groups to ensure that communities do not become divided along racial lines.

Cities Can Choose to Fail or Succeed

Jared Diamond proposed in his new book *Collapse: How Societies Choose to Fail or Succeed* that societies choose to kill themselves by their own governing decisions. So might it be for cities. He blames aggressive and profit-centered companies, agricultural and resource mismanagement, and bad governance by foolish leaders and the greedy ruling elite.

Diamond shows how some societies manage to reverse what might otherwise be a crucial mistake when beset by a range of problems and mounting failures. Let us and our city leaders counter decisions that will lead ultimately to the suicide of our cities. He noted that governments often have a short-term or 90-day focus, and mainly respond to crises. Thus crowd psychology pushes governmental authorities toward quick reactions as they try to maintain public approval. This is likely to reduce critical thinking and suppress painful realities just when they are needed.

As government, business and law enforcement agencies know, people imitate the behavior of their leaders. If leaders seek "yes" men and ask colleagues to minimize disagreements, they are likely to run into problems that nobody discussed. But if they ask colleagues to think critically and ask questions, they are likely to make better decisions and be more prepared for worst case scenarios.

The Role of the Church

In America's racial struggles and particularly in the struggle in Detroit, it is of interest that many key figures have been black ministers. In my friend Hubert Locke's book (a minister himself with a doctorate), *The Detroit Riot of 1967*, he points out:

> Nat Turner, leader of the famed Virginia slave revolt in the 1830s, was a Baptist cleric. Following his effort, slave states instituted a number of repressive measures against black slave religious movements. In some instances, it became illegal to teach slaves to read, especially the Bible, and unlawful for slaves to assemble for worship unless a white person was present.
>
> In the present century the slain civil rights leader and Nobel Peace Prize winner, Martin Luther King, Jr., also was a Baptist pastor; James Farmer, longtime leader of the Congress on Racial Equality, is a graduate of Howard University's School of Religion; and Channing Phillips, the first black man to

be nominated for President of the United States, is a militant Washington, D.C., clergyman. Even the Black Muslims, with their pronounced anti-white anti-Christian philosophy, interpret the goals and aspirations of black people with a religious context.

Similarly on the local (Detroit) level, Albert Cleage, for all his black nationalistic fervor, is nevertheless an Oberlin Seminary graduate and a clergyman in good standing in the United Church of Christ, although there are periodic rumors of attempts to oust him. Likewise, Roy A. Allen enjoys a position of prominence within Baptist circles in Detroit and serves on several commissions and boards...

To the extent that the racial struggle in America still finds its roots partially in religion, and that religious loyalties seem deep in the mass of black people in America, some see a sign of hope. The religious temperament may prove to be a corrective to the spirit of despair and nihilism that grips growing numbers of young black people in America.

Tamar Jacoby, author of *Someone Else's House: America's Unfinished Struggle for Integration,* while not exactly hopeful, has some suggestions of ways that Detroit and other cities wrestling with race issues can approach their problems.

She believes that the final answer involves integration, but how will that be accomplished? She proposes the usual solutions such as better leadership, incentives such as school choice, and acculturation where one learns to speak and write good English, and growing up in families where people are expected to get jobs. She also calls for improved public schooling, job training programs and apprenticeships in partnership with businesses.

Try to Walk in the Shoes of Others

It is important to understand how you would feel under treatment and circumstances that blacks encountered as slaves, then as free men but still afforded only second class or worse treatment. Understanding then may emerge about why many blacks became militants with increased rhetoric about "rebellion" and "revolution" with growing apathy toward integration and moves to self-segregation. Couple this with their problems with the "police system" (let me substitute here law enforcement) which I feel needs to be redefined in America.

How can we envision what it must have been like to be black in the days before understanding, enlightenment and new laws were enacted for civil rights for minorities?

Slavery—an abomination—leaves not only physical but psychological lingering effects throughout the years. The slaves, sold at auction, often branded, left families broken up, men being addressed as "boy", black women used sexually by their "owners", and numerous other consequences.

Indeed being black in America in the past meant a posture of humiliation, helplessness, defenselessness and dehumanization. Those who are not black Americans need to think about that, to picture that. I feel that many good Americans (non-blacks) understood much of this but their efforts were derailed by the riots of the 1960s and particularly in Detroit on that fateful day, July 23, 1967.

It must be hard for African Americans to want to be black and American when they are so angry at what the country has done to them. This distrust and anger creates an almost suicidal outlook in young people who tell interviewers that they don't expect to reach age 21 so they might as well do and take everything they can until then.

Consider the Two Kings

The story of Detroit is a painful summary of hopes dashed and applies to many other urban cities, to America and to its people—black, brown, red, yellow, white—who will face many challenges in the future. We all should examine and hearken to the lessons history has to teach us.

Will we eventually realize that urban turmoil, the inability or unwillingness to heal our nation's black/white issues can cause further decline and decay? I am reminded of two very different Kings: Rev. Martin Luther King, Jr. who preached non-violence and Rodney King, quite a different guy who was arrested and beaten by the Los Angeles Police Department.

Let me now remind you of how police sometimes cause riots. The Los Angeles riot after the Rodney King verdict was an example of a riot created because people thought that the officers who beat King were not punished sufficiently. The Los Angeles Police Department still has not recovered from the actions of their officers and the non-action of their chief, Daryl Gates. Is the fault with the rioters or with the police officers who acted badly and were not punished for it, or with their chief? Despite that, I can't forget the words of Rodney King, "Can't we all just get along?" To that I say We Must!

People see police departments and police as distinct from the people. I believe that the police and the community must cooperate to address problems within the community. The community, in effect, gets the police they deserve. Likewise, the police, by their actions, get the type of community they deserve. Good policing gets good citizens to do their part.

Final Words

I may be an old police visionary—some would say an irascible cross old curmudgeon. Now at 85, I feel great disappointment at what has happened to many American cities—particularly Detroit. Detroit and other cities must beware! If they don't change their police departments and put their police back in touch with the people, God knows how many Detroits there will be.

I've been a student and teacher of law enforcement and policing for much of my life. I've read many and maybe most of the important books on law enforcement, policing, sociology, psychology and history. I've taught at colleges, police academies and universities, and have written many newspaper columns and chapters for books on policing. This is my third book. My first two were *American Police Dilemma: Protectors or Enforcers?* and *American Law Enforcement Does Not Serve or Protect!*

This book explains what I believe has plagued Detroit, as well as what I tried to do in the New York City Police Department in command of Operations, as Police Commissioner for the City of Detroit, and as Sheriff of Oakland County, Michigan.

I have to admit that I'm losing faith in politicians to help the crime problem. Politics is a dirty business with power hungry people saying whatever leads to votes, with little true commitment to the ideals they profess to believe.

I'm losing faith in President Bush, some of our political leaders, some of our police, some of our media, some of our self-interest groups and even some of our youth to bring peace to our communities. I'm losing faith in business and industry where greed for the big dollars creates scandals (Enron, Halliburton, insider stock indiscretions) and a loss of interest in contributing to community improvement. Most distressing of all to me is that I am losing faith in our police with so many scandals, corruption, shortsightedness, and ineptitude.

Where are the creative ideas that might be helpful? We have a problem at Mexico-America border crossings with citizens who try to step up to help with problems they perceive. They are being called "vigilantes" by the President. They are really like a "Citizen Watch" or minutemen. There are 10 million people in our country illegally and some of our citizens want to do something about it rather than continuing to pay taxes to support them.

Why not train and use concerned citizens as volunteer deputies or reserve officers? Can we train and deputize these citizens to work properly with the Border Patrol? Why not develop a national identify card for travel for border crossings and even other purposes? Why not develop a system of six months or a year of national service for everyone at age 18 (male, female, rich, poor) like some other countries? Where is the media objectivity without pandering to the basest emotions to enhance sales? Where are the really good ideas of interest groups that go beyond seeking government handouts (reparations, grants, etc.)? Where are the creative ideas of our people who are caught in the middle of this madness and have the most to gain from suggestions made to leaders, police, groups, schools, etc.? They should not be silent.

Where are the creative ideas of police? I tried to come up with creative ideas from the beginning of my police career and the use of motor scooters was one of which I'm very proud. Police must be innovative, always looking for ways to do a better job. What would happen if they began to put "Law Enforcement and Protection Agency" on their buildings and their letterheads? What if police cars bore the slogan "It Takes a Team—You and Your Police"? What if an acronym of POLICE were spelled out on banners or police cars as "Protectors Of Liberty for Individuals and Community Equally"?

Do police demonstrate that they have become too afraid of the public by focusing only on weapons and pursuit vehicles? What about the value of motor scooters to promote community relations, a change that was instituted with considerable success in my three police agencies? What about enhancing prevention by adding new forms of police mobility? What about putting the police back in touch with the people?

What happened in Detroit reminds me of Colin Powell's comment about the advisability of starting war against Iraq because of Saddam Hussein. "If you break it, you own it." The black politicians and militants now own Detroit—they broke it.

But not all the blame can be laid at their feet. Since that terrible day, July 23, 1967, what has transpired because of police misconduct, political non-support of good policy, press and electronic media mostly serving their bottom line, people both black and white, white flight, malcontents (*nattering nabobs of negativism* in the late Spiro Agnew's words)?

The good people, black and white, who stayed, struggled to bring a once great city back, have seen business and industry leave for greener, less expensive pastures. Then there came the shopping malls in the outer perimeter, and the people went there. The chicken or the egg? Which came first? The people fleeing or industry and business following them. Now we have many smaller cities ringing the once proud city of Detroit.

Did it really happen because of the actions of a few police officers? Isn't that the story of riots, insurrections, racial tensions, turmoil generally caused or claimed to be caused by the improper actions of police—who should be there to defend and protect the city's citizens?

I had studied for promotions, studied in colleges and universities in police work—law enforcement. I knew about black-white skirmishes, insurrections, riots, and felt I knew why they happened. Whatever the underlying causes, and there are many, it is always the police and their actions that come under the penetrating and magnifying media glare and cause unforeseen ramifications.

That was why I took the position in Detroit. I felt that police had to change, should change and act differently. People have often said to me, you don't act like the police I know. I took it as a compliment. Well, how should the police act? Frankly, as the circumstances dictate. But why must they dictate, as they usually do? Why not change the circumstances sometimes. Why not give police a chance to act as helpers and protectors, not just as law enforcers?

Police should be different and act differently. They should protect liberty for the good decent people. Not all police can do that well. That's why I advocate a Dual Purpose police department, police force with cars that respond after the fact to arrest, incarcerate, etc. But there need also to be police protectors who are more knowledgeable, socially cognizant, able to communicate well, and able to gain cooperation from both young and old.

The foot patrol cop of old working the same beat came to know his people and exhibited many of these characteristics. But we can't afford that. That's why I put police on two-wheel scooters to work with the community, to watch, to correct the "broken windows" of the area. That's also why I believe women can be of greater assistance in the police force.

We also need technically trained police and firefighters in today's world since 9/11. Today this includes training to handle attacks of every kind (even biological and chemical), who are able to handle threats directed at our supplies of water, food, air, and resources. The protection and direction of police and firefighters will be vital in the case of attacks of anthrax, botulism, toxins, smallpox, Sarin gas (as in Japan), chlorine, mustard gas, etc., let alone other kinds of attacks.

As Rodney King said, "Why can't we all just get along?" We must all work to get along, to see and assist as "peace keepers". The police should not face daily a "lonely job of peace keeping". Somehow we must assist. We must consider others as members of "the human family" and act like good family members in all ways and at all times.

If we have grievances with others, let us work them out with respect, with patience, and with consideration for the feelings of others as if we could walk a bit in their shoes.

America needs better policing. Yes, policing must change! These are the thoughts of an irascible old curmudgeon. May God bless America.

About the Authors

Johannes Spreen, B.S., M.P.A., and Ph.D. (all but dissertation) was in law enforcement and police service from 1941 through 1984, interrupted by service in the U.S. Army Air Corps from 1943-1945 as Lieutenant Bombardier.

He was a career officer with the New York City Police Department, rising through the ranks to Inspector and Command of Operations.

After he retired from the NYPD, he became Police Commissioner of the City of Detroit. Later he was Sheriff of Oakland County, Michigan, for twelve years as the only Democrat at the County level.

Spreen was also Associate Professor at John Jay College in New York, Professor and Director of the Law Enforcement and Protection Program at Mercy College of Detroit. He was a columnist for the *Detroit News* and the *Port Huron Times Herald.*

Johannes Spreen instituted Scooter Patrols in New York City and Detroit and assisted the Washington, D.C., police with their scooter program.

He wrote the book *American Police Dilemma: Protectors or Enforcers* in 2003 and *American Law Enforcement Does Not Serve or Protect* in 2004.

Diane Holloway, Ph.D., was a Dallas psychologist and was appointed the first Drug "Czar" of Dallas by the Mayor. She also helped the Dallas Police Department develop their first police assessment center for upper ranks in 1987-8, and was an associate member of the International Association of Chiefs of Police and the Texas Police Association.

She wrote *Before You Say 'I Quit'; The Mind of Oswald; American History in Song; Analyzing Leaders, Presidents and Terrorists* and edited *Dallas and the Jack Ruby Trial.* She helped Johannes Spreen research and organize his previous books, *American Police Dilemma: Protectors or Enforcers?* and *American Law Enforcement Does Not Serve or Protect* as well as this work.

She said, "I enjoyed assisting Spreen, a top cop who believes that police should be better, talk better, act better, and backs it up by his own professionalism, moral courage, and clean language."

References

"A historian dissects Detroit's trouble." Editorial. *Detroit Free Press Jobs Page Academy* Summer 1998.

"African Americans and the UAW." Editorial. *African Americans on Wheels Magazine* Feb/Mar. 2000.

Aguilar, Louis. *The Detroit News* 23 Oct. 2004.

Angel, Cecil and Chastity Pratt. "Cosby tells parents to stop the foolishness", *Detroit Free Press* 14 Jan. 2005.

Aumente, Jerome "Detroit's Year Without News", *The Nation*, V. 207, Issue 0012, October 14, 1968.

"A Victory for Reason." Editorial. *Time Magazine* 19 Sep. 1969.

Aynesworth, Hugh "Sacking of Dallas police chief triggers fear of racial turmoil", *The Washington Times* 27 Aug. 2003.

Balaya, Gina "K.Everett", *U.S. Department of Justice*, Detroit, Michigan, Oct. 25, 2004.

Baulch, Vivian and Patricia Zacharias. "The Rouge plant, the art of Industry", *The Detroit News* online

Bayley, David H. *Police for the Future*. New York: Oxford University Press, 1994.

Bello, Marisol "As Detroit faces cuts, council pads own budget", *Detroit Free Press* 27 Jan. 2005.

Black Panther Party Newspaper Collection. *Maoist International Movement*, 11 May 1969 p. 7, Online at www.etext.org.

Blonston, Gary "How Detroit's militants are changing", *Detroit Free Press* 1 Oct. 1967.

Boyle, Kevin. "After the Rainbow Sign: Jerome Cavanagh and the 1960s" Speech delivered November 30, 1999 at *Walter P. Reuther Library of Labor and Urban Affairs*, Wayne State University, Detroit, Michigan.

"Guess who got the key to Detroit?" *CBS News* 26 Mar. 2003.

Chapman, Mark. *Christianity on Trial.* Maryknoll: Orbis Books, 1996.

Cheney, Bob. *Tragedy in Black and White.* San Jose: Authors Choice Press, 2001.

Cleage, Albert. *The Black Madonna.* New York: Sheed & Ward, 1969.

Cleaver, Eldridge. *Soul On Ice.* New York: Delta, 1999.

Conot, Robert. *American Odyssey.* New York: Bantam Books, 1973.

Conyers, John, Jr., "Tribute to the Trade Union Leadership Council." *House of Representatives* 30 Nov. 1995.

Cox, Mike. Attorney General Mike Cox Discusses Results of Investigation into Detroit Mayor Kwame Kilpatrick Press Conference June 24, 2003, *State of Michigan, Department of Attorney General,* www.michigan.gov.

Damren, Samuel. "The Keith Case", *The Court Legacy,* The Historical Society for the U.S. District Court for the Eastern District of Michigan, V. XI, No. 4, Nov. 2003,

Davenport, Christian. "Understanding Covert Repressive Action: The Case of the U.S. Government against the Republic of New Africa" *Journal of Conflict Resolution,* 49.1 (2005) 120-140.

DeLoach, Cartha. *Hoover's F.B.I.: The Inside Story.* Washington: Regnery Pub., 1995.

Diamond, Jared. *Collapse: How Societies Choose to Fail or Succeed.* New York: Viking, 2005.

Donner, Frank "A Special Supplement: The Theory and Practice of American Political Intelligence", *The New York Review of Books,* 16.7 (1971) 22 Apr.

Donner, Frank. *Protectors of the Privileged: Red Squad and Police Repression in Urban America.* University of California Press, 1992.

Elrick, M. L. "Detroit mayor names relative to direct construction", *Detroit Free Press* 3 Jul. 2002.

Elrick, M. L. and Schaefer, Jim "Mayor's family cashes in on charity", *Detroit Free Press* 29 Oct. 2004.

Farley, Reynolds, et al. *Detroit Divided.* New York: Russell Sage Foundation, 2000.

FBI, Investigative Programs, Organized Crime, www.fbi.gov)

"Final Report of the Select Committee to Study Government Operations with Respect to Intelligence Activities." *United States Senate* 23 Apr. 1976.

Fine, Sidney. *Violence in the Model City: The Cavanagh Administration, Race Relations, and The Detroit Riot of 1967.* Ann Arbor: University of Michigan Press, 1989.

Fogarty, Thomas. "Howard's link to separatist movement investigated", *Des Moines Register,* Des Moines, Iowa, 6/5/95.

Gado, Mark. *A Cry in the Night: The Kitty Genevese Murder,* Chapter 10: The Journey of Winston Moseley.

Georgakas, Dan and Marvin Surkin. *Detroit: I Do Mind Dying.* Cambridge: South End Press Classics, 1998.

"George Crockett Is Dead at 88". Editorial. *Detroit Free Press,* 1997.

Goodwin, Doris Kearns. *No Ordinary Time.* New York: Simon and Schuster, 1994.

Heinl, Jr., Col Robert D. "The Collapse of the Armed Forces." *Armed Forces Journal* 7 Jun. 1971.

Herman, Max. "Ethnic Succession and Urban Unrest in Newark and Detroit During the Summer of 1967". Joseph C. Cornwall Center for Metropolitan Studies, Rutgers University, Newark Campus, 2002.

Hersey, John. *Algiers Hotel Incident,* 1968.

Holloway, Diane. *American History in Song.* San Jose: Authors Choice Press, 2001.

—-. *Analyzing Leaders, Presidents and Terrorists.* San Jose: Writers Club Press, 2002.

—-. *Before You Say 'I Quit'.* New Orleans: Self Help Publishing Company, 2003.

—-. *Dallas and the Jack Ruby Trial: Memoirs of Judge Joe B. Brown, Sr.* San Jose: Authors Choice Press, 2001.

—-. *The Mind of Oswald.* Victoria, B.C.: Trafford Publishing Company, 2000.

Iacocca, Lee. *Iacocca: An Autobiography.* New York: Bantam Books, 1984.

Ingrassia, Paul and Joseph White. *Comeback: The Fall and Rise of the American Automobile Industry.* New York: Simon & Shuster, 1995.

Jacoby, Tamar. *Someone Else's House: America's Unfinished Struggle for Integration.* New York: Basic Books, 1998.

James Lafferty Collection, 1969-1973, ID#626, *Walter P. Reuther Library of Labor and Urban Affairs*, Wayne State University, Detroit, Michigan.

Johnson, James Weldon. *Along This Way.* New York: Da Capo Press, 2000.

Keith, Luther. "Bill Cosby clarifies his commentary", *The Detroit News* 26 Jul. 2004.

Keith, Luther. "Detroiters must team up to fight crime, violence", *The Detroit News* 21 Oct. 2004.

Kelley, Robin. "Identity Politics and Class Struggle", *New Politics.* 6:2 (1997) Winter.

Kerik, Bernard. *Lost Son.* New York: HarperCollins, 2001.

Lessenberry, Jack. "Hopes and horrors", *Metro Times Detroit* 31 Oct. 2001.

Lin, Judy. "Friends say Everett never ran away from her troubles", *The Detroit News* 28 Nov. 2004.

Lincoln, C. Eric. *The Black Muslims in America.* Boston: Beacon Press, 1961.

Lindberg, Richard C. "The Mafia in America", *Search International,* Schaumberg, Ill. 2005.

Locke, Hubert. *The Detroit Riot of 1967.* Detroit: Wayne State University Press, 1969.

Loven, Jennifer. "Farrakhan defends, forgives Barbara-Rose Collins" *AP, The Detroit News* 20 Jul. 1996)

McDonald, Maureen. "Movers and shakers: New Detroit brings racial understanding, economic help," *The Detroit News* 8 May 2002.

McGraw, Bill. "George Crockett is dead at 88" *Detroit Free Press* 9 Sep. 1997.

McGraw, Bill. "Hudson's name will fade, but family's legacy shines", *Detroit Free Press* 26 Jun. 2001.

Michigan Historical Colletions, Bentley Historical Library, University of Michigan. *John and Leni Sinclair Papers,* 1967-1979.

Mitchem, Stephanie. "Cross Currents: Sankofa—Black Theologies", *Journal of the Association for Religion and Intellectual Life,* Spring-Summer, 2000.

Moore, Natalie. "Detroit contractors must tell slave past." *The Detroit News* 25 Jun. 2004)

Morris, Julie and Jenny Nolan. "Sex, drugs, rock 'n' roll and plum street." *Detroit News* Rearview Mirror Online: History.

Morse, Chuck. "Communism in black American history." *Sierra Times.com* 12 Feb. 2001.

Owens, Frank. "Detroit, Death City." *Playboy Magazine* Aug. 2004.

Pepper, John (alias for Joseph Pogany). *American Negro Problems: A Program of Racial Strife for the United States.* Workers Library Publisher, Inc. 1928.

Police Use of Excessive Force: A Conciliation Handbook for the Police and the Community. Community Relations Service, U. S. Department of Justice, June, 1999, updated June, 2002.

Provenzano, Frank. "The beat moves on: Good-bye to Detroit icon" *Detroit Free Press* 26 Oct. 2003.

Raspberry, William. "How to reach black America", *Washington Post* 17 Jan. 2005.

Rieff, David. *Los Angeles: Capital of the Third World.* New York: Touchstone, 1991.

"Religion News in Brief." Editorial. *Belleville News Democrat,* May 29, 2003.

Report of the National Advisory Commission on Civil Disorders, New York: Bantam Books, 1968.

"Reporting the Detroit Riot." Editorial. *Detroit Free Press,* American Newspaper Publishers Assn., New York, 1968.

Riley, Rochelle. "Cosby bringing tough talk to Detroit", *Detroit Free Press* 17 Dec. 2004)

Salkowski, Joe and Enric Volente. "Mob faded locally long before key figure died", *AZ Daily Star* 19 May 2002.

Schneider, Daniel "Robert F. Williams vs. the Civil Rights Establishment", Student Term Papers, *John Carroll University,* Cleveland, November 19, 1998.

Shepardson, David and Darci McConnell, Darci. "Detroit police chief Oliver resigns", *The Detroit News* 31 Oct. 2003.

Shepardson, David and David Grant. "17 Detroit cops charged", *The Detroit News* 19 Jun. 2003.

Shepardson, David and Natalie Moore. "Everett faces bribery charges", *The Detroit News* 22 Oct. 2004.

Sherman, Lawrence. *The Quality of Police Education.* National Advisory Commission on Higher Education for Police Officers 1978.

Sherrill, Robert. "We Want Georgia, South Carolina, Louisiana, Mississippi and Alabama Right Now." *Esquire Magazine* Jan. 1969.

Simmons, Zena and Vivian Baulch. "Milestones in recent Detroit police history", *The Detroit News* 29 Jun. 2003.

Sinclair, Norman and Francis Donnelly. "Police brutality comes full circle: Force has a 30-year history of abuse," *The Detroit News* 29 Jun. 2003

Slivka, Judd. "Colleges bill dies in Senate", *The Arizona Republic* 6 Apr. 2005.

Smith, Robert. "Imari Obadele: The Father of the Modern Reparations Movement"

Spreen, Johannes. *American Law Enforcement Does Not Serve or Protect!* New York: iUniverse, Inc. 2004.

—-. *American Police Dilemma: Protectors or Enforcers?* iUniverse, Inc., New York, 2003.

Sugrue, Thomas J. *The Origins of the Urban Crisis.* Princeton: Princeton University Press, 1998.

"War on Campus, Michigan State." Editorial. *Vietnam*, August 1995, p. 28.

Thompson, Heather Ann. *Whose Detroit? Politics, Labor and Race in a Modern American City.* New York: Cornell University Press, 2002.

Thottam, Jyoti et al. "The worst mayors in America" *Time,* April 24, 2005.

Trautman, Neal. "The Corruption Continuum: How Organizations Become Corrupt", *National Ethics Institute*, June 21, 2004.

Tully, Edward J. "Regional Consolidaton of Law Enforcement Services in the United States", *National Executive Institute Associates*, Jan. 2002.

Vitullo-Martin, Julia. "Detroit Fights Back", The Manhattan Institute, *City Journal,* Summer 1995

Volkman, Ernest. *Gangbusters: The Destruction of America's Last Great Mafia Dynasty.* New York: Faber & Faber, 1998.

Washington, James, Ed. *I Have a Dream: Writings.* San Francisco: HarperSanFrancisco, 1992)

Welch, Neil J. and David Marston. *Inside Hoover's F.B.I.* New York: Doubleday Books, 1984.

Wendland, Mike. "Spam king lives large off others' e-mail troubles" *Detroit Free Press* 22 Nov. 2002.

Widick, B. J. *Detroit: City of Race and Class Violence.* Detroit: Wayne State University Press, 1984.

Wilde, Harold R. and James Q. Wilson. "The Urban Mood", *Commentary Magazine,* 48:4 (1969) Oct.

Williams, Robert. *Negroes With Guns.* Detroit: Wayne State University Press, 1962.

Wilson, James Q. "The Closing of the American City," *The New Republic*, 11 May, 1998.

Young, Bob. "Kobe, money can't buy love" *Arizona Republic* 26 Apr. 2005.

Appendix A

The New Yorker article "T.S.U.", Feb. 5, 1966

"The radio-equipped motor scooter is a comparatively slow-moving protective device that fills the gap between the foot patrolman, who covers a neighborhood in depth but cannot always get to the scene of a crime fast enough, and the patrol car, which moves rapidly but has a limited field of observation. Scooters provide mobility and flexibility. They reduce the opportunity for crime, because they can reach any part of a precinct in a matter of minutes." This pithy pronouncement was made to us by Inspector Johannes Spreen, the man in charge of the experimental motor-scooter program launched last summer by the Police Department.

The scooters have proved so effective in dealing with parking violations and with crime on the streets that the Department has decided to expand the program, and the 1966 budget has asked for funds with which to acquire a total of 685 scooters, the present total being 59. The expansion has included a nod in the direction of Johannes Spreen, a huge, rather rumpled-looking man who, as a captain and later as a deputy inspector, fought for the scooter program over a period of five years; as a sign of his and its success, he was promoted to full inspector late in November.

"Scooters have been used in Central Park and Prospect Park for the past two years," Inspector Spreen told us. "At the moment, we have nine scooters patrolling the parks, 30 on traffic duty in midtown Manhattan, and 20 assigned to what we call our Tactical Scoot Units, for experimental work. Each T.S.U. consists of seven men and six Vespas—the spare man fills in when a regular rider is off duty, sick, or in court. The men wear the usual police uniform, plus a light-blue Fiber-glas helmet, and they have a two-way Motorola radio slung over the shoulder, and carry a nightstick, either in the hand or fitted into a rack on the Vespa.

"The scooterman is basically a more mobile foot patrolman. He takes his orders direct from the precinct house, unlike the radio prowl car, which is controlled by a borough-wide communications unit. The scooter itself is very nimble. It can weave through stalled traffic, jump the curb and travel along the sidewalk, cut through a narrow alley, and patrol a park that is chockablock with benches and playground equipment. Moreover, it is relatively cheap. I estimate that a man on a scooter, which costs us $300, and equipped with a two-way radio, which costs us $700, can patrol from 10 to 15 foot posts in a quarter of an hour. We may never be able to afford sufficient manpower to put a policeman on every corner, but, with scooters, we can have a policeman coming around every corner. This could cut our crime rate by as much as 30%."

Inspector Spreen suggested that we watch an experimental T.S.U. in action, and soon we found ourself in the back of an unmarked patrol car with Sgt. James P. Marron, of the Central Park scooter squad, who had been assigned to evaluate the unit. The unit was operating, for the first time, in the Seventh Precinct, on the lower East Side; on this occasion, only four of the scootermen happened to be on hand, the others being off duty (the unit operates from 10 a.m. to 6 p.m. seven days a weeks) or in court to testify on arrests made earlier in the week.

Sgt. Marron said the four men, working in pairs, would have to patrol the entire precinct, an area of about 20 blocks. "At first, they'll be working out sweep patterns," he said. "This helps them to learn the neighborhood and also to test the reception on their radios—sometimes we run into dead spots. In any event, we like to keep them moving around as much as possible; we think they reduce crime simply by being so visible."

Sgt. Marron's car was equipped to pick up scooter calls, and the first call we heard was for Scooter 20 to check on a noisy motor reported to be outside 54 Ludlow Street. By the time our car reached that address, Scooters 20 and 59 were parked at the curb, and the men had dismounted and were rapping on the windows of an enormous refrigerator truck, who motor was indeed making a fearful racket. The scootermen roused the driver, who was taking a snooze, and advised him to move his truck along to a non-residential area.

As they remounted, another radio call ordered them to the site of a sidewalk injury, at 94 Orchard Street. Our car followed the scooters as far as the corner of Canal and Orchard Streets, where a trailer truck that had failed to round a sharp turn was blocking the intersection. The scooters nipped up onto the sidewalk and disappeared down the street. The trailer truck eventually unscissored itself and freed the intersection; by then the scootermen had long since reached 94 Orchard

Street, and we found them giving first aid to a young truck driver who had injured himself in an unloading accident.

In the course of the next couple of hours, the scootermen flagged down a woman who had driven through a red light, and handed her a summons; broke up a disorderly group of wine-bibbers at the corner of Suffolk and Broome Streets; checked a complaint by a woman that her black raincoat had been spattered with paint from a painter's bucket standing on a windswept scaffold; and completed a special sweep of the warehouse district down by the river—a favorite dumping ground for stolen automobiles.

We were just about to call it a day when Sgt. Marron's radio crackled into life and we heard one of the scootermen asking precinct headquarters for a license-plate check of two automobiles parked on Monroe Street. A few minutes later, the precinct dispatcher reported that one of the plates belonged to a stolen car. "Mobility and good communications," Sgt. Marron said. "That's what it takes, and that's what the scooters give us."

Appendix B

Declaration of Independence
Of
Republic of New Africa

We, the Black People in America, in consequence of arriving at a knowledge of ourselves as a people with dignity, long deprived of that knowledge; as a consequence of revolting with every decimal of our collective and individual beings against the oppression that for three hundred years has destroyed and warped the bodies and minds and spirits of our people in America, in consequence of our raging desire to be free of this oppression, to destroy this oppression wherever it assaults mankind in the world, and in consequence of our inextinguishable determination to go a different way, to built a new and better society in a new and better world do hereby declare ourselves forever free and independent of the jurisdiction of the United States of America and the obligations which that country's unilateral decision to make our ancestors and ourselves paper-citizens placed upon us.

We claim no rights from the United States of America other than those rights belonging to human beings anywhere in the world, and these include the right to damages, reparations, due us for the grievous injuries sustained by our ancestors and ourselves by reason of United States lawlessness.

Ours is a revolution against oppression—our own oppression and that of all people in the world. And it is a revolution for a better life, a better station for mankind, a surer harmony with the forces of life in the universe. We, therefore, see these as the aims of our revolution:

- To free black people in America from oppression;

- To support and wage the world revolution until all people everywhere are so free;

- To build a new Society that is better than what we now know and as perfect as man can make it;

- To assure all people in the New Society maximum opportunity and equal access to that maximum

- To promote industriousness, responsibility, scholarship and service

- To create conditions in which freedom of religion abounds and man's pursuit of God and/or the destiny, place and purpose of man in the Universe will be without hindrance;

- To build a black independent nation where no sect or religious creed subverts or impedes the building of the New Society, the New State Government, or the achievement of the aims of the Revolution as set forth in this Declaration;

- To end exploitation of man by man or his environment;

- To assure equality of rights for the sexes;

- To end color and class discrimination, while not abolishing salubrious diversity, and to promote self-respect and mutual respect among all people in the Society;

- To protect and promote the personal dignity and integrity of the individual, and his natural rights;

- To assure justice for all;

- To place the major means of production and trade in the trust of the State to assure the benefits of this earth and man's genius and labor to society and all its members, and

- To encourage and reward the individual for hard work and initiative and insight and devotion to the revolution.

In mutual trust and great expectation, we the undersigned, for ourselves and for those who look to us but are unable personally to fix their signatures hereto, do join in this solemn Declaration of Independence. And to support this Declaration and to assure the success of our Revolution we pledge without reservation ourselves, our talents and all our worldly goods.

APPENDIX C

New Bethel Incident
Detroit Police Officers
Association Ad April 15, 1969

Detroit Police Officers Association
God Bless You George!
The Complete Story of the Assassination of Patrolman Czapski
    Time: 11:40 p.m.; Date: Saturday, March 29th; Patrolman Mikchael Czapski, age 22 and Patrolman Richard Worobec, age 28, cruising near Linwood and Euclid observed ten to twelve men dressed in green military fatigue uniforms with leopard skin epaulets armed with rifles and carbines in front of the New Bethel Baptist Church.
    They immediately stopped the scout car and got out to investigate. Neither drew his gun. Upon seeing the officers, the would-be killers in guerilla fashion, turned and fired. Patrolman Czapski, fatally wounded, fell. Patrolman Worobeck, although critically wounded, managed to crawl to the scout car and call for assistance. Patrolman Czapski, brutally shot seven times, was dead upon arrival at Ford Hospital. The scout car was riddled with bullets. Patrolman Worobec barely escaped with his life. The assassins ran straight into the New Bethel Baptist Church. Patrolman Worobeck's cries for help were heard over the police radio.
    Within seconds supporting scout cars arrived on the scene. Black as well as white officers responded. Fellow officers removed Czapski and Worobec under fire from the Church. A ranking officer at the scene pounded repeatedly on the locked door of the Church and demanded entry. The only answer received was gunfire. The officer then broke into the darkened, barricaded building. Immediately they were fired upon from the center of the altar by a rifleman. The man dove for cover behind an overturned table near the pulpit. Shots were being fired from all over. One sniper fired at officers from a loft located near a corner of the

building. When the officers returned his fire, the sniper fell along with his loaded automatic.

Other officers came in and turned on the lights. Everyone was ordered to stand with their hands up. Slowly they began to rise as directed. One hundred forty-two adults including five injured persons, as well as five juveniles, were in the building. The majority, both men and women, were wearing paramilitary fatigues with leopard skin epaulets and combat boots, the uniform of the Republic of New Africa. Requests for information brought only silence. Not one person offered assistance or cooperation. Nine weapons, including rifles, hand guns, gas ejecting spray and quantity of ammunition was recovered from inside the church building. Narcotics were also found.

The ranking officers at the scene ordered all those present arrested. Why?

1. Because one officer was critically wounded and another apparently dead;

2. Because the assassins wore military uniforms;

3. Because the police were shot at from the church;

4. Because the police had to break into the church;

5. Because the lights were off when they finally got in the church;

6. Because they were fired upon after they entered;

7. Because people wearing uniforms identical to the assassins were in the church;

8. Because no aid was given to the officers once they secured the church;

9. Because several weapons were found in the church;

10. Because of threat of further neighborhood disturbance.

Police busses were called even before the premises were completely secured, and within 40 minutes the busses arrived at police headquarters. Arrangements were immediately made for detectives on duty to remain and additional detectives were called in to process the prisoners as quickly as possible.

The prisoners were taken into the garage on the ground floor of police headquarters and from there in small groups they were sent to the scientific laboratory. Nitrate tests were conducted to find traces of gunpowder. Then, the prisoners were taken to the Robbery Breaking and Entering Bureau for fingerprints and other identification procedure. They were finally sent to the 9th floor where they were registered for arrest.

A detective sergeant from the Homicide Bureau was placed in charge. The case began to take shape as the patrolmen involved arrived to make their reports. At 5:30 a.m. when the detective in charge first learned that Judge Crockett was in the building, several patrolmen still had not completed their preliminary reports. Some had yet to arrive from the scene. Of the 142 people arrested, only 40 had been completely processed. Detectives were working quickly. Possibly some were wanted criminals, but there was no time to determine this.

At 5:45 a.m. the Police Dept. was ordered to stop everything and produce all prisoners before Judge Crockett in a makeshift court set up on the first floor of police headquarters. Security arrangements had to be made quickly to comply with Judge Crockett's orders.

By 6:35 a.m. the prisoners started arriving downstairs in the makeshift courtroom already occupied by Judge Crockett, representative James Del Rio and an Assistant Prosecutor. As the prisoners started to enter Judge Crockett's makeshift courtroom, Representative Del Rio was seen running in and out of the room. Mutual greetings were exchanged between Del Rio and the prisoners in line.

By the time Prosecutor Cahalan arrived Judge Crockett had released 15 prisoners. During this time the press was excluded from the floor. While releasing prisoners, Judge Crockett never inquired whether or not they were fugitives. The prisoners were released without requiring cash bonds. Unfortunately, no court stenographer was present.

When Prosecuting Attorney William Cahalan arrived, he and the Judge, along with Del Rio, had a short but private conference. Cahalan and Judge Crockett returned to the makeshift courtroom.

For the first time the press was allowed near the courtroom. On at least one occasion Representative Del Rio appeared to be holding a press conference in a corner. Then he ran back into the courtroom. During this time patrolmen standing guard were jeered by the prisoners who were anticipating their immediate release. Remarks such as, "We'll only be here a short time, Whitey," were directed to the officers.

Then, suddenly, Milton Henry, with what appeared to be two guards following close behind, burst into the side door of the building and pushed past the police to the prisoners. Again, mutual greetings were exchanged. Henry then entered the courtroom, and exited. He left the building and then returned with his guards close behind. This reassured the prisoners who were by this time making "black power gestures." He also conferred briefly with Representative Del Rio and then left the building.

When a prisoner identified as James Wheeler was brought before Crockett, Prosecutor Cahalan asked him to be held. Judge Crockett released the prisoner on his promise to appear in court at noon. The Prosecutor pleaded with the Judge to reconsider, whereupon the Judge cited him for contempt, ordered his reappearance at noon, declared the hearing terminated, and stormed out of the building. The remaining prisoners were then taken to the 9th floor of police headquarters where they remained until the hearing at noon in Judge Crockett's courtroom.

At the hearing held in Recorder's Court the Assistant Prosecutor requested all prisoners be held until it could be determined whether or not they were fugitives. The Judge refused. Only two were held. Six had traces of gunpowder on their hands, but only two were held. It was later determined that a number of the persons arrested had prior felony arrests including three persons convicted of conspiracy in the planned slaying of Roy Wilkens, President of the N.A.A.C.P. and Whitney Young, Director of the National Urban League.

At the time of the incident the Church was not being used for religious services. It had been rented to the Republic of New Africa, R.N.A. The R.N.A. is a militant race-oriented organization founded on March 31st, 1968, by former followers of Malcolm X (Malcolmites). Its avowed purposes are:

1. Formation of paramilitary units of blacks for armed seizure of the states of Mississippi, Louisiana, Alabama, Georgia and South Carolina.

2. Upon seizure to defend the territory against the federal government.

3. Establishment of diplomatic relations with Communist China and Cuba.

4. To organize guerilla warfare in the northern cities of the United States.

5. Removal of all whites from territories seized.

The leaders of this organization are Milton Henry and his brother, Richard B. Henry. Milton Henry, a licensed attorney, on many occasions has attacked the courts and so-called "White Man's Justice." In a pamphlet put out by the organization entitled War in America, written by Brother Imari, slave name Richard B. Henry, published in August 1968, by the Malcolm X Society, Box 697, Detroit, Michigan 48206, it is stated on page 32, that the unions have been the constant enemy of black unity and black progress, because they successfully used their power to deprive George Crockett of an important endorsement in his candidacy for Judge.

Judge Crockett apparently claims that the officers acted illegally in arresting the persons in the church. Yet, the law provides:

1. It is unlawful and constitutes the crime of riot for five or more persons acting in concert to wrongfully engage in violent conduct, and thereby intentionally or recklessly cause or create a serious risk of causing public terror or alarm.

2. It is further unlawful for persons intending to cause or to aid or abet the institution or maintenance of a riot, to do an act or engage in conduct that urges other persons to commit acts of unlawful force or violence, or the unlawful burning or destroying of property, or the unlawful interference with a police officer.

3. It is further unlawful for a person to assemble or act in concert with four or more persons for the purpose of engaging in conduct constituting a crime of riot, or to be present at an assembly that either has or develops such a purpose, and to remain there with intent to advance such purpose.

In view of what happened, the police certainly knew murder had been committed and had probable cause to believe an assembly was being conducted which potentially created a serious risk of causing public terror and alarm.

Judge Crockett maintains that he issued a Writ of Habeas Corpus on his own motion because he felt the arrested persons were illegally restrained of their liberty and that the administration of tests for nitrates upon detained individuals without the assistance of counsel and prior to their being warned of their right to counsel is unconstitutional. The applicable cases, however, don't even remotely support the Judge's position. Further, the case the Judge relies on, *U.S. v. Wade, 338 U.S. 218 (1967)*, expressly indicates that it is inapplicable to the type of scientific test here involved.

Judge Crockett maintains that he is objective and wants to see justice done. This is hard for us to swallow in view of his previous actions. For example, on Saturday, November 16, 1968, a Detroit Police Officer with a home and family in Detroit and with no previous criminal record, was arraigned before Judge Crockett on charges of felonious assault growing out of the Veterans Memorial Incident. The prescribed standards for the release of a prisoner and consideration of bail are as follows:

1. The seriousness of the offense.

2. The likelihood of return, predicated upon the man's ties in the community.

3. The accused's previous criminal record, or lack thereof.

Judge Crockett set bond in this case in the sum of $5,000, almost unheard of in this kind of case where the Defendant has no previous record. The same day Judge Crockett arraigned 19 other defendants who were not police officers in crimes ranging from Assault with Intent to Commit Rape, Armed Robbery, Sale and Possession of Narcotics, to Receiving Stolen Property. In many of these cases the defendants had prior felony convictions. Except for one bond that was reduced by Judge Crockett from $50,000 to $10,000, the highest bond he set that day was $2,500. He granted personal bonds in two narcotics cases, five breaking and entering cases, one received stolen property case, one larceny in a building case, and the highest bond he set, other than the patrolman's was $2,500.

Justice that is either all Black or all White is not justice at all. On Sunday, April 6, 1969, the following advertisement appeared in the "personal" section of *The Detroit News* on page 2C: "God bless you George. We thank you for your aid and encouragement last Sunday morning. We all love you. Brothers Richard and Milton."

Need more be said! Anyone wishing to assist in petitioning for the removal of Judge Crockett or in the demanding for changes in the present laws or court procedures, or interpretation of the laws, contact DPOA, 2899 W. Grand Blvd., Detroit, Mich. 48202. Phone: 873-0404. Detroit Police Officers Association.

APPENDIX D

Responses to My Resignation as Detroit Police Commissioner

I was overwhelmed by a thousand or more letters in response to the news that I wanted to remove my name as police commissioner from Mayor-elect Roman Gribbs, after he talked with me and did not indicate that he wanted me to continue in my position.

These letters, which I will excerpt below, gave me some idea of what had been most valuable to citizens. These comments served as a guide to what citizens expected and valued from their police force.

Since I did not expect to write a book, I obtained no permission from any of these people to use their quotations. I will not violate their privacy by revealing their exact identity.

Mrs. Hazel F. wrote: "Last week I saw two young patrolmen walking the beat on Whittier and Kelly. It gave me a wonderful feeling and I told them so.... These two officers seemed very pleased and wished that more people would tell them how they felt about them. The fact that they were there is another credit to you. How long will they be around when you are gone?"

A black officer I met on the night we stopped the riot, patrolman Crear M., wrote: "Coach, the city had a great season under your leadership...It was great being on the same team with you."

A resident of Windsor, Canada, wrote: "As a former Detroit resident, I am taking the liberty of writing to voice my regrets on your resignation. I am 70 years young, retired, living in Windsor. I worked and lived in Detroit for 40 years. Fear drove me to reside in Windsor.... From one who appreciates the time and effort you gave so freely to make Detroit a better place to live."

A Redford High School student, Sherry W. wrote: "You are really 'with it' as shown by your groovy 'love-in,' in which Detroit gained some good favorable national publicity for a change. I am 15 and I think it is terrible that some of the other teens call the police 'pigs'. I feel that without police everyone would be pigs!"

Michael A. Y. wrote: "I think you have brought a warm heart to the leadership of the police department and thereby helped to humanize our idea of the police. There remains, it is true, a wide gap between our black citizens and our police, but I believe this gap has been reduced, at least among the moderate segments of the black community. Unquestionably, you have been the 'people's choice' in the white areas of our city."

Linda and Gary G. wrote: "I was very sorry to hear of your resignation. My husband and I feel that you have done a fantastic job in bucking up the Detroit Police Department. You have taken a badly beaten department and transformed it into something we both are proud of....
Now that you have made the Detroit Police Department something to be proud of, the job of Commissioner becomes a political plum."

Mr. and Mrs. George L. J. wrote: "My husband and I are two of many people in Detroit who are concerned for our children, our homes and our city. You gave us hope that the police can work in and with the community and perhaps there is hope and a reason for staying in Detroit. You made part of the news interesting and more exciting in that we knew something was being done to help us and our city."

James D. M. of Townline Realty wrote: "I am not or never have been a resident of Detroit but I know that what happens to Detroit directly affects us here in the suburbs and all of Michigan eventually. Thanks for a job well done."

Mrs. John Theodorou wrote after her policeman husband died in a Detroit shooting: "I am the widow of the late John Theodorou who lost his life from one of the shootings Friday November 22nd, 1969....
I doubt if you remember but you met John and his little old brown dog in DeSantis's Parking lot when you paid your respect to another policeman who lost his life, Paul Begin. John was very impressed by you and told me he hoped you

were going to stay on in your present position. I now add my hopes to his that you will not want or have to desert our bullet shattered, blood spattered, body strewn aching and tired city." I did remember her husband well and wrote her about my memories of her husband.

John A. M., coordinator of the law enforcement program of the State of Connecticut, wrote: "I just read in the newspaper about Pat Murphy accepting your job. I'm sorry that you have lost out in the game of politics and hope that you have a suitable position to go to. If not, please contact me and I would see that you got the September 1970 faculty vacancy on our law enforcement staff."

Every student of the fourth grade at Sumter School wrote me and a sample of one of their letters is from Bradley Scott D. "Mrs. Green's fourth grade class would like to tell you how much we appreciate your fine work. We are sad you are retiring. We wish you good luck in the future. We hope people stop calling you policemen bad names…"

Attorney Walter S. N., whom I had seen many times in court, wrote: "More than 75% of our contact has been on the basis where I was advocating the position of a client or clients. This letter has nothing to do with advocacy. In my judgment, your stay in Detroit was all too short. You accomplished much to increase the possibility of the Detroit Police Department becoming a fully professional institution within the foreseeable future. You have been the primary salesman in the community for the concept that just law enforcement is the only means by which the rights of all citizens, be they police officers or not, can be assured. Your constant seeking for recognition of the fact that with rights and power go equal and concomitant responsibilities has been inspiring."

Jay and Mary Lou L. wrote: We need more people like you in leadership positions, who are not afraid to talk about love and bringing people together."

Harold G. D., who owned a bookkeeping and tax service, wrote: "I wish to express my personal thanks for your efforts to encourage law and order in Detroit. Also your constant reminders of the principles of 'love they neighbor as thyself.'…Your police program has directed attention to our social reform program."

Mrs. James K. P. wrote: My family and I have enjoyed more trips downtown and into Detroit this past year than we had in the several previous years and I feel that it has a lot to do with our feeling that we had nothing to fear, thanks to the Detroit Police. If you haven't done anything else, it is so reassuring to see the policemen on duty either in patrol cars or on foot.... I liked your Buck Up the Police idea and contributed to it."

Brian P. C. wrote: "I am 19 years old and a student at Wayne State University...It is so sad and yet somehow so sickeningly inevitable that you be victimized by that utterly detestable group of pseudo-political hot dogs that infest city hall...For in a world of such hypocrisy and self-seeking public service, the sincerity, creativity, and fair-minded justice you have exhibited are truly an inspiration."

Pete K. wrote: "I am twenty years of age and a college student. I would like you to know that for the first time in almost two years I went downtown to see the auto show. You know what? It really felt safe down there for the first time."

Bonnie J. wrote: "I've never written a fan letter before, but I've been a fan of yours since you took office as Detroit's Police Commissioner.... You've brought a new vitality and enthusiasm to the Police Department. Your ideas have been refreshing and original. And you've helped give the police of this city a new, more humane image, which they really deserve."

Frank W. wrote: "Thank you for a job well done. You had style! You had flair! Your scooter program, the helicopter, the 'buck up your police', and the 100-day love-in were just great. I am truly glad you're staying in Detroit. History, later on, will bear testimony that you were right and the obstinate council, who had no guts, no vision, were wrong. The council couldn't turn the green light on. 'Hey, look about you' a saying my daughter told me about from Camp Dearborn last summer, reminded me of you. Soul is what it was. You made us all look up and around, and lifted our spirits high."

Physician Henry J. V., M.D. wrote: "I am certain you have laid a foundation for the development of a greatly improved department and respect for it by the people."

Mrs. Betty L. wrote: "One of the things I especially liked about you was the way you stood up for the men of your department. The police of Detroit have a very hard job and I think knowing you stood behind them boosted their morale and made them a better department. Another thing I like was the way you got out among the people letting them know you cared about them and about the community they lived in."

Judge John H. G. of the State of Michigan Court of Appeals wrote: "I am convinced that you have rendered a great service to the City of Detroit and have been one of the outstanding police commissioners Detroit has had over the past thirty years. The innovations that you have commenced with the Department are many. You have served during a most troublesome period and I think had there been a different commissioner, the racial tension would have been much greater."

A telegram from Dr. John F. B., the Wayne County Medical Examiner, read: "Your reasons for resignation are well-founded however I hope you will reconsider since the city needs you. You have done the best job yet."

President Rand H. of the Mayor's Committee "Keep Detroit Beautiful" wrote: "We had been so pleased with all you had accomplished for our city and were hoping you would continue with us."

Father William Breandan of St. Dominic's Church wrote: "I am a catholic priest of the Dominican Order and not in the habit of writing fan letters...

I felt an obligation to tell you that I think you performed an outstanding service for the community of Detroit. So many times people in public service seem to get nothing but abuse. To me you gave every indication of dedication to your profession. The causes of crime are pride, greed, envy and lust. To eradicate these is more in line with my work than yours and if there is greater love of God among our people then crime will lessen. Once a man looks upon his fellow man as a person created by God and knows he must live that way then he will treat his neighbor as one of noble birth regardless of the color of his skin or the size of his bankroll. Poverty of this world's good may be one thing which helps a person to find riches in crime but I do know for certain that poverty of the love of God causes crime."

Alison B. wrote: "I am a girl, fourteen to be exact, who is planning to be a policewoman. I read in the newspaper and saw on T.V. that you are leaving office. You will be a great loss to the police department. You're a very great man in my eyes. You have done so much to help combat crime in our streets. You have also proposed many good bills to make me wish I was of voting age to vote 'yes' on them....

Here is a copy of a poem I wrote that my mom wanted me to send along. Being a Policewoman is what I want to be very, very much....

Being a policewoman means helping not only those you love but helping all of mankind regardless of race, creed or religion."

Edward John "Jack" R., pastor of the Metropolitan Baptist Church, wrote: "Your contribution to Detroit will some day be equated to that of industry."

Joseph J. W. wrote: "I am the son of a Detroit police sergeant who retired several years ago, so perhaps I have more empathy for the kinds of situations you have had to deal with in your job. Both my wife and I are native Detroiters who love our home town, but who also moved to the suburbs before you took over. Although we can no longer vote in Detroit, my wife travels into town each day and I come in two evenings a week to study at Wayne. Therefore we both feel very grateful to you because you have done the best job possible to keep the streets of our home town safe."

Elaine H., secretary to Queen's Blue Collar Workers of America, wrote: "As a result of your efforts to promote a better understanding between the police-citizens and the inner city, many are recognizing the importance of the attempts to establish this line of communication."

Walter E. W., Service Director of the Marine Corps League, wrote: "May I commend you on a job well done and I am sure that had you stayed on as our Police Commissioner, this City would have become a safer one with less crime on our streets."

Mayor Donald R. Cronin of Flint, Michigan, wrote: "I want to take this opportunity to thank you very sincerely for the help you have given me and our own Police Chief, James R., while you were in office in Detroit. The scooter patrol innovation that you instituted in the 12th precinct worked effectively for you, and based upon your recommendations, we here in Flint utilized it to a great advantage this past year. It was so successful here in Flint that Chief R. has requested 35 additional scooters for the forthcoming year, and we are trying at this time to find funds for his request."

Thomas S. A. wrote: "I am a black man who has never written to a public official in all my 47 years. I feel impelled, however, to congratulate you for your efforts in regard to our police department and city as a whole. The best wishes of many thousands of blacks and whites go with you and your family regardless of destination."

Harrison E. B., Vice President and Treasurer of the Great Lakes Mutual Life Insurance Company wrote: "I made several contributions to your 'Buck Up Your Cop' program with which to establish some of the equipment before denied you by the establishment. Detroit can hardly afford to lose men of your level regardless of capacity."

Dwight Havens, President of the Greater Detroit Chamber of Commerce, wrote: We have always felt here at the Greater Detroit Chamber of Commerce, that you were the man to guide us out of the wilderness of law and order problems. Our committees and the members of the staff have enjoyed greatly their association with you. We have admired your work and hope the new innovations you introduced and ideas you developed will continue to contribute effectively to the situation here in Detroit."

Mrs. Mamie M. wrote: "I only wish I could speak for the whole black race....
Whoever takes the job you are leaving whether his skin is black blue green white or grizzly would have to be a magician to deal with all the things I see going on in this world."

Annabelle L. wrote: "It is most refreshing to see my daughter return home from classes at Presentation Grade School and related almost a one to one contact with the motor scooter patrolman who had a class conversation with these children and give the image of the policeman that I knew in my childhood....
I am black but live in a world of human beings who benefit based on merit and not color. We also marvel as a community that policemen are no longer in cars but are walking and talking and meeting people."

A twenty-year city employee who did not sign her name wrote: "I am so sad. I am black. I feel you have done and are doing a grand job and that you have a real interest in the City of Detroit. You care!"

Ann M. K. wrote: "It is policemen on scooters, policemen walking and talking and smiling policemen everywhere...
Actually life in Detroit has a new beginning."

Judith B. wrote: "It would be safe to assume that the bookmakers in 1967 would have given the Lord Jesus better odds in bringing back Lazarus from the dead than you had in breathing life back into the Detroit Police Department. The men in blue are finally beginning to enjoy more public support and respect, all of which must be attributed to your community-oriented programs."

Charles R. N., elevator starter, wrote: "You may recall me as the elevator starter at the Hotel Ponchartrain....
I believe I am one of the few who have moved from the suburbs back to Detroit to gain independence and enjoy the many things and places that Detroit has to offer...
Meeting the many guests and customers at my hotel, I extol the many virtues of our city in the way of museums, the fine Civic Center, theaters, parking and our fine zoo and shopping area and urge them to make use of them without fear...
In a recent visit to Cleveland to visit old friends, I was dismayed to hear from them that they refused to visit downtown because of the black problem....
My sixteen year old son has never had any trouble and remarks about the frequency of police patrols on foot and in cars and scooters."

An officer whom I knew, Jim K., wrote: "I am proud to have served the Department under your leadership and I am especially proud that you were the Commissioner that handed me my new badge on 11-21-69."

Mrs. L. R. C. wrote: "On Nov. 30, we drove our family downtown to see the lovely displays and decorations. I can say with all honesty we felt safe, we have always gone down before, but we never could get out of the car. We were just plain scared. This year was different. We saw policemen walking and two others on their scooters."

Of course, I had some letters from detractors. Mr. John G. B. wrote: "You certainly know how to blow your own horn, at least statistically. Have you ever been mugged or your children threatened if they didn't bring some money back to school with them after lunch? Guess not. Every time Spreen comes on my screen I could scream from pain in my spleen. This writer thinks Detroit will be better off without you and your grandiose ideas."

I wrote him, as I did the others, thanking him for his comments and explaining that my daughter went to a racially integrated school in the heart of Detroit.

Appendix E

Police Executives Must Be Role Models Even If It Means Going to Jail

Every top cop has had many defining experiences when he had to make tough choices. Those choices may get him in one kind of trouble or another. When the media covers a top cop "in trouble", the image goes out to his men and women and they must decide whether they should use him as a role model.

I went to jail when I felt I had to stand firm for my decision to not have a bad law enforcement officer on my force, even if it cost me my freedom. I hoped, at the time, that my stand would be depicted by the media correctly so that the issues would be clear for the public and my officers to see. I especially wanted everyone to get the message that we don't want bad cops or bad deputies on the payroll, and that police executives should not and would not cover up their crimes. Here's what happened.

I was the Oakland County Sheriff, top cop in Michigan's second most populous county. I was arrested and jailed for refusing to obey a court order to reinstate a sheriff's deputy whom I had fired the year before. You see, on March 11, 1976, I fired Detective Sergeant Keith Lester, 33, after he was charged with larceny by conversion for failing to turn over $200 a court gave him to pay a crime victim. He had pocketed $200 of a $750 restitution payment made by three youths in a larceny case in which they stole a trailer. The restitution was to be collected by Lester and given to the victims.

The charge against Lester was dismissed in February, however, and he sued for reinstatement of his job and back pay of $20,000. Judge Thorburn had dismissed the case because he said Lester should have been charged with embezzlement, not with larceny by conversion. Judge Beer granted the request to dismiss the case.

My view was that the charge against Lester had been improperly dismissed and that Lester was guilty. If I reinstated Lester, it would have lowered morale in the department. Besides that, Lester should have followed normal channels of appeal through the county employee appeal process to regain his job before he went to court.

The Oakland County Circuit Judge William Beer ordered me to be jailed indefinitely on contempt charges. He said I would stay in jail until I changed my mind and intended to lodge me in my own county in a local jail. Sheriff John O'Brien of Genesee County heard the news and sent his administrative assistant to suggest to Judge Beer that I be taken to the Genesee County jail in Flint, Michigan. I was grateful.

The judge's order came late after a day of legal haggling. I had appeared at a press conference with a toothbrush in my pocket, saying that I was ready to be locked up for my principles. I told the reporters, "I never thought I would see such a day when I myself would be charged with a crime. But I'd rather be right than free." The Oakland County deputies later presented me with a plaque that contained those lines.

Judge Beer, 67, who had been a judge for 20 years, said that I had violated the separation of powers doctrine by refusing to obey his order. The judge told reporters, "Judges' orders, even if distasteful, must be obeyed."

Judge Beer denied my request to delay the jailing from Friday to Monday so that I could make arrangements to take care of my wife, who was by that time an invalid, suffering with multiple sclerosis and curvature of the spine. She had undergone six operations during the last year and I wanted to spend Mother's Day with her instead of in jail.

When he denied the request, he said, "That has already been fully discussed."

Just before being sentenced by Judge Beer, there was a graduation ceremony in my jail for inmates who had attained their G.E.D. We had the Pontiac School system in our jail, teaching inmates so they could acquire the G.E.D. and pursue a better life. I had been scheduled to give the graduation address.

I had felt that a motivational type speech was in order. The inmates did not know that I was myself going to be jailed that very afternoon. I praised their efforts, told them they were started on a better road, and to keep going.

I then related the story of my life starting as a little immigrant lad from Germany who could not speak the English language. I wound up telling them about growing up in a Depression, gathering old newspapers to sell for a few cents, shoveling snow, lugging boxes of wood to make a little money because we were so poor. I described how I helped my father make cigars by stripping tobacco, how my parents didn't speak English very well, and that I never went to college until I was 35 years old. I congratulated ones getting their GEDs and added, "If I can do it, you can do it."

I told them to keep on and said, "When you get out, I don't want to see you back. Go out. Be a success. You can do it."

At the conclusion of my remarks, I informed them that I would immediately become an inmate like them. I was very touched when they all stood and gave me applause that continued until I left the room.

Before going to the jail, I called my wife and told her that if she felt she needed me, I would acquiesce to Judge Beer's order.

She said very crisply, "Stick to your guns, Sheriff. We're all right." I'll never forget that remark. She really would be all right. A contingent of officers from the Sheriff's Office was already at our home to offer assistance to my wife and daughter.

I turned my gun over to my undersheriff, John Nichols, and was taken into custody by Kenneth McArdle, administrative assistant to the Genesee County Sheriff, John O'Brien. O'Brien, a fellow Democrat, arranged for an attorney for me. I wasn't handcuffed, but the Judge had cautioned McArdle that I was to be treated "just as any other prisoner in jail."

When I arrived at the jail, Sheriff O'Brien welcomed me and we chatted for fifteen minutes before I was taken to the booking area and fingerprinted.

A deputy checked my personal property, which included a wallet with $54, an uncashed paycheck, sheriff's badge, checkbook, tie, tiepin and shoes. I said, "I never violated a court order before. To me, this is kind of like a comedy, but it's a tragedy. All I know is my 35 years in law enforcement seem to be going up in smoke."

My wife had packed clothes into a small suitcase, which I was not able to take along. My attorney, Robert White of Grand Rapids, began working on an emergency appeal of Beer's order. White told reporters that I might be released the next day if he could get the appellate judges to hear the case.

They let me keep my civilian clothes rather than wearing a prison uniform. I was placed in a cell apart from other prisoners, a 10-foot square room. The room had a bed, a desk, two barred windows, and was usually used for intake. I was in "solitary confinement for my own protection." The idea was that some of the 303 prisoners serving time for murder or robbery might like to show a sheriff or a policeman what jail is like.

Prisoners on the floor above me called officers with shotguns to control a disturbance during the 24 hours I served in jail. A group of inmates had overpowered a guard and stole his keys but they returned to their cells after they found that the guard's keys did not fit doors that would let them out. I was thinking, suppose they can't contain it? Suppose it gets down here? Would I be considered friend or foe?

I slept from about 1 a.m. to 4 a.m. and then decided that was no good way to spend time. So I got up and made some notes. I thought a lot about freedom while I was deprived of it. I'd never been in jail before where I couldn't get out. It kind of gives you a feeling of standing in the other guy's shoes. Being behind bars yourself, you maybe develop a little bit of understanding, a little bit of empathy. Here's what I wrote at 4:00 a.m. on May 7th, 1977.

> You do a lot of thinking in jail. You think about how long you may be in, how long you will stay behind bars. You realize the importance of freedom. You think of your loved ones, particularly when they are dependent upon you and you cannot be there to help.
>
> In my case, you think of why you are here. How can you as a sworn servant of the law possibly be in jail for violating that law? You wonder at the strange turn of events, this strange paradox that has led me down this particular road ending up behind bars. Have I really flouted the law of my country? I guess I have but that was never my intention. And I would not say I flouted, I respectfully differed.
>
> How strange, I hear the sounds of people and traffic passing by and yet I cannot leave and join it Why? My thoughts were on the protection and service of the people, under the law of our land. To do so with the best possible service under my constitutional obligation as the chief peace officer of the county.
>
> Yet this has led me into a collision course where principle met principle head on. Where I as an officer of the court had to object to its ministrations. I felt for the public good and the people I serve.
>
> Yet I am sure those same motives were in the mind of the judge who put me here. How odd; we are both attempting to do our job. Is there a greater morality over the legal letter of the law?
>
> I do not feel I really violated a law violently. I wanted to pursue another road but that was apparently impossible. I do not feel unclean inside. I do not feel wrong. I did what I felt was right.
>
> It is unusual that my 35 years in law enforcement and my earnest belief in proper and professional law enforcement has led me tonight to a barred cell in the Genessee County jail.

I also kept thinking about my decision. It was the first time in my 35-year career as a policeman that I had not lived by the law. I thought, "Did I flout the law?" I guess I did but I only meant to respectfully disagree with it.

When Mayor LaGuardia gave me the oath of office in 1941, he said there would be rough times ahead. He said I'd be looking down the barrel of a gun. But he never said I'd be looking through cell bars as a prisoner.

Supporters and well-wishers sent some 30 telegrams and made 74 calls on my behalf while I was in jail. One telegram from my own department read, "We are proud of you. Hang in there. The department stands taller because of your action."

Another telegram sent by the administrator of the Criminal Justice Institute in Detroit said, "All professional law enforcement personnel salute you as an administrator and as a man." That was very gratifying. I put myself out there on a limb, and it could have been cut off.

I arrived after supper had been served so they got me a hamburger from a nearby Burger King. Saturday I ate the normal prisoner fare of cereal for breakfast and hot dogs and beans for lunch. I talked with several of the inmates at meals. One, who was in for non-payment of child-support, told me he would be perfectly willing to pay if his wife would use the money for the child and not for herself and her boyfriend. I thought it odd that we put a man in jail where he could not earn any money for child support. There has to be a better way.

Through the night, a 30-page appeal was delivered to a court clerk Saturday morning. By early afternoon, a three-judge panel of the state Court of Appeals freed me on personal bond. They met Saturday and granted my motion to postpone the Circuit Court order pending appeal after I served 23 ½ hours. The judges set no date for the appeal hearing.

I told a couple of the jail trustees who befriended me that they ought to continue their education. I said that if I could overcome hardship, so could they. The reporters who covered this said that I was often accused of being more of an educator than a police administrator.

I was 57 at the time but I did what I felt was important and necessary. I believed I had an obligation to law enforcement to try to upgrade the profession. I felt that Keith Lester had violated a trust and to restore him would be wrong. We would have no confidence in him. The public would have no trust in him.

I'll never forget that when I came home, my wife and daughter had draped yellow ribbons across the bushes and a large sign on the garage declaring "Way to go, Pa." I was able to spend Mothers' Day at home with them after all.

I was vindicated two months later by the Michigan Court of Appeals, which ruled that I should not have been jailed for refusing to rehire a fired deputy. At the press conference after the ruling, I told reporters that the judge made a number of mistakes but it sure was nice to be right and to be free. Especially when I learned that Deputy Lester was not only fighting his dismissal but was arrested on another criminal charge of willful neglect of duty.

The brief tenure in jail sort of rounded out my education. I told some of those who greeted me that I hoped I never had to take advantage of Sheriff O'Brien's hospitality again, or reciprocate.

Part of my fervor against rehiring Lester came from previous orders from the appeals board and the courts forcing me to rehire four other deputies. I couldn't have that because after awhile, half the department would be less than satisfactory.

Later we found out a very interesting thing about the Judge who had sentenced me. Judge Beer was discovered to have had nine kids in all, three by his first wife and six by his secretary. He led a double life for years until it was discovered after one of his children died. One of his kids (by the secretary) wrote a kind of gossip column in the *Detroit News*. Judge Beer, to his credit, later appeared as a party held a restaurant for a fundraiser saying to all that Johannes Spreen was a decent, honorable man, in effect that he had been wrong. Jim Ellison wrote a book about Beer called *Judicial Indiscretion* that was made into an NBC movie of the week.

My Undersheriff, John Nichols, when I was placed in jail, wrote a letter to the *Oakland Press*. Here is an excerpt of that letter.

> In your editorial of May 10, 1977, you either failed to get the facts, failed to check the validity of those facts as you received them, or ignored the basic facts entirely. The unfortunate point is that the whole premise and tenor of your offering was based on this erroneous belief! That being that Sheriff Johannes Spreen ignored the law without availing himself of the proper channel of legitimate appeals. THIS IS NOT TRUE!! The Michigan Court of Appeals had been petitioned and the case accepted, Docket No. 77-1485, when the Sheriff was sentenced for contempt. The appeal which you described as made while "Spreen was in jail" was, in fact, the *second* appeal including a Petition for Release from that jail. Thus Sheriff Spreen had quietly followed normal procedure.
>
> The Sheriff's contention was and is that his (Lester's) discharge was proper under the rules as they are written. The dismissal by the court was not a finding of innocence as attested to by the trial judge's statement quoted by you...I shall not attempt to convince you that Sheriff Spreen did not "in effect, put himself in jail." I do point out that the judge had other options open to deal with the violation. Those same options he has exercised countless times in other cases before him, both civil and criminal. Fines, suspensions of sentence, probation, all were open to him. He chose jail. That was his right, his prerog-

ative, but not his mandate. Yes, Mr. Munro, I do agree with you on one point. Courts are not perfect.

I shall mention, only in passing, the economic motivation for the Sheriff's "defiance" which you did not consider, apparently. Some $21,000 in County funds would have been spent to repay the defendant officer. The Sheriff protested not only in behalf of police professionalism but as a taxpayer, in the interest of the taxpayer, against premature if not improvident expenditure of these funds.

Index

978-0-595-35798-7
0-595-35798-9

www.ingramcontent.com/pod-product-compliance
Lightning Source LLC
Chambersburg PA
CBHW030257290526
45785CB00001B/116